Social Sensing
Building Reliable Systems on Unreliable Data

Social Sensing
Building Reliable Systems on Unreliable Data

Dong Wang

Tarek Abdelzaher

Lance Kaplan

AMSTERDAM • BOSTON • HEIDELBERG • LONDON
NEW YORK • OXFORD • PARIS • SAN DIEGO
SAN FRANCISCO • SINGAPORE • SYDNEY • TOKYO

Morgan Kaufmann is an imprint of Elsevier

Acquiring Editor: Todd Green
Editorial Project Manager: Lindsay Lawrence
Project Manager: Priya Kumaraguruparan
Designer: Mark Rogers

Morgan Kaufmann is an imprint of Elsevier
225 Wyman Street, Waltham, MA, 02451, USA

ISBN: 978-0-12-800867-6

Library of Congress Cataloging-in-Publication Data
A catalogue record for this book is available from the Library of Congress.

British Library Cataloguing-in-Publication Data
A catalogue record for this book is available from the British Library.

For information on all Morgan Kaufmann publications
visit our website at www.mkp.com

Working together
to grow libraries in
developing countries

www.elsevier.com • www.bookaid.org

To Na, Guangsen, Haixia, and Xuezeng
D.W.

To Ann
T.A.

To Gail and Ariana
L.K.

Contents

Acknowledgments

This book would not have been possible without the encouragement, support, and hard work of many individuals who contributed in different ways to the journey of discovery described within. The authors are grateful to all the colleagues, students, and researchers who dedicated their time to developing theory, building systems, running experiments, and generally advancing the state of the art in social sensing, as well as the agencies funding their work.[*]

The need for a book on social sensing first occurred to the authors after a collaboration between Mani Srivastava, Tarek Abdelzaher, and Boleslaw Szymanski, who together wrote a survey on Human-centric Sensing. The survey, published in the Philosophical Transactions of the Royal Society, in January 2012, offered the view that social networks may be the future sensor networks, highlighting the link between the two fields. At the time, very little analytic foundations existed for reliably exploiting social networks as networks of sensors. Special thanks goes to Mani and Boleslaw for kick-starting the crosspollination of ideas from social and sensor networks that ultimately led to this book.

It was not until Dong Wang and Tarek Abdelzaher discussed social sensing with Lance Kaplan, however, that the research leading to the book was started. The reliability foundations described in this book came out of two different communities: Problem formulations borrowed from data mining were subjected to solution techniques borrowed from estimation theory. Among the authors, it was Lance Kaplan who represented the sensor fusion community and who first devised approaches for extending traditional fusion techniques to soft social sensing data. He thereby formulated the direction of this research from the very beginning. The authors are grateful to their colleagues in the data mining and machine learning communities who shared insights and offered advice on early directions of this research. Special thanks goes to Dan Roth, Jiawei Han, Charu Aggarwal, and Mudhakar Srivatsa for their help in understanding the related research landscape in data mining and machine learning, and what a new book may contribute to that landscape.

Much of the research described in this book was done under the Network Science Collaborative Technology Alliance (NS CTA). The authors are grateful to their NS CTA collaborators William Dron, Alice Leung, Ramesh Govindan, Thomas LaPorta, Amotz Barnoy, Heng Ji, Prasant Mohapatra, John Hancock, Sibel Adali, Debra Jones, Tobias Hollerer, Cleotilde Gonzalez, Arun Ayengar, and John O'Donovan

[*]Research reported in this book was sponsored, in part, by the Army Research Laboratory and was accomplished under Cooperative Agreement W911NF-09-2-0053, DTRA grant HDTRA1-10-10120, and NSF grants CNS 09-05014, CNS 10-35736, and IIS 14-47795. The views and conclusions contained in this document are those of the authors and should not be interpreted as representing the official policies, either expressed or implied, of the Army Research Laboratory or the U.S. Government. The U.S. Government is authorized to reproduce and distribute reprints for Government purposes notwithstanding any copyright notation here on.

for their input. Many thanks also goes to Alex Kott, Ananthram Swami, Reginald Hobbs, Gregory Cirincione, Paul Tandy, Peter Vendeventer, Robert Kehlet, Sue Kase, Elizabeth Bowman, Barbara Broome, Clare Voss, Timothy Hanratty, Tien Pham, Jonathan Bakdash, Jemin George, Stephen Tratz, Jamal Laoudi, Douglas Briesch, Lisa Scott, Norbou Buchler, Kevin Chan, and Kelvin Marcus for their discussions on social sensing and for offering an application perspective.

The authors would further like to acknowledge Hieu Le, Raghu Ganti, Jeff Pasternack, Shiguang Wang, Hossein Ahmadi, Tanvir Al Amin, Eunsoo Seo, Yusuf Uddin, Lu Su, Hangchang Liu, Shen Li, Shaohan Hu, Prasanna Giridhar, Siyu Gu, and Chenji Pan for taking part in building systems, developing theory, and running social sensing experiments described in this book.

Finally, the book would not have been possible without the support of our friends and family, who encouraged us to complete this work, and put up with the late nights, missed promises, and rescheduled obligations it took to do so.

Authors

DONG WANG

Dong Wang is currently an Assistant Professor at the Department of Computer Science and Engineering, the University of Notre Dame. He received his Ph.D. in Computer Science from University of Illinois at Urbana Champaign (UIUC) in 2012, an M.S. degree from Peking University in 2007 and a B.Eng. from the University of Electronic Science and Technology of China in 2004.  Dong Wang has published over 30 technical papers in conferences and journals, including IPSN, ICDCS, IEEE JSAC, IEEE J-STSP, and ACM ToSN. His research on social sensing resulted in software tools that found applications in academia, industry, and government research labs. His work was widely reported in talks, keynotes, panels, and tutorials, including at IBM Research, ARL, CPSWeek, RTSS, IPSN, Carnegie Mellon University, and the University of Michigan, to name a few. Wang's interests lie in developing analytic foundations for reliable information distillation systems, as well as the foundations of data credibility analysis, in the face of noise and conflicting observations, where evidence is collected by both humans and machines.

TAREK ABDELZAHER

Tarek Abdelzaher is currently a Professor and Willett Faculty Scholar at the Department of Computer Science, the University of Illinois at Urbana Champaign. He has authored/coauthored more than 200 refereed publications in cyber-physical systems, distributed computing, sensor networks, and control, with emphasis on human-in-the-loop challenges.  He is an Editor-in-Chief of the Journal of Real-Time Systems, and has served as Associate Editor of the IEEE Transactions on Mobile Computing, IEEE Transactions on Parallel and Distributed Systems, IEEE Embedded Systems Letters, the ACM Transaction on Sensor Networks, and the Ad Hoc Networks Journal.

Abdelzaher's research interests lie broadly in understanding and controlling performance properties of computing systems that interact with both a physical environment and social context in the face of increasing complexity, distribution, and degree of embedding in the physical world.

LANCE M. KAPLAN

Lance M. Kaplan received the B.S. degree with distinction from Duke University, Durham, NC, in 1989 and the M.S. and Ph.D. degrees from the University of Southern California, Los Angeles, in 1991 and 1994, respectively, all in Electrical Engineering. From 1987 to 1990, Dr. Kaplan worked as a Technical Assistant at the Georgia Tech Research Institute. He held a National Science Foundation Graduate Fellowship and a USC Dean's Merit Fellowship from 1990 to 1993, and worked as a Research Assistant in the Signal and Image Processing Institute at the University of Southern California from 1993 to 1994. Then, he worked on staff in the Reconnaissance Systems Department of the Hughes Aircraft Company from 1994 to 1996. From 1996 to 2004, he was a member of the faculty in the Department of Engineering and a senior investigator in the Center of Theoretical Studies of Physical Systems (CTSPS) at Clark Atlanta University (CAU), Atlanta, GA. Currently, he is a researcher in the Networked Sensing and Fusion branch of the U.S. Army Research Laboratory. Dr. Kaplan serves as Editor-In-Chief for the IEEE Transactions on Aerospace and Electronic Systems (AES). In addition, he recently served on the Board of Governors of the IEEE AES Society and on the Board of Directors of the International Society of Information Fusion. He is a three time recipient of the Clark Atlanta University Electrical Engineering Instructional Excellence Award from 1999 to 2001. His current research interests include signal and image processing, automatic target recognition, information/data fusion, and resource management.

Foreword

Technology has impacted all our lives. Whether it is technological advances in medicine, transportation, manufacturing, agriculture, defense, entertainment or just about any area whatsoever, there is sometimes a resulting major change in how we live, work, and socialize. The Internet is a prime example of this phenomenon. Today, combining the Internet capabilities with the proliferation of sensors is producing a new revolution, called *social sensing*. This book is at the forefront of this emerging set of capabilities.

At the center of this new area is the concept of real-time, person centric broadcasting. An important characteristic of social sensing is the ability for an individual to have connectivity to information while he is on the move. TV and radio stations are a small number of information sources that broadcast to the masses. With social sensing each person can become both a broadcaster and consumer of information in almost any location. This fundamentally changes how we exchange information. However, important questions must be resolved for this paradigm to become useful. The major issues are reliability, trustworthiness, coverage, security, privacy, and real-time availability of the data being broadcast by individuals.

Fortunately, this book makes major progress at resolving many of these issues. For example, many individuals may report on a situation such as a major traffic accident, by tweeting, taking pictures, and recording sounds in the area of the situation. Is the sensor data reliable? Perhaps the microphone has a poor quality sensor which fails to record key information sounds. Are the pictures taken trustworthy? Perhaps a person fakes the photo. Is there enough information to obtain a complete picture of the incident and current state of the accident? How soon will the information be available to interested parties? This book begins to develop theoretical foundations for social sensing analytics that tackles many of these issues. It does this by combining machine learning, information fusion, data mining, and statistics to support reliability and trustworthiness.

One major value of this book is the comprehensive review of the analytical theories and frameworks underlying this area. Another is the lucid way that confidence is addressed for social sensing. The book also uniquely describes participatory and opportunistic sensing, together with social data scavenging, and demonstrates how these social sensing trends contribute to social sensing.

While research results in this area of social sensing have been accelerating, the literature is disjoint and often fails to take a comprehensive view. The book is remarkable in that it synthesizes the concepts and fundamentals found in the research and goes much beyond a summary by putting forth new and exciting solutions and directions.

It is also important and instructive to place social sensing in the larger context of wireless sensor networks (WSN) and cyber physical systems (CPS). To date most WSNs and CPSs collect information from physical sensors. These sensors may be noisy, in error, or even unavailable at times (e.g., devices go into sleep mode to save energy). Many techniques(e.g., Kalman filters) have been developed to deal with these stochastic situations. With social sensing there is now the ability to provide a potentially large number of sensing streams based on human provided inputs. What is the equivalent set of techniques to attain confidence in the sensing results? This book gives analytic results that explain how to attain guarantees in these social sensing scenarios. With this capability it seems that our next generation WSNs and CPSs can be improved by social sensing.

Over the years there have been many results and studies involving humans-in-the-loop. For example, the most common situation is supervisory control. In supervisory control, involvement of humans takes place in two ways. In one case, the process runs autonomously. Humans intervene with the control algorithm when it is necessary, typically by adjusting set points. These control problems are well understood. In the other case, the process accepts a command, carries out the command autonomously, reports the results and waits for further commands to be received from the human. As a concrete example, human-in-the-loop control is used in a wheelchair-mounted robotic arm to retrieve an object from a shelf. In this feedback control system, human provides input via a touch screen or joystick which is analyzed by a vision processing system to position the robotic arm to retrieve the object. In these cases the human is the controller. The human has also been the system. Here physiological properties (blood pressure, lung volume, heart rate) of a human are monitored and controlled by some device or drug. Social sensing now focuses on the human being a sensor. This potentially supports the creation of many new applications and capabilities, especially in the WSN, CPS, and Internet of Everything (IOE) systems.

Many research communities can play a role in advancing the social sensing field, including, WSN, CPS, IOE, signal processing, machine learning, data mining, and natural language processing. While many of these related areas are obvious contributors, the book adds important clarifications that articulate the distinctions between sensing and data mining, and how natural language processing solutions are needed.

In summary, this is an exciting book; the first of its kind. It addresses a new and emerging field of social sensing in a comprehensive and analytical manner. You will enjoy reading it!

John A. Stankovic
BP America Professor
Department of Computer Science
University of Virginia

Preface

In the late 1990s, multimedia streaming research was popular, and algorithms for delivering improved quality-of-service (QoS) over the Internet were at a high point. This was also the Ph.D. thesis topic of Tarek Abdelzaher, the second author of this book.

"When I was approaching graduation," Abdelzaher recalls, "I remember being asked on one of my interviews 'Won't your multimedia streaming research career be short?'". Abdelzaher did not understand the question and asked the interviewer why he thought this should be the case. His reply was very insightful: "Your research is about improving human experience by streaming higher quality content through limited resources. Humans, however, have a sensory saturation limit—a maximum bandwidth beyond which improvements are simply not perceptible. Sooner or later, technology will catch up and we shall have enough raw bandwidth to saturate the human receiver's senses. What will you do with your career then?". Abdelzaher considered the question carefully, then replied "I will then find another information bottleneck". We wrote this book because we believe that this new information bottleneck has finally arrived!

The question did haunt Abdelzaher for a long time. Indeed, projecting current trends into the future is not enough. One should also look for natural limits and break points in those trends. It is those limits that help us predict when a trend will cease to be, and allow us to prepare for the shift when shift occurs. The book explores the implications that current trends in information generation, combined with limits on human cognition, might have on information services of the future, and offers a reliability solution for the subset of services we call *social sensing*.

As far as multimedia QoS goes, today, more than fifteen years after that interview, the advent of entertainment devices such as D-Box in modern movie theaters, probably suggests that the industry is finally getting close to saturating the human perception as far as audio-visual stimuli alone are concerned (at least on 2-D screens). While Netflix can still use more research on QoS algorithms to reproduce the IMAX experience at home over modern Internet bandwidth, a far more severe bottleneck is unfolding that will dramatically affect future information services, devices, applications, and communication options. This bottleneck is brought about by the age of sensors and democratized real-time broadcast.

It is not point-to-point connections that will saturate our senses. Rather it is the point-to-multipoint information exchange! Traditionally, information such as the news was disseminated by a few trustworthy sources. Today, one has access to numerous blogs that provide orders of magnitude increases in the number of news sources. However, the reliability of these sources can be suspect. Now that each of us can send messages for the entire world to read, such as tweets, or upload pictures for the entire world to see, thanks to social networks that support information broadcast, the amount of real-time information out there far exceeds our cognitive capacity to consume it. Adding to that the growing volume of information generated by sensors that are getting more widely deployed and capable of generating information continuously in real-time, the picture becomes clear. The pace at which technological advances increase the rate of information generation far outstrips the rate at which our own cognitive capacity evolves to consume it. We still read and comprehend information at the same rate that our ancestors did. A widening gap is created between the information production and consumption capacity. New algorithms are needed to bridge this gap while preserving the quality of information (QoI) for the receivers as much as possible.

Today, thanks to social networks and sensors, each of us can be a broadcast source. Collectively, we constitute a unique state observer of ongoing events. We call this act, *social sensing*. To bridge the widening gap between data generation and consumption rates, new algorithms must cut noise from unreliable sources and focus receiver attention on a small subset of relevant and credible observations. In this book, we focus on the reliability aspects of this data distillation process. Extracting reliable information from large noisy social sensing data sets is not as easy as it seems. Wide-spread rumors, for example, can give rise to what appears to be highly corroborated claims. Nevertheless, the claims in question could be false. A mathematical framework is needed to correctly analyze the reliability of observations originating from generally unvetted or unreliable sources, interconnected by complex social, cultural, and geographic links. Such a framework is developed in this book.

Using mathematical techniques described in this book, the reader is familiarized with analytic machinery needed to produce reliable conclusions from unreliable social sensing data. These techniques will allow use of crowd-sensing to gather information from untrained, unvetted sources, without compromising reliability guarantees needed for mission-critical applications. Much in the same way that Kalman Filters allow us to recover state estimates from noisy data while rigorously quantifying the estimation error, the techniques described in this book allow us to recover ground truth from social sensing data while quantifying reliability bounds. The uniqueness of humans as highly individualized sensors of unknown specifications makes the process more challenging. The book takes the reader on a journey of discovery through the mathematical underpinning of building reliable systems on unreliable data. We hope that techniques developed in this book will become part of the solution space in dealing with information explosion in the age of broadcast. These techniques can help eliminate unnecessary redundancy, cut noise, and focus receiver attention in the next generation of sensory-analytics, intelligence, and cyber-physical applications.

A new information age

Twenty years ago, your best bet to find information was to go to a library, search through a pile of index cards, find your way through rows of shelves, and borrow a book. Ten years ago, your best bet to let your friends know of your latest endeavors was to call them. These days are long gone.

One of the most remarkable advances in the last decade was the advent of an age of real-time broadcast. An author of this book remembers a recent ride in a hot air balloon that he happened to share with a newly-wed couple. They were taking a lot of pictures. When the ride was over, they were met with friends. The first question they asked their friends was: "Have you seen our air pictures on Facebook?." Indeed, information about the experience had already preceded them to the ground.

The age of modern broadcast is enabled by a confluence of three technological advances. First, we now have an unprecedented connectivity on the move, apparently, even while in a hot air balloon. Second, we have an increasingly rich set of options for broadcasting information. Twitter, Facebook, YouTube, Instagram, Flickr, and Foursquare are just a few examples. Finally, we live in a world of information acquisition (i.e., sensing) devices that we use on daily basis. Cameras, GPS devices, fitbits, smart watches, and Internet-connected cars are generating significant amounts of data that we may or may not choose to share.

A direct consequence of the age of broadcast is information overload. In point-to-point communication (such as a phone call), a minute consumed by the initiator corresponds to a minute consumed by the responder. Hence, a balance exists between the collective capacity consumed at sources and the collective capacity consumed at sinks. In contrast, on broadcast channels, for every minute consumed at the broadcast source, hours may be collectively consumed by the community of receivers. For example, if a 1-minute broadcast message is read by 1000 recipients, then 1000 minutes are collectively consumed at the receivers for the one minute spent at the source. This is fine when the number of sources is a lot smaller than the number of receivers (e.g., think of the number of radio stations compared to the number of listeners). However, in the current age of democratized real-time broadcast, everyone can be a source. A survey in 2014, suggested that more than 1 Billion users were on Twitter, more than 1.3 Billion on Facebook, and more than 1.5 Billion on Google+. On Twitter, your message is visible to all. The underlying paradigm is one of global broadcast. Given that everyone can be a broadcast source, the balance between production and consumption is disrupted. The proliferation of sensing devices further exacerbates the imbalance. Consequently, a gap widens between the capacity of sources to generate information and the capacity of sinks to consume it. This widening gap heralds a new era of services whose main function is to summarize large amounts of broadcast data into a smaller amount of actionable information for receivers.

A key class of summarization services in the new age of real-time broadcast are services that attain situation awareness. Much of the information uploaded on social media constitutes acts of sensing. In other words, sources report observations they made regarding their physical environment and found worthwhile to comment on. We call this phenomenon, *social sensing*. In their raw form, however, these observations are not very useful and generally lack reliability. There are conflicting sentiments, conflicting claims, missing data, purposeful pieces of misinformation, and other noise.

Table 1.1 shows examples of tweets collected from Syria on Twitter in August 2013, in the week following the sudden deaths of thousands of citizens in Ghouta; a suburb near the capital, Damascus. It can be seen that many different claims are posted, some of which are true but others are pure conjecture, rumors, or even intentionally planted misinformation. Hence, the use of social sensing data, such as tweets on Twitter, for enhancing situation awareness must be done with care. A key problem is to extract reliable information from large amounts of generally less reliable social sensing data. Recently, significant advances were made on this topic.

We formally define social sensing as the act of collection of observations about the physical environment from humans or devices acting on their behalf. Assessing data reliability is a fundamental research challenge in this field. This challenge, if successfully addressed, may engender a paradigm shift in situation awareness by allowing development of dependable applications with guaranteed correctness properties that rely on the collective observations of untrained, average, and largely unreliable sources. In this chapter, we introduce this problem, go over the underlying technical enablers and motivations of social sensing applications, and discuss several key challenges and state-of-the-art solutions. We then review the organization of the book, chapter by chapter, to offer a reading guide for the remainder of the book.

1.1 OVERVIEW

The idea of leveraging the collective wisdom of the crowd has been around for some time [1, 2]. Today, massive amounts of data are continually being collected and shared (e.g., on social networks) by average individuals that may be used for a myriad of societal applications, from a global neighborhood watch to reducing transportation delays and improving the efficacy of disaster response. Little is analytically known about data validity in this new sensing paradigm, where sources are noisy, unreliable, erroneous, and largely unknown. This motivates a closer look into recent advances in social sensing with an emphasis on the key problem faced by application designers; namely, how to extract reliable information from data collected from largely unknown and possibly unreliable sources? Novel solutions that leverage techniques from

Table 1.1 A Twitter Example

Medecins Sans Frontieres says it treated about 3,600 patients with 'neurotoxic symptoms' in Syria, of whom 355 died http://t.co/eHWY77jdS0
Weapons expert says #Syria footage of alleged chemical attack "difficult to fake" http://t.co/zfDMujaCTV
U.N. experts in Syria to visit site of poison gas attack http://t.co/jol8OlFxnf via @reuters #PJNET
Syria Gas Attack: 'My Eyes Were On Fire' http://t.co/z76MiHj0Em
Saudis offer Russia secret oil deal if it drops Syria via Telegraph http://t.co/iOutxSiaRs
Long-term nerve damage feared after Syria chemical attack http://t.co/8vw7BiOxQR
Syrian official blames rebels for deadly attack http://t.co/76ncmy4eqb
Assad regime responsible for Syrian chemical attack, says UK government http://t.co/pMZ5z7CsNZ
Syrian Chemical Weapons Attack Carried Out by Rebels, Says UN (UPDATE) http://t.co/lN4CkUePUj #Syria http://t.co/tTorVFUfZF
US forces move closer to Syria as options weighed: WASHINGTON (AP) – U.S. naval forces are moving closer to Sy...http://t.co/F6UAAXLa2M
Putin Orders Massive Strike Against Saudi Arabia If West Attacks Syria http://t.co/SFLJ9ghwbt
400 tonnes of arms sent into #Syria through Turkey to boost Syria rebels after CW attack in Damascus – > http://t.co/KLwESYChCc
UN Syria team departs hotel as Assad denies attack http://t.co/O3SqPoiq0x
Vehicle of UN #Syria #ChemicalWeapons team hit by sniper fire. Team replacing vehicle & then returning to area.
International weapons experts leave Syria, U.S. prepares attack. More http://t.co/4Z62RhQKOE
Military strike on Syria would cause retaliatory attack on Israel, Iran declares http://t.co/M950o5VcgW
Asia markets fall on Syria concerns: Asian stocks fall, extending a global market sell-off sparked by growing ...http://t.co/06A9h2xCnJ
Syria Warns of False Flag Chemical Attack!
UK Prime Minister Cameron loses Syria war vote (from AP) http://t.co/UlFF1wY9gx

machine learning, information fusion, and data mining recently offer significant progress on this problem and are described in this book.

In situations, where the reliability of sources is known, it is easy to compute the probability of correctness of different observations. Among other alternatives, one can use, say, Bayesian analysis to fuse data from sources of different (known) degrees of reliability. The distinguishing challenge in social sensing applications is that the reliability of sources is often unknown. For example, much of the chatter on social networks might come from users who are unknown to the data collection system. Hence, it is hard to assess the reliability of their observations. The same is true of situations, where individuals download a smartphone app that allows them to contribute to a social sensing data collection campaign. If anyone is allowed to participate, the pool of sources is unvetted and the reliability of individual observers is generally unknown to the data collector. It is in this context that the problem of ascertaining data reliability becomes challenging. The challenge arises from the fact that one neither knows the sources, nor can immediately verify their claims. What can be rigorously said, in this case, about the correctness of collected data? More specifically, how can one jointly ascertain data correctness and source reliability in social sensing applications? The problem is of importance in many domains and, as such, touches upon several areas of active research.

In sensor networks, an important challenge has always been to derive accurate representations of physical state and physical context from possibly unreliable, non-specific, or weak proxies. Often one trades off quantity and quality. While individual sensors may be less reliable, collectively (using the ingenious analysis techniques published in various sensor network venues) they may yield reliable conclusions. Much of the research in that area focused on physical sensors. This includes dedicated devices embedded in their environment, as well as human-centric sensing devices such as cell-phones and wearables. Recent research proposed challenges with the use of humans as sensors. Clearly, humans differ from traditional physical devices in many respects. Importantly to our reliability analysis, they lack a design specification and a reliability standard, making it hard to define a generic noise model for sources. Each human is its own individual with different model parameters that predict how good that individual person's observations are. Hence, many techniques that estimate probability of error for sensors do not apply, since they assume the same error model for all sensors.

Humans also exhibit other interesting artifacts not common to physical sensors, such as gossiping. It is usually hard to tell where a particular observation originated. Even if we are able to unambiguously authenticate the source, who we received some observation from, it is hard to tell if the source made that observation themselves, or heard it from another. Hence, the original provenance of observations may remain uncertain. Techniques described in this book offer analytic means to determine source reliability and mitigate uncertainty in data provenance.

Reputation systems is another area of research, where source reliability is the issue. The assumption is that, when sources are observed over time, their reliability is eventually uncovered. Social sensing applications, however, often deal with scenarios, where a new event requires data collection from sources who have not previously participated in other data collection campaigns, or perhaps not been "tested" in the unique circumstances of the current event. For example, a hurricane strikes New Jersey. This is a rare event. We do not know how accurate the individuals who fled the event are at describing damage left behind. No reputation is accumulated for them in such a scenario. Yet, it would be desirable to leverage their collective observations to deploy help in a more efficient and timely manner. How do we determine which observations to believe?

In cyber-physical systems (CPS) research, an important emphasis has always been on ensuring validity and on proving that systems meet specifications [3–5]. The topics of reliability, predictability, and performance guarantees receive much attention. While past research on CPS addressed correctness of software systems (even in the presence of unverified code), in today's data-driven world, a key emerging challenge becomes to ascertain correctness of data (even in the presence of unverified sources). The challenge is promoted by the need to account for the humans in the loop. Humans are the drivers in transportation systems, the occupants in building energy management systems, the survivors and first responders in disaster response systems, and the patients in medical systems. It makes sense to utilize their input when trying to assess system state. For example, one can get a more accurate account of current vehicular traffic state and more accurate prediction of its future evolution, if driver input was taken into account in some global, real-time, and automated fashion. This is assuming that the inputs are reliable, which is not always the case. The reliable social sensing problem, if solved, would enable the development of dependable applications in domains of transportation, energy, disaster response, and military intelligence, among others, where correctness is guaranteed despite reliance on the collective observations of untrained, average, and largely unreliable sources.

Techniques described in this book are also of relevance to business analytics applications, where one is interested in making sense out of large amounts of unreliable data. These techniques can thus serve applications in social networks, big data, and human-in-the-loop systems, and leverage the proliferation of computing artifacts that interact with or monitor the physical world. The goal of this book is to offer the needed theoretical foundations that exploit advances in social sensing analytics to support emerging data-driven applications. The book also touches on contemporary issues, such as privacy, in a highly interconnected and instrumented world.

1.2 CHALLENGES

Social sensing described in this book broadly refers to three types of data collection: (i) *participatory sensing*, (ii) *opportunistic sensing*, and (iii) *social data scavenging*. In participatory sensing, individuals are explicitly and actively involved in the sensing process, and choose to perform some critical operations (e.g., operating the sensors, performing certain tasks, etc.) to meet application requirements. In opportunistic sensing, individuals are passively involved, for example, by pre-authorizing their sensing device to share information on behalf of the owner whenever contacted by the indicated data collection agent to meet application requirements [6]. Social data scavenging refers to a sensing paradigm, where individuals remain unaware of the data collection process. An example is where social networks are treated as sensor networks. Public data posted on social networks (e.g., Twitter) are searched for relevant items. In social data scavenging, the participants "agree" to the fact that their posts are in the public domain and they are simply unaware how the public may actually use their information.

A classical example of a social sensing application is geo-tagging campaigns, where participants report conditions in their environment that need attention (e.g., litter in public parks), tagged by location. More recent examples of social sensing applications include enhancing real-time situation awareness in the aftermath of disasters using online social media, and traffic condition prediction using GPS traces collected from smartphones.

We henceforth call the challenge of jointly ascertaining the correctness of collected data and the reliability of data sources the *reliable social sensing* problem. In traditional sensing scenarios such as participatory and opportunistic sensing, data sources are sensors, typically in human possession. In the data scavenging scenario, individuals are represented by sensors (data sources) who occasionally make observations about the physical world. These observations may be true or false, and hence can be viewed as binary claims.

The term, participant (or source) reliability is used to denote the odds that a source reports a correct observation. Reliability may be impaired because of poor sensor quality, lack of sensor calibration, lack of (human) attention to the task, or even intent to deceive. Data collection is often open to a large population, where it is impossible to screen all participants (or information sources) beforehand. The likelihood that a participant's measurements are correct is usually unknown a priori. Consequently, it is challenging to ascertain the correctness of the collected data. It is also challenging to ascertain the reliability of each information source without knowing whether their collected data are correct or not. Therefore, the main questions posed in the reliable social sensing problem are (i) whether or not one can determine, given only the measurements sent and without knowing the reliability of sources, which of the reported observations are true and which are not, and (ii) how reliable each source is without independent ways to verify the correctness of their measurements. This also requires one to address how reliability is formally quantified.

1.3 STATE OF THE ART

Prior research on social sensing can be mainly classified into three categories (i.e., discount data fusion, trust and reputation systems, and fact-finding techniques) based on whether the prior knowledge of source reliability and claim correctness or credibility is known to the application. We discuss the state-of-the-art techniques in these categories in detail below.

1.3.1 EFFORTS ON DISCOUNT FUSION

When we have prior knowledge about the reliability of the sources but no prior knowledge of the correctness or credibility of the claims (information), one can filter the noise in the claims via fusion. This is a classic case for the target tracking community where disparate sensor systems (the sources) generate tracks that must be combined. The tracks are estimates of the kinematic state of the target, and the reliability of the sources is expressed as a state covariance error for the tracks. The expression for the fused state estimate by accounting for all the sensors as a function of the tracks and error covariances is well known [7–11]. When the sensor tracks are uncorrelated, the fused track can be interpreted as a weighted average of the senor tracks where the weights are proportional to the inverse of the error covariances for the sensors. The general expression for correlated tracks is slightly more complicated, but it is reasonable to interpret the track fusion process as discounting the tracks based on their reliability followed by a combining process. The difficulty in track fusion is determining which tracks for the various sensors associate for the fusion process. Techniques for track-to-track association do exist [12, 13], but they rely on understanding the correlation of tracks from different sensors. Unfortunately, it is not known how to determine this correlation when the tracks are formed for each sensor in a distributed manner.

In the information fusion community, belief theory provides the mechanism to combine evidence from multiple possibly conflicting sources [14–16]. The concept of discounting beliefs based upon source reliability before fusion goes back to Shafer [14]. Recently, subjective logic has emerged as a means to reason over conflicting evidence [17]. Subjective opinions are formed from evidence observed from individual sources. When incorporating multiple opinions, the subjective opinions need to be discounted similar to Dempster-Shafer theory before consensus fusion. In essence, this form of discount fusion can be interpreted as a weighted sum of evidence where the weights are proportional to the source reliabilities. The consensus fusion operation in subjective logic assumes the evidence used to form the subjective opinions of the sources are independent. Current research is investigating the proper fusion rule when the sources incorporate correlated evidence.

1.3.2 EFFORTS ON TRUST AND REPUTATION SYSTEMS

When we have prior knowledge of the correctness or credibility of claims (information) but no prior knowledge on the reliability of sources, a lot of work in trust and reputation systems make efforts to assess the reliability of sources (e.g., the quality of providers) [18–21]. The basic idea of reputation systems is to let entities rate each other (e.g., after a transaction) or review some objects of common interests (e.g., products or dealers), and use the aggregated ratings to derive trust or reputation scores of both sources and objects in the systems [18]. These reputation scores can help other entities in deciding whether or not to trust a given entity or purchase a certain object [19]. Trust and reputation scores can be obtained from both individual and social perspectives [22, 23]. Individual trust often comes from experiences of direct interaction with transaction partners while social trust is computed from third-party experiences, which might include both honest and misleading opinions. Different types of reputation systems are being used successfully in commercial online applications [24–27]. For example, eBay is a type of reputation system based on homogeneous peer-to-peer systems, which allows peers to rate each other after each pair of them conduct a transaction [24, 25]. Amazon on-line review system represents another type of reputation systems, where different sources offer reviews on products (or brands, companies) they have experienced [26, 27]. Customers are affected by those reviews (or reputation scores) in making purchase decisions. Various techniques and models have also been developed to detect deceitful behaviors of participants [28, 29] and identify discriminating attitudes and fraudulent activities [30, 31] in the trust and reputation systems to provide reliable service in an open and dynamic environment. Recent work has investigated consistency of reports to estimate and revise trust scores in reputation system [32, 33].

1.3.3 EFFORTS ON FACT-FINDING

Given no prior knowledge on the reliability of sources and the credibility of their claims (information), there exists substantial work on techniques referred to as *fact-finders* within data mining and machine learning communities that jointly compute the source reliability and claim credibility. The inspiration of fact-finders can be traced by Google's PageRank [34]. PageRank iteratively ranks the credibility of pages on the Web, by considering the credibility of pages that link to them. In fact-finders, they estimate the credibility of claims from the reliability of sources that make them, then estimate the reliability of sources based on the credibility of their claims. *Hubs and Authorities* [35] established a basic fact-finder model based on linear assumptions to compute scores for sources and claims they asserted. Yin et al. introduced *TruthFinder* as an unsupervised fact-finder for trust analysis on a providers-facts network [36]. Other fact-finders enhanced these basic frameworks by incorporating analysis on properties [37–39] or dependencies within claims or sources [40–43]. More recent works came up with some new fact-finding algorithms designed to handle the background knowledge [44, 45] and multi-valued facts [46], provide semantics to the credibility scores [47], and use slot filling systems for multi-dimensional fact-finding [48]. A comprehensive survey of fact-finders used in the context of trust analysis of information networks can be found in [49].

The book reviews in great detail a comprehensive analytical framework that optimally (in the sense of maximum likelihood estimation, MLE) solves the reliable social sensing problem and rigorously analyzes the accuracy of the results, offering correctness guarantees on solid theoretical foundations [50]. It is the notion of quantified correctness guarantees in social sensing that sets the purpose of this book apart from other reviews of data mining, social networks, and sensing literature. The developed techniques can be applied to a new range of reliable social sensing applications, where assurances of data correctness are needed before such data can be used by the application, in order to meet higher level dependability guarantees.

1.4 ORGANIZATION

The rest of this book familiarizes the reader with recent advances in addressing the reliable social sensing problem. These contributions help establish the foundations of building reliable systems on unreliable data to support social sensing applications with correctness guarantees.

- Chapter 2 reviews the emerging social sensing trends and applications. In this chapter, we outline several recent technical trends that herald the era of social sensing. Some early research in participatory and opportunistic sensing are first reviewed. We then describe social data scavenging, a new social sensing data collection paradigm that is motivated by the popularity of online social networks and large information dissemination opportunities. At the end of the chapter, we discuss the prospective future of social sensing.
- Chapter 3 reviews mathematical foundations and basic technologies that we will use in this book. These foundations include basics of information networks, Bayesian analysis, MLE, expectation maximization (EM), as well as bounds and confidence intervals in estimation theory. The chapter concludes with an analytical framework that allows us to put all these foundations together.
- Chapter 4 reviews the state-of-the-art fact-finders with the emphasis on an analytically-founded Bayesian interpretation of the basic fact-finding scheme that is popularly used in data-mining literature to rank both sources and their asserted information based on credibility values. This interpretation enables the calculation of correct probabilities of conclusions resulting from information network analysis. Such probabilities constitute a measure of quality of information (QoI), which can be used to directly quantify participant reliability and measurement correctness in social sensing context.
- Chapter 5 reviews a MLE scheme that casts the reliable social sensing problem into an EM framework which can be solved optimally and efficiently. The EM algorithm makes inferences regarding both participant reliability and measurement correctness by observing which observations coincide and which do not. It was shown to be very accurate and outperforms the state-of-the-art fact-finders.
- Chapter 6 reviews the work to obtain the confidence bounds of the MLE presented in Chapter 5. In particular, we first setup the reliability assurance problem in social sensing and then review real and asymptotic confidence bounds in participant reliability estimation of the EM scheme. The confidence bounds are computed using the Cramer-Rao lower bound (CRLB) from estimation theory. In addition to the confidence bounds, we present a rigorous sensitivity analysis of such confidence bounds as a function of information network topology. This analysis offers a fundamental understanding of the capabilities and limitations of the MLE model. Finally, we review a real world case study that evaluates the confidence bounds presented in this chapter.
- Chapter 7 reviews a generalization of the basic MLE model presented in previous chapters to address conflicting observations and non-binary claims. The basic model presented in Chapter 5 assumes only corroborating observations from participants. In this chapter, we review the work that generalizes the basic model to solve more complex problems, where conflicting observations exist. This effort was motivated by the fact that observations from different participants in social sensing applications may be mutually contradicting. A real world case study is presented to evaluate the generalized model in a real world

social sensing application. Another assumption of the basic model is that the claims were assumed to be binary. We review the work that further generalizes the theory for conflicting observations and non-binary claims.

- Chapter 8 reviews recent work that leverages the understanding of the underlying information dissemination topology to better solve the reliable social sensing problem. What makes this sensing problem formulation different is that, in the case of human participants, not only is the reliability of sources usually unknown but also the original data provenance may be uncertain. Individuals may report observations made by others as their own. Therefore, we review a novel abstraction that models humans as sensors of unknown reliability generating binary measurements of uncertain provenance. This human sensor model considers the impact of information sharing among human participants through social networks on the analytical foundations of reliable social sensing. We also review a real-world case study that evaluates the human sensor model using Twitter as the experimental platform.

- Chapter 9 reviews work that explores physical dependencies between observed variables to improve the estimation accuracy of reliable social sensing. The observed variables reported in social sensing applications that describe the state of the physical world usually have inherent dependencies. We review a cyber-physical approach to solve the problem by exploiting the physical constraints to compensate for unknown source reliability. These physical constraints shape the likelihood function that quantifies the odds of the observations at hand. We show that the maximum likelihood estimate obtained by this new approach is a lot more accurate than one that does not take physical constraints into account. At the end of the chapter, we review a real world case study to showcase the cyber-physical approach in a crowd-sensing application.

- Chapter 10 reviews the work in recursive fact-finding that is designed to address the real-time streaming data challenges in social sensing. The original EM scheme is an iterative algorithm that is mainly designed to run on static data sets. However, such computation is not suited for streaming data because we need to re-run the algorithm on the whole dataset from scratch every time the dataset gets updated. We review a recursive EM algorithm for streaming data that considers incremental data updates, and updates past results in view of new data in a recursive way. The recursive EM algorithm was shown to achieve a nice performance tradeoff between estimation accuracy and the algorithm execution time.

- Chapter 11 points readers to further readings in related areas of social sensing. These areas include estimation theory, data quality, trust analysis, outlier and attack detection, recommender systems, surveys, and opinion polling. The point of this chapter is to help readers better place the work reviewed in this book in the context of broader literature from different communities. Readers are encouraged to investigate beyond the recommended work, identify new problems, and advance the state-of-the-arts in social sensing.

- Chapter 12 concludes the book with a summary of theories, techniques, and methods presented. It provides the readers an opportunity to recap the key problems and solutions presented in each chapter as well as the overall picture of the entire book. At the end of this chapter, we also outline remaining challenges that need to be appropriately addressed in future social sensing applications. These directions can potentially serve as topics for future graduate theses, course projects, and publications.

With this book, we hope to bridge several communities: for CPS researchers, we would like to draw the parallel between system reliability and data reliability, and argue for the growing importance of investigating the latter to support crowd-sensing, humans in the loop, and emerging data-driven CPS applications of the foreseeable future. This should hopefully encourage collaborations between CPS, machine learning, and data mining fields. For sensor networks researchers, we would like to offer the analogy between sensors and humans who happen to share their observations. The book presents a model of humans as sensors that allows rigorous data fusion theory to be applied, while capturing some essential properties of human behavior. For individuals involved in business analytics, we would like to offer a range of solutions that extract reliable and actionable information from large amounts of unreliable data. This will hopefully encourage collaboration between sensor network, social network, and data fusion researchers, in both academia and industry. The outcome could be to disseminate knowledge on building new sensing and data analytics systems that effectively combine inputs from humans and machines, while offering rigorous reliability guarantees, similar to those obtained from physical (hard) data fusion and signal analysis.

Social sensing trends and applications

2

2.1 INFORMATION SHARING: THE PARADIGM SHIFT

Humans are indeed the most versatile sensors. They can make judgments, where traditional sensing technology falls short. They are already embedded in spaces that are interesting to measure. They are good at understanding context, detecting anomalies, interpreting complex scenes, and prioritizing information transfer. Hence, leveraging their help can lead to a better understanding of many human-centric eco-systems, such as urban spaces, transportation systems, agricultural processes, human-operated supply chains, and residential energy consumption, to name a few. Several surveys appeared in recent literature that offer different visions for the social sensing landscape [51, 52]. There are many ways humans can be involved in sensing systems. For example, they may serve as:

- **Information sources:** The versatility of humans as sophisticated observers of their surroundings has led to their exploitation as information sources since the early days of civilization. Military intelligence, for example, has relied on human sources long before the introduction of physical sensors. The recent advent of social networks reaffirms the importance of humans as an information source. Coupled with technological advances that enable instantaneous global information transfer, media that collect grassroots human observations are supplanting the news in delivery of timely information. The author has recently been in a conversation with a friend from California, who confessed that when experiencing what feels like an Earthquake, he first turns to Twitter. Chances are, if this is not a false alarm, the social network will already be teaming with real-time tweets announcing the event.

- **Sensor operators:** Humans can alternatively operate sensors such as cameras or geotagging apps. In this case, we still leverage the versatility of humans in identifying what sensory observations to report. However, the act of sensing itself is carried out by another device, under human control. Early participatory sensing applications adopt this model. A common application in that category is geotagging. Humans would participate in geotagging campaigns, where the goal is generally to record locations of observations of interest. For example, a campaign might record locations of invasive species in a park, or locations of offensive graffiti on city walls. The human would have to observe the item of interest, then take a picture or push a button on their phone to record the current location.

- **Sensor conveyors:** Humans increasingly serve as sensor conveyances. For example, they carry smartphones that now come equipped with an impressive array of sensors, they drive cars that have many sensors of their own, and they wear smart pieces such as watches and vision devices (e.g., Glass), that can record events on the move. The exploitation of human mobility for ferrying sensors is natural in applications that aim at measurements of social spaces. It offers coverage of the space and has a natural tendency to deliver more measurements from more heavily utilized (and hence, typically more important) areas.

- **Sensor data processors:** It is common for humans to process sensory data as well. For example, tagging your friend in a picture on Facebook is an act of sensory data processing. In this act, the potentially complex scene in the original picture (which itself is a sensor output) is processed by you. The processing results in the generation of additional metadata (the tags) that can, in principle, be exploited by collection applications downstream. Individuals post comments on photos, which also constitute sensory data processing for the same reason. The emergence of crowd-sourcing platforms, such as the Mechanical Turk [53], enables large-scale application of human capabilities to sensor data processing tasks. Humans can also perform data fusion and analysis, producing their own inferences and opinions regarding the underlying observations, and sharing information of higher semantic content. For example, they may recognize a video to indicate that "police attacks demonstrators" or that "demonstrators attack police," a distinction that is harder to do in an automated fashion by a machine.

In addition to the role humans play in sensing, it is often interesting to distinguish the manner in which they participate. For example, they may explicitly and intentionally join a sensing campaign or may simply be sharing data on social media with no awareness of the sensing application. They may share data on their own, out of conviction to do a public good, or may be incentivized to do it in exchange for a benefit. As mentioned earlier, a confluence of three social and technology trends explains the increasing ubiquity of social sensing. Those trends are:

- *Sensing device proliferation:* The first trend that fuels social sensing applications is the commercial proliferation of sensing systems that are commonly accessible to large consumer populations. Active RFIDs, smart residential power meters (with a wireless interface), camera cell-phones, in-vehicle GPS devices, accelerometer-enhanced entertainment platforms (e.g., Wii-fit), and activity monitoring sportsware (e.g., the Nike+iPod system) have all reached mature market penetration, offering unprecedented opportunities for data collection.

- *Mobile connectivity:* The second trend lies in ubiquitous mobile Internet access available to sensing platforms on the move. This untethered connectivity allows events to be measured and reported in real time, anytime, anywhere. A clear example is the case of GPS measurements and pictures taken by cell-phones. Besides GPS and cameras, modern smartphones currently host myriads of other sensors as well, such as accelerometers, magnetometers, and gyroscopes, and offer 3G/4G, WiFi, and Bluetooth network access, which enables sharing their data. Vehicular Internet access, is also becoming available, for example, Chrysler and BMW were some of the earliest car manufacturers to enable applications that exploit network connectivity. The vehicular OBD-II interface is already being used by services such as OnStar for remote diagnostics. Other applications may perform traffic statistics, alert to nearby accidents, or detect emergency conditions. In medical spaces, significant investments have been made in sensor technology for longitudinal monitoring. Microsoft HealthVault was one early example of an initiative to automate collection of and access to medical information. A significant number of vendors announced wearable health and biometric monitoring sensors that automatically upload user data to HealthVault. WiThings, a company that offers a variety of WiFi enabled health and fitness monitoring devices is another example of sensors in social spaces. The proliferation of sensing devices with Internet connectivity that collect data in social spaces makes it feasible to build human-centric data collection and sharing applications that augment human capabilities and improve situation awareness.
- *Social networks:* The existence of sensors and Internet connectivity, however, would not have been sufficient, by itself, to support social sensing in the mainstream. The third key trend that fueled social sensing was the increased popularity of mass information dissemination channels, afforded by social networks. Twitter, Flickr, Twitpic, YouTube, and other networks allow individuals to globally broadcast their observations. It is this global dissemination opportunity that makes it easy to build large-scale applications that utilize commonly-available sensors, upload data in real-time, and share the observations at scale.

The above opportunities have generated significant interest in the research community in building application prototypes that rely on observations made by humans or by sensors in their vicinity. Below, we present an application taxonomy then outline recent work related to social sensing, and conclude with a note on privacy.

2.2 AN APPLICATION TAXONOMY

One can generally divide social sensing applications into three types, depending on their functionality. The three types differ in the level of complexity of data processing done to the measurements.

- *Data-point-centric applications:* The first and simplest social sensing application is one where individuals share single data points (the observations) that are then made available to clients or decision-makers. An example is geo-tagging applications, where individuals share pictures (tagged by location) of entities of relevance to the application. For example, a sensing campaign might ask participants to document locations of invasive species in a park, or locations of garbage on a beach. These observations (and pictures) can then be displayed on a map, or offered to municipal decision-makers for appropriate action.
- *Statistics-centric applications:* The second type of social sensing applications is one where statistics are computed from the data. An example might be a traffic speed monitoring or a pollution monitoring application where the speed or pollution levels measured by different individuals are used to compute statistics such as averages and probability distributions. Many early examples of social sensing belong in that category. For example, traffic patterns were monitored in a city to help drivers avoid congestion areas [54], bike route data were collected by biking enthusiasts to help them pick better routes [55], and hiker encounters were recorded on mountain trails to help locate missing hikers [56]. These applications offer useful statistics about a given locale that are of interest to individuals in that locale.
- *Model-centric applications:* A third and most general type of social sensing applications has been described in literature, where *generalizable models* are learned from sensory data collection, that can be used to affect human decision making outside of the collection locale. For example, sharing data collected by smart energy meters installed in some households, together with relevant context, can lead to a better understanding of energy consumption in contemporary homes and best practices that increase energy efficiency elsewhere around the nation. Similarly, sharing data collected by activity sensors among fitness enthusiasts can lead to lifestyle recipes that promote healthier behaviors for multitudes of others. Also, sharing data on environmental pollutants and personal well-being (e.g., locations and incidents of asthma attacks) can establish links between likelihood of attacks and exposure to specific contaminants, which may help individuals reduce their exposure to those contaminants. In a recent study of vehicular fuel-efficiency, a model predicts the total fuel consumption for a vehicle on a road segment as a function of several variables such as road speed, degree of congestion, and vehicle parameters. Once the model is known, it is possible to optimize human decisions by offering better (GPS) navigation advice for any vehicle on any street.

2.3 EARLY RESEARCH

An early overview of social sensing applications is presented in [57]. Some early applications include CenWits [56], a participatory sensor network to search and rescue hikers in emergency situations, CarTel [54], a vehicular sensor network for traffic monitoring and mitigation, CabSense [58], an application that analyzes GPS data from NYC taxis and helps you find the best corner to catch a cab [59] and BikeNet [55], a bikers sensor network for sharing cycling related data and mapping the cyclist experience. More recently, social sensing applications in healthcare have become popular. Numerous medical devices have been built with embedded sensors that can be used to monitor the personal health of patients, or send alters to the clinic or through the patient's social network when something unexpected happens. Such social sensing can be used for activity recognition for emergency response [60], long term prediction of diseases [61–63], and life-style changes that affect health [64, 65].

Early work in social sensing focused on challenges such as preserving privacy of participants [66, 67], improving energy efficiency of sensing devices [68, 69] and building general models in sparse and multi-dimensional social sensing spaces [70, 71]. Examples include privacy-aware regression modeling, a data fusion technique that produces the same model as that computed from raw data by properly computing non-invertible aggregates of samples [66]. Authors in [67] gave special attention to preserving privacy over time-series data based on the observation that a sensor data stream typically comprises a correlated series of sampled data from some continuous physical phenomena. Acquisitional Context Engine (ACE) is a middleware that infers unknown human activity attributes from known ones by exploiting the observation that the values of various human context attributes are limited by physical constraints and hence are highly correlated [68]. E-Gesture is an energy efficient gesture recognition architecture that significantly reduces the energy consumption of mobile sensing devices while keeping the recognition accuracy acceptable [69]. The sparse regression cube is a modeling technique that combines estimation theory and data mining techniques to enable reliable modeling at multiple degrees of abstraction of sparse social sensing data [70]. A further improved model to consider the data collection cost was proposed in [71].

The concept of sensing campaigns have been introduced in literature, where participants are recruited to contribute their personal measurements as part of a large-scale effort to collect data about a population or a geographical area. Examples include documenting the quality of roads [72], measuring the level of pollution in a city [73], or reporting locations of garbage cans on campus [74]. In addition, social sensing covers scenarios where human sources spontaneously report data without prior coordination, such as data describing important events. Examples include large volumes of reported observations of political unrest, riots, and natural disasters on Twitter. Recent research attempts to understand the fundamental factors that affect the behavior of these emerging social sensing applications, such as analysis of characteristics of social networks [75], information propagation [76], and tipping points [77].

A critical question about trustworthiness arises when the data in social sensing applications are collected by humans whose "reliability" is not known. In social sensing, anyone can contribute data. Such openness greatly increases the availability of the information and the diversity of its sources. On the other hand, it introduces the problem of understanding the reliability of the contributing sources and ensuring the quality of the information collected. Trusted Platform Module (TPM), commonly used in commodity PCs, can be used to provide a certain level of assurance at the expense of additional hardware [78]. YouProve is a recent technique that relies on trust analysis of derived data to allow untrusted client applications to verify that the meaning of source data is preserved [79]. Trust analysis can also be performed at the server side by building a likelihood function for sensed data to provide a quantifiable estimate of both source reliability and the correctness of observations. A rich set of work that are referred to as fact-finders have been developed to perform trust analysis in information networks by jointly assessing the reliability of sources and the credibility of facts reported by them. A detailed review of literature on fact-finders is provided in Chapter 4.

2.4 THE PRESENT TIME

Information distillation (or reduction of large amounts of data into smaller amounts of actionable information) is an increasingly important interaction modality between humans and data. Information distillation services are made popular by a shift in the digital information landscape. This shift is from a web of slowly updated cross-linked objects (e.g., Web pages) to streams of continually generated real-time data emitted by humans and sensors. The availability of real-time data offers both new opportunities and new challenges. There are unprecedented opportunities for building real-time situation awareness applications such as disaster-response services that help first-responders assess current damage, transportation advisories that help individuals avoid traffic bottlenecks, and citizen-science tools that collect and process data from speciality sensors (such as rain gauges or pollution sensors) owned by interested individuals. Reliable information must be distilled from unreliable data. Applications that use the data must address modeling challenges, in order to offer predictive services that learn from past observations. Several categories of sensing applications were discussed ranging from those where humans collect data points that are individually significant to those where models or statistical properties of aggregates are sought.

Many other challenges remain topics of current research. Those include front-end challenges (e.g., energy consumption), coordination challenges (e.g., participatory sensing campaign recruitment), back-end challenges (e.g., modeling and prediction), and challenges in the overall understanding of the emergent behavior of social sensing systems at large. While a significant amount of research has already been undertaken along those fronts, much remains unsolved. New interdisciplinary research is needed to bring about better solutions for a better theoretical understanding of emerging social sensing systems in a future sensor- and media-rich world. In the rest of this book, we focus on one such challenge: namely, the challenge of ascertaining data reliability.

2.5 **A NOTE ON PRIVACY**

A discussion of social sensing would not be complete without commenting on a topic that lies at the crux of information sharing; namely, that of user privacy. What do advances in social sensing mean in terms of privacy expectations of individuals? There has been significant advances in research on user privacy, but the problem is by no means solved. It is the authors' belief, however, that privacy will be solved through legal protection and not by technical means.

It is interesting to observe that modern society has already given up on privacy in very significant ways. For example, while most would consider a credit card number to be private data, they share that number voluntarily with complete strangers on regular basis; often multiple times a day! Every time we use a credit card at a restaurant, a waiter we might have never seen before disappears with our card but we prefer to use our cards instead of cash. The reason is simple: we trust the legal system to be efficient at catching credit card fraud. Our liability due to fraud is limited, and credit cards are far more convenient than cash, which can attract even more crime.

Our phone's location services offer another example of loss of privacy. Most of us have gotten used to turning on navigation on our smartphones when driving in an unfamiliar locale. Clearly, turning on a location service reveals our location, but many people are accustomed to that and do not mind it in exchange for the perceived benefit of not having to use paper maps. In fact, some car manufacturers advertise loss of privacy as a feature. Their cars, they say, will transmit their location to get help should any problem or accident occur. The reason we have grown to accept some loss of privacy is in part the perceived benefit and in part the protection associated with the service. Should private information be somehow misused, the user has a legal recourse. Hence, good business practice suggests that privacy be respected.

Storage of our private email is another example of voluntary loss of privacy. Many of us use providers, such as Microsoft and Google, to handle email. Such email becomes observable to various analytics engines that can mine the text of that email. Nevertheless most people are comfortable using these services because we trust the providers.

Our trust in providers, good business practices, and the legal system is not a new development. Several hundred years ago, much of human society lived in small towns and rural areas. In a small town everyone knows everyone else's business. It is very hard to hide. Residents of little towns did not have privacy expectations. The reason was simple. While it is possible for others to know much about you, it is hard for them to get away with crimes that exploit such data. After all, everyone does know everyone else's business, so perpetrators will be caught.

Over the centuries, little towns grew into bigger cities, where it became possible for perpetrators to hide. Privacy became an issue. We conjecture that the advent of communication technology, sensing, and data analytics will eventually produce a world, where distances are drastically reduced, and the city turns again into a village—a global village, if you will, where data may be shared but crimes are not committed because it is hard to hide from the ubiquitous eye of data-centric crime-detection and investigation systems, backed by legal protection of the individuals' right to share data without fear of misuse. Hence, privacy, as a technical problem, is not discussed in the rest of this book.

Mathematical foundations of social sensing: An introductory tutorial

3.1 A MULTIDISCIPLINARY BACKGROUND

The inspiration for developing mathematical foundations for reliability of social sensing systems comes from multiple research communities. Many of these communities do not interact. They have different research objectives, different applications, and different publication venues. As a result, some opportunities were missed for connecting the dots between their advances. Jointly, these advances offer the needed foundations for leveraging unreliable social sensing sources, while offering collective reliability guarantees.

In the sensor fusion community, well established results exist that describe estimation algorithms using noisy sensors and quantify the corresponding estimation error bounds. It is possible to exploit Bayesian analysis to combine evidence and use estimation theory to rigorously compute confidence intervals as a function of reliability of input sources, even in the presence of noise and uncertainty. These results have typically been applied to the estimation of physical signals and tracking dynamic state such as trajectories of mobile targets. Given a physical model of how a target behaves, and given some observations, theory was developed on how to infer hidden variables that are not directly observed. Since sensor fusion deals with measuring state of the physical world, a key concept that threads through the research is the existence of a unique ground truth (barring, for the moment, the quantum effects and Schrodinger's cat). The existence of a unique ground truth offers a non-ambiguous notion of error that quantifies the deviation of estimated state from ground truth. In turn, the existence of a non-ambiguous notion of error lends itself nicely to the formulation of optimization problems that minimize this error. Such problems were formulated for estimating the state of physical systems, usually given by well-understood models, from noisy indirect observations. However, they have seldom been applied to the estimation of parameters of social sources and reliability of social observations.

Data mining researchers, on the other hand, do not usually exploit physical models of targets. This is because of the nature of the data mining problems. Rather than

21

dealing with well-defined and well-understood objects for which physical dynamic models exist, data mining research tries to understand very large systems, and infer relations that are observed to hold true in the data. Much advances were made in data mining on representing very large data sets as abstract graphs of heterogeneous nodes, and inferring interesting new properties of the underlying systems from the topology of such graphs. This area is referred to as heterogeneous network mining. The analysis techniques described in that space are mostly heuristic, but have the power of producing interesting insights starting with no prior knowledge about the system whose data are collected. Importantly, since the system in question is often very complex and not well-understood, much of the work stops at computing different properties, without defining a notion of error. In many cases, ground truth cannot be defined. For example, when clustering individuals according to their beliefs into liberals and conservatives, it is really hard to define a rigorous and unbiased notion of what ground truth means, and offer a non-ambiguous notion of error. As a consequence of the difficulty in defining error for solutions of data mining problems, few problems are cast as ones of error optimization. Rather, data mining problems are often cast as minimizing internal conflict between observations. Hence, data mining literature does not usually offer bounds on error of data mining algorithms.

Machine learning researchers take a different approach to extracting properties of poorly understood systems. They typically propose a generative model for how the system behaves. Unlike researchers in sensor data fusion who often exploit representations of the exact dynamics of their targets, in machine learning the generative model has hidden parameters that are estimated only empirically. Machine learning literature describes techniques for learning model parameters using algorithms such as expectation maximization (EM).

The above body of results, put together, suggests an approach to reliable social sensing. Namely, we borrow from data mining the techniques used for knowledge representation. Specifically, we represent sources and observations by graphs that allow us to infer interesting properties of nodes. We then borrow from machine learning the idea of using generative models with hidden parameters to be estimated. Hence, we propose simple models for behavior of individual nodes in those graphs, such as lying, gossiping, or telling the truth. These models allow us to compute likelihood of observations as a function of model parameters of nodes. Finally, once a generative model is present, we are able to use the body of results developed in sensor data fusion to design optimal estimators and assess estimator error and confidence intervals. Specifically, we find model parameters that maximize the likelihood of the specific graph topology borne out from our data. Note specifically that, since the final outcome of this work is to decide which of a large number of social observations are true, we are able to define a rigorous notion of ground truth. After all, the observations we are interested in are those concerning the physical state of the world. Hence, ground truth exists (although is not known). A non-ambiguous notion of error therefore exists as well, and we are able to rigorously cast reliable social sensing as an error optimization problem.

Below, we first survey the foundations of social sensing borrowed from aforementioned different communities. We then bring it all together and discuss our problem formulation.

3.2 BASICS OF GENERIC NETWORKS

A generic network represents an abstraction of our real world with a focus on the objects (normally represented by *nodes*) and the interactions between the objects (normally represented by *links*) [80]. Our world is an interconnected world. A large number of information and physical entities (e.g., individual agents, social groups, web pages, genomes, vehicles, computers, etc.) are interconnected or interact with each other and form numerous, large-scale, and sophisticated networks. Some well-known examples of generic networks include World Wide Web, social networks, biological networks, transportation networks, epidemic networks, communication networks, healthcare networks, electrical power grids, and so on. Due to its prevalence and importance, the analysis of generic networks has gained a wide attention from researchers from different disciplines (e.g., computer science, sociology, biology, physics, economics, health, and so on).

Considering the node and link types, generic networks in general can be classified into two main categories: *homogeneous* and *heterogeneous*. Homogeneous networks usually represent the networks where the nodes are the objects of the same type and links are the relationships from the same type. A popular example of such networks is the web page network, which is the fundamental abstraction of Google's PageRank algorithm [34]. In this network, entities are all of the same type (i.e., web pages) while links are also of the same type (i.e., hyperlinks). In contrast, heterogeneous networks are the networks where the nodes and links are of different types. For example, in a university network, we may have different types of nodes to represent professors, students, courses, and departments as well as different types of links to represent their interactions such as teaching, course registration, or departmental association. Hence, we need to treat different nodes and links in heterogeneous networks as appropriate types to better capture the essential semantics of the real world [81].

Numerous techniques and methods have been developed to analyze both homogeneous [82–85] and heterogeneous [36, 86–88] networks. Many homogeneous network problems are related with World Wide Web and social networks. Examples include ranking [82], community detection [83], link prediction [84], and influence analysis [85]. State-of-the-art research developments in heterogeneous networks explore the power of links to mine hidden information related with both nodes and links in the network. Examples include fact-finding [36], rank-based clustering [86], relationship prediction [87], and network evolution [88]. In this chapter, we focus on a special type of heterogeneous networks that are usually used in fact-finding literature [35–37] and relate that to the data reliability problem in social sensing. In its simplest form, this special type of heterogeneous networks can be represented by bipartite graphs. Nodes on one side of the graph represent information sources and nodes on the other side represent information entities. The links in the graph connecting two types of nodes describe which source contributes/claims which information entity. The goal of the problem is to find the attributes of the nodes in the graph. For example, what is the likelihood of a source to generate a correct information entity? What is the probability of a given entity to be true? This bipartite graph can be generated to model more complex networks where links between sources and links between information entities are considered.

In the rest of this chapter, we will first review several basic concepts and methods from statistics and estimation theory that will be used throughout this book. They include Bayesian analysis in Section 3.3, maximum likelihood estimation (MLE) in Section 3.4, EM in Section 3.5 and confidence intervals in Section 3.6. Then we will put everything together under a framework that studies the aforementioned heterogeneous network in Section 3.7.

3.3 BASICS OF BAYESIAN ANALYSIS

Bayesian analysis (also called Bayesian inference or Bayesian statistics) is a method of analysis where the Bayes' rule is used to update the probability estimate of a hypothesis as additional data is observed [89]. In this section, we review the basics of Bayesian analysis. Let us start with a simple example. Suppose a 50-year-old patient has a positive lab test for a cardiac disease. Assume the accuracy of this test is 95%. That is to say given a patient has a cardiac disease, the probability of positive result of this test is 95%. In this scenario, the patient would like to know the probability that he/she has the cardiac disease given the positive test. However, the information available is the probability of testing positive if the patient has a cardiac disease, along with the fact that the patient had a positive test result.

Bayes' theorem offers a way for us to answer the above question. The basic theorem simply states:

$$p(B|A) = \frac{p(A|B) \times p(B)}{p(A)} \tag{3.1}$$

where event B represents the event of our interests (e.g., having a cardiac disease) and A represents an event related to B (e.g., positive lab test). $p(B|A)$ is the probability of event B given event A, $p(A)$ and $p(B)$ is the unconditional marginal probability of event A and B, respectively. The proof of Bayes' theorem is straightforward: we know from probability rules that $p(A, B) = p(A|B) \times p(B)$ and $p(B, A) = p(B|A) \times p(A)$. Given the fact that $p(A, B) = p(B, A)$, we can easily obtain:

$$p(A|B) \times p(B) = p(B|A) \times p(A) \tag{3.2}$$

Then we divide each side by $p(A)$, we obtain Equation (3.1). Normally, $p(A|B)$ is given in the context of applications (e.g., the lab test accuracy in our example) and $p(B|A)$ is what we are interested to know (e.g., the probability of having a cardiac disease given a positive lab test result). $p(B)$ is the unconditional probability of the event of interests, which is usually assumed to be known as prior knowledge (e.g., the probability of a 50-year-old to have a cardiac disease in the population). $p(A)$ is the marginal probability of A, which can be computed as the sum of the conditional probability of A under all possible events of B in its sample space Ω_B. In our example, the sample space of B is whether a patient has a cardiac disease or not. Formally, $p(A)$ can be computed as:

$$p(A) = \sum_{B_i \in \Omega_B} p(A|B_i) \times p(B_i) \tag{3.3}$$

Now, let us come back to our cardiac disease example to make the theorem more concrete. Suppose that, in addition to the 95% accuracy of the test, we also know the false positive rate of the lab test is 40%, which means the test will produce the positive results with a probability of 40% given the patient does not have the cardiac disease. Hence, we have two possible events for B: B_1 represents the event that the patient has the cardiac disease while B_2 represents the negation. Given the accuracy and false positive rate of the test, we know $p(A|B_1) = 0.95$ and $p(A|B_2) = 0.4$. The prior knowledge $p(B)$ is the marginal probability of a patient to have a cardiac disease, not knowing anything beyond the fact he/she is a 50-year-old. We call this information prior knowledge because it exists before the test. Suppose we know from previous research and statistics that the probability of a 50-year-old to have a cardiac disease is 5% in the population. Using all above information, we can compute $p(B|A)$ as follows:

$$p(B|A) = \frac{0.95 \times 0.05}{0.95 \times 0.05 + 0.4 \times 0.95} = \frac{0.0475}{0.0475 + 0.38} = 0.111 \tag{3.4}$$

Therefore, the probability of a patient to have a cardiac disease given the positive test is only 0.111. In Bayesian theorem, we call such probability the *posterior probability*, because it is the estimated probability after we observe the data (i.e., the positive test result). The small posterior probability is somewhat counter-intuitive given a test with so-called "95%" accuracy. However, if we look at the Bayes' theorem, a few factors affect this probability. First is the relatively low probability to have the cardiac disease (i.e., 5%). Second is the relatively high false positive rate (i.e., 40%), which will be further enlarged by the high probability of not having a cardiac disease (i.e., 95%).

The next interesting question to ask is: what happens to Bayes theorem if we have more data. Suppose that, in the first experiment, we have data A_1. After that we repeat the experiment and have new data A_2. Let us assume that A_1 and A_2 are conditionally independent. We want to compute the posterior probability of B after two experiments: $p(B|A_1, A_2)$. This can be done using the basic Bayes' theorem in Equation (3.1) as follows:

$$p(B|A_1, A_2) = \frac{p(A_1, A_2|B) \times p(B)}{p(A_1, A_2)}$$

$$= \frac{p(A_1|B) \times p(A_2|B) \times p(B)}{p(A_1) \times p(A_2|A_1)}$$

$$= \frac{p(B|A_1) \times p(A_2|B)}{p(A_2|A_1)} \tag{3.5}$$

The above result tells us we can use the posterior of the first experiment (i.e., $p(B|A_1)$) as the prior for the second experiment. The process of repeating the experiment and recomputing the posterior probability of interest is the basic process in Bayes' analysis. From a Bayesian perspective, we start with some initial prior probability of some event of interests. Then we keep on updating this prior probability with a posterior probability that is computed using the new information we obtained from experiment. In practice, we continue to collect data to examine a particular hypothesis. We do not start each time from scratch by ignoring all previously collected data. Instead, we use our previous analysis results as prior knowledge for the new experiment to examine the hypothesis.

Let us come back to our cardiac example again. Once the patient knows the limitation of the test, he/she may choose to repeat the test. Now the patient can use Equation (3.5) to compute the new $p(B)$ after each repeated experiment. For example, if the patient repeats the test one more time, the new posterior probability of having a cardiac disease is:

$$p(B|A) = \frac{0.95 \times 0.111}{0.95 \times 0.111 + 0.4 \times 0.889} = \frac{0.10545}{0.10545 + 0.3556} = 0.229 \qquad (3.6)$$

This result is still not very affirmative to claim the patient has a cardiac disease. However, if the patient chooses to keep on repeating the test and finding positive results, his/her probability to have a cardiac disease increases. In the following repeated test, subsequent positive results generate probabilities: test 3 = 0.41352, test 4 = 0.62611, test 5 = 0.79908, test 6 = 0.90427, test 7 = 0.95733, test 8 = 0.98158, test 9 = 0.99216, test 10 =0.99668. As we can see, after enough tests and successive positive test results, the probability to make an affirmative conclusion is pretty high. Note that the above is a toy example to demonstrate the basic Bayesian analysis. It assumes that the results of all tests are statically independent conditioned on B, which may not always be true in actual medical tests.

3.4 BASICS OF MAXIMUM LIKELIHOOD ESTIMATION

In statistics and estimation theory, MLE is a method to estimate the parameters of a statistical model in a way that is asymptotically most consistent with the data observed. Let us start with a simple example to explain the intuition of this method. In this example, we have a random number generator $G(T)$. It can generate a random integer number from 1 to T with a uniform probability distribution (i.e., it has the same probability to generate every number in its range). Let us first suppose that T only has two possible values: 10 and 20. After one run, the generator generated a number: 5. The question is: which of the two values does T equal to? Many people guess T is 10. Their reason is that 5 is more likely to come up when T is 10 (i.e., the probability is 0.1) than T is 20 (i.e., the probability is 0.05). Now suppose T can be any integer value, the generated number is still 5. What is the most likely value of T? I guess you already get the answer: 5. The reason is simple: in the case $T < 5$:

the probability to generate 5 is 0; in the case $T > 5$: the probability to generate 5 is smaller than the case of $T = 5$. The above reasoning follows the basic principle of MLE: make the guess of estimated parameters for which the observed data are least surprising.

In general, for a fixed set of data and given statistical model, the MLE method searches for the set of values of the model parameters that maximize the likelihood of the selected model matching the observed data. Formally, suppose $X_1, X_2, \ldots, X_n$ are statistically *independent* random variables with a family of distributions represented by $f(X_i|\theta)$, where θ is the unknown vector of estimation parameters that determines the distribution. For continuous random variables, $f(X_i|\theta)$ represents the probability density function of X_i. For discrete variables, $f(X_i|\theta)$ represents the probability mass function (pmf) $p(X_i|\theta)$. To use the MLE method, one first need to specify the joint density function of all observations. Let us denote the observed values $X_1 = x_1, \ldots, X_n = x_n$. The joint density function is:

$$f(x_1, x_2, \ldots, x_n|\theta) = f(x_1|\theta) \times f(x_2|\theta) \times \cdots \times f(x_n|\theta) \tag{3.7}$$

The above joint density function can be seen from a different perspective. One can consider $x_1, x_2, \ldots, x_n$ as the fixed "parameters" of the above function and consider θ as the "variable" of the function that can change freely. Then we can rewrite the above function as follows:

$$L_n(\theta; x_1, x_2, \ldots, x_n) = f(x_1|\theta) \times f(x_2|\theta) \times \cdots \times f(x_n|\theta) = \prod_{i=1}^{n} f(x_i|\theta) \tag{3.8}$$

The above function is called the *likelihood function*. It represents the joint probability of observing the data values $X_1 = x_1, \ldots, X_n = x_n$ as a function of the parameter θ. The *MLE* $\hat{\theta}_n$ is the estimated value of θ that maximizes the likelihood function (i.e., $L(\hat{\theta}_n) \geq L(\theta)$ for all θ). Since it is easier to deal with sums than products, we usually use the logarithm of the likelihood function in practice. We call this function *log-likelihood function*:

$$\ln L_n(\theta; x_1, x_2, \ldots, x_n) = \sum_{i=1}^{n} \ln f(x_i|\theta) \tag{3.9}$$

The derivation of the log-likelihood function is called *score function*:

$$V_n(\theta) = \frac{\partial}{\partial \theta} \ln L_n(\theta; x_1, x_2, \ldots, x_n) = \sum_{i=1}^{n} \frac{\partial}{\partial \theta} \ln f(x_i|\theta) \tag{3.10}$$

Usually we can find the MLE by setting the score function to 0 (i.e., $V_n(\theta) = 0$ for $\hat{\theta}_n$)). $V_n(\theta)$ is a random function of θ and the solution $\hat{\theta}_n$ is a random variable.

Now let us review the basic concepts and ideas of MLE by walking through a simple example. In this example, we consider the following binomial distribution:

$$P(x|n, p) = \binom{n}{x} p^x (1 - p)^{(n-x)} \tag{3.11}$$

where $P(x|n,p)$ represents the probability of x successes in a sequence of n Bernoulli experiments, each of which yields success with probability p. For example, suppose $p = 0.7$ and $n = 10$, we can use the above equation to answer the question: "what is the probability to have 4 successful experiments in 10 trials?" However, we can look at the problem from a different perspective: suppose we do not know the value of p before the experiments, but after 10 trials, we know that there are 4 successful experiments. Then our question is: "what is the most likely value of p?" This is a MLE problem: now the data x are fixed, we view Equation (3.11) as a function of parameter p, and use it to compute the MLE of p. Thus we define the likelihood function of our problem as:

$$L(p|n,x) = \binom{n}{x} p^x (1-p)^{(n-x)} \tag{3.12}$$

which is essentially the same function as Equation (3.11), but it is now viewed as a function of p. The MLE of p is the value of p that maximizes the function $L(p|n,x)$. It is easier to maximize the logarithm of the likelihood function, which is:

$$\log L(p|n,x) = \log \binom{n}{x} + x \log p + (n-x)\log(1-p) \tag{3.13}$$

We set the derivative of the above function to 0 with respect to p, and solve for p the value that maximize the likelihood function. It turns out that in this case, the MLE of p is $\hat{p} = \frac{x}{n}$, which matches with our intuition.

The negative second derivative of the likelihood function is called *observed information* $I(\theta)$, which is defined as follows:

$$I_n(\theta) = -\frac{\partial^2}{\partial \theta^2} \ln L_n(\theta) = -\sum_{i=1}^{n} \frac{\partial^2}{\partial \theta^2} \ln f(x_i|\theta) = \frac{\partial}{\partial \theta} V_n(\theta) \tag{3.14}$$

The observed information in general depends on the observe data, and is also a random variable. The *Fisher information* is defined as the expectation of the observed information, which is a way of measuring the amount of information the observed random variable X carries about the unknown estimation parameter θ upon which the probability of X depends. It can be proved that expected value of the score function $V_n(\theta)$ is 0 and the variance of $V_n(\theta)$ is the Fisher information at θ [90]. Also the fisher information and score function can be used in a recursive method to estimate the model parameters efficiently [91].

The MLE has several nice properties. The first one is called *consistent*: $\hat{\theta}$ converges to the true value of θ (i.e., θ_0) both in weak and strong convergence. The second one is called *asymptotic normality*: as the sample size n increases, the distribution of MLE tends to be the Gaussian distribution with mean as θ_0 and covariance matrix equals to the inverse of the Fisher information matrix. The third one is called *efficiency*: as the sample size goes to infinity, the MLE achieves the least mean squared error among all consistent estimators. Its performance can be characterized by Cramer-Rao lower bound (CRLB), which will be discussed in details in Section 3.6. For the proofs of the above properties, one can refer to [92] for details.

3.5 BASICS OF EXPECTATION MAXIMIZATION

In statistics and estimation theory, EM is an iterative algorithm that is used to find the maximum likelihood or maximum posteriori estimation of parameters of statistical models, where the data are "incomplete" or the likelihood function involves latent variables [93]. The latent variables (sometimes also called hidden variables) are defined as the variables that are not directly observed from the data we have but can rather be inferred from the observed variables. Here is a simple example of Binomial Mixture Model: we have two binary number generators which generate either 1 or 0 in a trial. Suppose the probability of generating 1s of two generators are p_1, p_2, respectively. Every trial we choose the first generator with probability q and the second one with probability $1 - q$. Suppose that, we used the two generators to generate a sequence of binary numbers $x = 1, 0, 0, 1, 0, 1, 1, 0, 1, 1, 1, 0$. Our goal here is to jointly estimate $\theta = (p_1, p_2, q)$ from the data we observed (i.e., x). This problem is a bit tricky because we do not know which generator was used in every trial to generate numbers and p_1, p_2 can be different. However, this problem is much easier to formulate if we just choose to add a latent variable Z_i for trial i to indicate which generators was used. We will come back to this example after we review the basics of EM algorithm.

Intuitively, what EM does is iteratively "completes" the data by "guessing" the values of hidden variables then re-estimates the parameters by using the guessed values as true values. More specifically, EM algorithm contains two main steps: (i) an expectation step (E-step) that computes the expectation of the log-likelihood function using the current estimates for the parameters; (ii) a maximization step (M-step) that computes the estimate of the parameters to maximize the expected log-likelihood function in E-step. As we discussed in the previous section, finding the solution to a MLE problem generally requires taking derivatives of the likelihood function with respect to unknown variables (including both the estimation parameters and latent variables) and solving the resulting equations. However, in statistical models with latent variables, such approach is often not possible: the result is typically a set of inter-locking equations where the solution of the parameters requires the values of the latent variables and vice-versa, but substituting one set of equations into another produces unsolvable equations. Based on the aforementioned observation, the EM algorithm provides a numerical way to solve the two sets of inter-locking equations. It starts by picking arbitrary values of one of two sets of unknowns, use them to estimate the second set, then use the new values of the second set to better estimate the first set, and then keep iterating between the two until estimation converges.

The following is a more formal description of EM algorithm. Given a statistical model consisting a set of observed data X, a set of unobserved or missing data Z, and a vector of unknown estimation parameters θ to be estimated. The likelihood function $L(\theta; x)$ is given by:

$$L(\theta; x) = p(x|\theta) = \sum_z p(x, z|\theta) \tag{3.15}$$

As we discussed earlier, the log-likelihood function is normally used to compute the MLE. Hence, we denote the log-likelihood function $l(\theta;x) = \log L(\theta;x)$. Let us first consider the following inequality:

$$l(\theta;x) = \log p(x|\theta) = \log \sum_z p(x,z|\theta)$$

$$= \log \sum_z q(z|x,\theta) \frac{p(x,z|\theta)}{q(z|x,\theta)}$$

$$\geq \sum_z q(z|x,\theta) \log \frac{p(x,z|\theta)}{q(z|x,\theta)} = F(q,\theta) \tag{3.16}$$

where $q(z|x,\theta)$ is an arbitrary density function over Z. The above inequality is called Jensen's inequality, which basically states for a real continuous concave function: $\sum_x p(x)f(x) \leq f(\sum_x p(x)x)$. Instead of maximizing $l(\theta;x)$, the EM algorithm maximizes its lower bound $F(q,\theta)$ through following two steps:

$$q^{(t+1)}(z|x,\theta^{(t)}) = \arg\max_q F(q,\theta^{(t)}) \tag{3.17}$$

$$\theta^{(t+1)} = \arg\max_\theta F(q^{(t+1)}(z|x,\theta^{(t)}),\theta) \tag{3.18}$$

The above two steps is another interpretation of the E-step and M-step. We can start with some random initial value of parameters $\theta^{(0)}$ and iterate between the above two steps until the estimation converges. Solving Equation (3.17) while fixing θ, we can obtain $q^{(t+1)} = p(z|x,\theta^{(t)})$. To compute Equation (3.18), we fix q and note that:

$$F(q^{(t+1)},\theta) = \sum_z q^{(t+1)}(z|x,\theta^{(t)}) \log \frac{p(x,z|\theta)}{q^{(t+1)}(z|x,\theta^{(t)})}$$

$$= \sum_z q^{(t+1)}(z|x,\theta^{(t)}) \log p(x,z|\theta^{(t)}) - \sum_z q^{(t+1)}(z|x,\theta^{(t)}) \log q^{(t+1)}(z|x,\theta^{(t)})$$

$$= Q(\theta|\theta^{(t)}) + H(q^{(t+1)}) \tag{3.19}$$

As we mentioned earlier, maximizing $l(\theta;z)$ is equivalent to maximizing its lower bound $F(q,\theta)$. Maximizing $F(q,\theta)$ with respect to θ is equivalent to maximizing $Q(\theta|\theta^{(t)})$ with respect to θ. Now, we can re-interpret Equations (3.17) and (3.18) as follows:

$$\mathbf{E-step}: \quad \text{Compute} \quad Q(\theta|\theta^{(t)}) = E_{p(z|x,\theta^{(t)})} \log p(x,z|\theta) \tag{3.20}$$

$$\mathbf{M-step}: \quad \theta^{(t+1)} = \arg\max_\theta Q(\theta|\theta^{(t)}) \tag{3.21}$$

Equations (3.20) and (3.21) are the E-step and M-step of the EM algorithm. In E-step, we compute the expectation of the log-likelihood function with the distribution of the latent variables that depends on the observed data and $\theta^{(t)}$. In M-step, we compute the estimation of the θ in next round as the ones that maximize the expectation function in E-step. The algorithm iterates between the above two steps until convergence. Note that, in order to show that the EM converges to a local maximal of the likelihood surface, one need to show that $log(p(x|\theta^{(t+1)})) \geq log(p(x|\theta^{(t)}))$, which is an easy proof [94].

After introducing the EM algorithm, let us come back to the Binomial Mixture Model example we mentioned at the start of this section and apply the EM to solve it. Let us specify the definition of the latent variable: $Z_i = 1$ if the first binary number generator was used in the ith trial and 0 otherwise. We start by writing down the expected log-likelihood function of our problem.

$$Q(\theta|\theta^{(t)}) = E\left[\log \prod_{i=1}^{n} [q \times p_1^{x_i} \times (1-p_1)^{(1-x_i)}]^{z_i} \times [(1-q) \times p_2^{x_i} \times (1-p_2)^{(1-x_i)}]^{1-z_i}\right]$$

$$= \sum_{i=1}^{n} E[z_i|x_i, \theta^{(t)}][\log q + x_i \log p_1 + (1-x_i)\log(1-p_1)]$$

$$+ (1 - E[z_i|x_i, \theta^{(t)}])[\log(1-q) + x_i \log p_2 + (1-x_i)\log(1-p_2)] \quad (3.22)$$

Then we can compute $E[z_i|x_i, \theta^{(t)}]$ for E-step as:

$$Z(i,t) = E[z_i|x_i, \theta^{(t)}] = p(z_i = 1|x_i, \theta^{(t)})$$

$$= \frac{p(x_i|z_i, \theta^{(t)})p(z_i = 1|\theta^{(t)})}{p(x_i|\theta^{(t)})}$$

$$= \frac{q^{(t)} \times [p_1^{(t)}]^{x_i} \times [(1-p_1^{(t)})]^{(1-x_i)}}{q^{(t)} \times [p_1^{(t)}]^{x_i} \times [(1-p_1^{(t)})]^{(1-x_i)} + (1-q^{(t)}) \times [p_2^{(t)}]^{x_i} \times [(1-p_2^{(t)})]^{(1-x_i)}} \quad (3.23)$$

Following M-step, we maximize $Q(\theta|\theta^{(t)})$ with respect to θ, we obtain:

$$\frac{\partial Q(\theta|\theta^{(t)})}{\partial p_1} = 0 : \quad p_1^{(t+1)} = \frac{\sum_i Z(i,t)x_i}{\sum_i Z(i,t)}$$

$$\frac{\partial Q(\theta|\theta^{(t)})}{\partial p_2} = 0 : \quad p_2^{(t+1)} = \frac{\sum_i (1-Z(i,t))x_i}{\sum_i (1-Z(i,t))}$$

$$\frac{\partial Q(\theta|\theta^{(t)})}{\partial q} = 0 : \quad q^{(t+1)} = \frac{\sum_i Z(i,t)}{n} \quad (3.24)$$

3.6 BASICS OF CONFIDENCE INTERVALS

In statistics, a *confidence interval* provides an estimated range of values which is likely to include an unknown estimation parameter [95]. The confidence interval is calculated from a given set of sample data and used to indicate the reliability

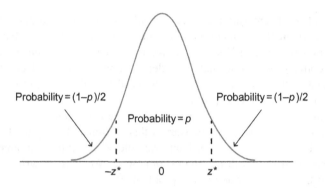

FIGURE 3.1

Confidence interval for a standard norm distribution.

of the estimate. *Confidence limits* are the lower and upper bounds of a confidence interval, which define the range of the interval. *Confidence level* is the probability that the confidence interval contains the true value of the estimation parameter given a distribution of samples. For example, when we say, "we are 95% confident that the true value of the estimation parameter is in our confidence interval," what we really mean is 95% of the observed confidence intervals will capture the true value of the parameter. However, once a sample is taken, the true value of the population parameter is either in or outside the confidence interval, it is not a matter of chance. If a corresponding hypothesis test is performed, the confidence level is the complement of the significance level (i.e., 95% confidence interval reflects a significance level of 0.05).

Now let us go through a simple example of norm distribution to better illustrate the above concepts. Suppose that a simple random sample of size n is drawn from a norm population with unknown mean μ and known standard deviation σ. Then the sample distribution is $N(\mu, \sigma/\sqrt{n})$. Then we can use the standard norm distribution $N(0, 1)$ to compute the confidence interval for the confidence level $p = 95\%$ as shown in Figure 3.1. Here we need to introduce one more concept: standard score (also called z score). It represents the number of standard deviations that an observation is away from the mean. For example, the z score for the 95% confidence level of a standard norm distribution is 1.96. For this problem, we use the sample mean $\bar{x}$ as an estimate for μ, then the 95% confidence interval is:

$$\left(\bar{x} - z^* \frac{\sigma}{\sqrt{n}}, \bar{x} + z^* \frac{\sigma}{\sqrt{n}} \right) \tag{3.25}$$

In estimation theory and statistics, the CRLB is defined as the inverse of Fisher information and describes a lower bound on the estimation variance of any unbiased estimator [96]. An unbiased estimator that achieves CRLB actually achieves the lowest possible mean squared error among all unbiased estimators and is said to be *efficient*. To give an intuitive explanation, we provide an inform proof as follows. Let us start with the definition of an unbiased estimator $\hat{\theta}(X)$:

$$E[\hat{\theta}(X) - \theta|\theta] = \int [\hat{\theta}(x) - \theta] \times L(x;\theta)\, dx = 0 \tag{3.26}$$

where $L(x;\theta) = p(x|\theta)$ is the likelihood function we discussed in the previous section. Intuitively, if the likelihood is strongly dependent on θ (e.g., sharply peaked w.r.t. to changes in θ), it is easy to estimate the correct value of θ, and hence the data contains a lot of information about parameters. On the contrary, if the likelihood is weakly dependent on θ (e.g., flat and spread-out w.r.t. to changes in θ), then it would take many samples of data to estimate the correct value of θ. Hence the data contain much less information about the estimation parameter.

We take the derivative of Equation (3.26) with respect to θ, we get:

$$\frac{\partial}{\partial\theta}\int [\hat{\theta}(x) - \theta] \times L(x;\theta)\, dx = \int [\hat{\theta}(x) - \theta] \times \frac{\partial L(x;\theta)}{\partial\theta}\, dx - \int L(x;\theta)\, dx = 0 \tag{3.27}$$

Given the fact that $L(x;\theta)$ is a probability, we know that $\int L(x;\theta)\, dx = 1$. From calculus, we know that $\frac{\partial L}{\partial\theta} = L\frac{\partial \log L}{\partial\theta}$. We can rewrite Equation (3.27) as:

$$\int [\hat{\theta}(x) - \theta] \times L(x;\theta) \times \frac{\partial \log L(x;\theta)}{\partial\theta}\, dx = 1$$

$$\int [\hat{\theta}(x) - \theta] \times \sqrt{L(x;\theta)} \times \sqrt{L(x;\theta)} \times \frac{\partial \log L(x;\theta)}{\partial\theta}\, dx = 1 \tag{3.28}$$

If we square the above equation and use Cauchy-Schwarz inequality, we can obtain:

$$\left[\int [\hat{\theta}(x) - \theta]^2 \times L(x;\theta)\, dx\right] \times \left[\int \left[\frac{\partial \log L(x;\theta)}{\partial\theta}\right]^2 \times L(x;\theta)\, dx\right] \geq 1 \tag{3.29}$$

The right most factor is the Fisher information as we mentioned in Section 3.4: $I(\theta) = \int \left[\frac{\partial \log L(x;\theta)}{\partial\theta}\right]^2 \times L(x;\theta)\, dx$. The left most factor is the expected mean squared error (i.e., variance) of our estimation $\hat{\theta}$:

$$Var(\hat{\theta}) = E[(\hat{\theta}(x) - \theta)^2|\theta] = \int [\hat{\theta}(x) - \theta]^2 \times L(x;\theta)\, dx \tag{3.30}$$

Finally, we can show from the above derivation:

$$Var(\hat{\theta}) \geq \frac{1}{I(\theta)} = CRLB(\theta) \tag{3.31}$$

This equation re-states the definition of CRLB we introduced earlier, which provides an fundamental bound to quantify the estimation accuracy on the parameter θ of an unbiased estimator like MLE.

Now let us revisit the binomial example we discussed in Section 3.4 to give a concrete example of computing CRLB. The experiments in this example include n independent Bernoulli trials, with x trials succeed. The probability of each trial to succeed is p, which is the estimation parameter of our problem. We already showed the MLE $\hat{p} = \frac{x}{n}$. In the following we compute the Fisher information to obtain the CRLB for our estimate. We denote the likelihood function as $L(x; p) = \binom{n}{x} p^x (1-p)^{(n-x)}$

$$I(p) = -E\left[\frac{\partial^2}{\partial p^2} \log(L(x; p)) | p\right]$$

$$= -E\left[\frac{\partial^2}{\partial p^2} \log\left(p^x(1-p)^{(n-x)} \frac{n!}{x!(n-x)!}\right) \bigg| p\right]$$

$$= -E\left[\frac{\partial^2}{\partial p^2}(x \log p + (n-x)\log(1-p)) | p\right]$$

$$= -E\left[\frac{\partial}{\partial p}\left(\frac{x}{p} - \frac{n-x}{1-p}\right) \bigg| p\right]$$

$$= E\left[\left(\frac{x}{p^2} + \frac{n-x}{(1-p)^2}\right) \bigg| p\right]$$

$$= \frac{np}{p^2} + \frac{n(1-p)}{(1-p)^2}$$

$$= \frac{n}{p(1-p)} \tag{3.32}$$

Hence, the CRLB is the inverse of Fisher information, which is $\frac{p(1-p)}{n}$ in this case.

3.7 PUTTING IT ALL TOGETHER

After we reviewed several concepts and methods from statistics and estimation theory in previous sections, we will discuss, in this section, a generic network model for social sensing where we can put everything together under the same framework.

As we discussed earlier, in social sensing, a group of participants (sources) with unknown reliability collectively report observations about the physical world. Since we usually are not certain about the correctness of the observations, we call the collected data claims. This basic data collection paradigm can be represented by a graph model as shown in Figure 3.2. In this model, nodes on the left represent participants (sources) and nodes on the right represent claims. The links connecting two types of nodes in the graph describe "who said what." For simplicity, in the basic model, claims are assumed to be binary (either true or false). This network abstraction belongs to heterogeneous networks that are discussed in Section 3.2 since there are two types of nodes in the network. What we are interested in social sensing context is the attributes of the nodes in the network. For example, what is the reliability of sources (i.e., the likelihood of a particular source to generate true claims)? What is

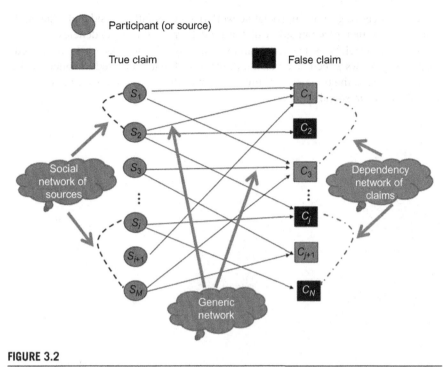

FIGURE 3.2

Generic network model for social sensing.

the correctness of claims (i.e., the probability of a particular claim to be true)? This problem is trivial if we either know the source reliability or the claim correctness in advance. However, one key challenge in social sensing is that we are aware of *neither* the source reliability *nor* the claim correctness a priori.

This book reviews a series of recent work that address the data reliability challenge under the same analytic framework. In particular, Chapter 4 reviews the sate-of-the-art fact-finders as well as a Bayesian interpretation of the basic fact-finding scheme used in generic network analysis. To overcome some fundamental limitations of the basic fact-finding scheme, Chapter 5 reviews a MLE framework by leveraging the MLE principle discussed in Section 3.4. This MLE framework allows applications to jointly estimate both the reliability of sources and the correctness of claims to obtain the optimal solutions that are most consistent with the data observed. In order to quantify the accuracy of the MLE, Chapter 6 reviews a quantification scheme based on CRLB discussed in Section 3.6. After that, we will review the work that study different extensions and generalizations of the basic MLE model. Chapter 7 reviews the extension of the basic model where observations can be conflicting and claims can be non-binary. Chapter 8 reviews the generalization of the model where dependencies between sources (e.g., links in social networks) are explicitly considered. Chapter 9 reviews the further generalization of the model where the dependencies between claims (e.g., correlations between variables in physical network) are considered. Chapter 10 reviews a recursive version of the model that is tailored to better handle streaming data. In the remaining of this book, we will review these exciting progress and discoveries in social sensing.

Fact-finding in information networks

4

4.1 FACTS, FACT-FINDERS, AND THE EXISTENCE OF GROUND TRUTH

Fact-finders are an interesting class of algorithms whose purpose is to recognize "truth" from observations that are noisy, conflicting, and possibly incomplete. As such, they are quite fundamental to our quest to build reliable systems on unreliable data. The majority of fact-finders can be thought of as algorithms that combine two fundamental components, whose use is prevalent in data mining literature. Namely, fact-finders intertwine the use of *clustering* and *ranking* components. Informally, the clustering component combines together pieces of evidence in support of the same facts. The ranking component weights the trustworthiness, credibility, authority, or probability of correctness of different clusters of evidence. Different fact-finders vary in how they perform the ranking and clustering steps. While both ranking and clustering are well-researched areas in data mining, the fact-finding problem itself is a bit of a special case, because, unlike most other data mining problems, fact-finders typically deal with situations, where a unique externally defined ground truth exists.

To appreciate what the above statement means, let us first elaborate on what we mean by *externally defined ground truth*. This is a concept we inherit from sensing and data fusion, where the objective is always to estimate the state of some *external* system; the system being monitored. That system is assumed to have state that is independent of what the sensing and data fusion algorithms are doing. That state is unique and unambiguous. While the sensors may be noisy and the estimation algorithms might make simplifying assumptions about how the monitored system behaves, once an estimate of the state is obtained, this estimate can, in principle, be compared to a unique and unambiguous *actual* state. Any difference between the actual and estimated states would constitute a unique and unambiguous measure of estimation error.

Note that, many algorithms can define their own set of assumptions. Under this set of assumptions, they may reach optimal conclusions. While the algorithms may be optimal in that sense, they may or may not do well in terms of estimation error. It all depends on how well their simplifying assumptions approximate the real world.

The International Society of Information Fusion, being the copyright holder, grants permission to reprint Figure 1, Figure 2 and Figure 3, page 6, and text of the article, D. Wang, T. Abdelzaher, H. Ahmadi, J. Pasternack, D. Roth, M. Gupta, J. Han, O. Fatemich, H. Le, and C. Aggarwal, "On Bayesian Interpretation of Fact-finding in Information Networks", Proceedings of *The 14th International Conference on Information Fusion*, Chicago, U.S.A, July, 2011.

Now, let us go back to our previous statement. We pointed out that the existence of a unique externally defined ground truth in fact-finding problems makes them different from many other clustering and ranking problems. Consider, for example, community detection. The goal is usually to identify different communities (clusters of nodes) based on node interaction patterns. The solution consists of the clusters that have been identified. It is generally hard to compare these clusters to a metric of ground truth. It could be, for example, that communities were split across belief boundaries, such as liberals versus conservatives. However, it is not straightforward to define what exactly constitutes a liberal and what exactly constitutes a conservative. Hence, it is hard to tell in an unambiguous way whether the resulting clusters are consistent with "ground truth" or not. In some sense, the formed clusters define their own ground truth. An optimal solution to a clustering problem simply says that according to the distance metric used for clustering, the resulting clusters are optimal and constitute the best answer to the problem.

The same lack of an externally defined ground truth can be said about many ranking problems as well, investigated in data mining literature. For example, recent work in data mining develops algorithms for combined ranking and clustering [86]. The algorithm is used to rank the top 10 conferences and the top 10 authors in several fields. The results are intuitive in that the best conferences and the most recognized authors indeed come on top. However, it is hard to define an objective measure of error because it is hard to quantify ground truth. After all, how would one define a top author? Is it the number of publications they have? Is it the number of citations to their work? Is it their success in technology transfer from published research? There is no single, unique, agreed-upon metric and therefore no single, unique, agreed-upon ground truth. The ranking algorithm defines its own ground truth based on some assumed model. For example, under the simplifying assumption that better authors have more papers, one can come up with a unique and unambiguous ranking. However, there is no unique external reference to compare this resulting ranking to in order to determine how accurate exactly the simplifying assumption underlying the ranking was. It is precisely the existence of an external reference (for what is considered "true") versus the lack thereof that is the distinction we are trying to draw between problems for which an externally defined ground truth exists and problems for which it does not.

Now, by contrast, consider the problem of fact-finding. Let the goal of the fact-finder be to identify which of a set of facts claimed by some unreliable sources actually occurred in the physical world. The fact-finding algorithm can make simplifying assumptions about how sources behave. Based on those assumptions some answers are given. Once the answers are given, it is in principle possible to define an error based on a comparison of what the fact-finder believed and what was actually true in the external physical world. The distinction is important because it allows us to formulate fact-finding problems as ones of minimizing the difference between exact and estimated states of systems. In other words, we cast them as sensing problems and are thus able to apply results from traditional estimation theory.

It remains to make two more points clear. First, the assumption of the existence of an externally defined unique ground truth does not necessarily mean that this ground truth is available to the fact-finding algorithm. In fact, most of the time, it is not. By analogy with target tracking algorithms, when the position of a target is estimated, one can define the notion of an estimation error even if this error is not available in practice because the data fusion system does not know the exact location of the target. (After all, if it did, we would not need to do the estimation in the first place.) The point is that the target has a unique and unambiguous location in the physical world at any given time. The deviation of the estimate from that actual location is the error. Estimation theory quantifies bounds on that error under different conditions.

The second point is that the existence of ground truth versus lack thereof does not constitute an advantage of one set of problems or solutions over another. The discussion above simply sheds light on an interesting difference between many problems addressed in data mining and problems addressed in sensing. Philosophically speaking, data mining is about discovery of uncharted territory. Hence, by definition, no agreed upon models for ground truth need to exist. If anything, the goal is to discover what ground truth might be. Sensing, on the other hand, is about reconstruction of an existing physical world in cyberspace. Therefore, by definition, sensing is only as good as the accuracy to which it reconstructs world state, compared to ground truth. In this book, the problem addressed is fundamentally one of *sensing*, although it does use inspiration from data mining literature. We define a notion of error and set up the fact-finding problem as one of minimizing this error. First, however, we take a look at previous literature in the area.

4.2 OVERVIEW OF FACT-FINDERS IN INFORMATION NETWORKS

In this section, we first review several state-of-the-art fact-finders used in information network analysis. Some early fact-finder models include *Sums* (Hubs and Authorities) [35], *TruthFinder* [36], *Average Log*, *Investment*, and *Pooled Investment* [37]. *Sums* developed a basic fact-finder where the belief in a claim c is $B^i(c) = \sum_{s \in S_c} T^i(s)$ and the truthfulness of a source s is $T^i(s) = \sum_{c \in C_s} B^{(i-1)}(c)$, where S_c and C_s are the sources asserting a given claim and the claims asserted by a particular source, respectively. Both $B(c)$ and $T(s)$ are normalized by dividing by the maximum values in the respective vector to prevent them from going unbounded. *TruthFinder* is the first unsupervised fact-finder proposed by Yin et al. for trust analysis on a providers-facts network [36]. It models the fact-finding problem as a graph estimation problem where three types of nodes in the graph represent providers (sources), facts (claims), and objects, respectively. They assumed multiple mutual exclusive facts are associated with an object and providers assert facts of different objects. The proposed algorithm iterates between the computation of trustworthiness of sources and confidence of claims using heuristic based pseudo-probabilistic methods.

In particular, the algorithm computes the "probability" of a claim by assuming that each source's trustworthiness is the probability of it being correct and then average claim beliefs to obtain trustworthiness scores. Pasternack et al. extended the *Sums* framework by incorporating prior knowledge into the analysis and proposed several extended algorithms: *Average Log, Investment, and Pooled Investment* [37]. *Average Log* attempts to address the trustworthiness overestimation problem of a source who makes relatively few claims by explicitly considering the number of claims in the trustworthiness score computation. In particular, it adjusts the update rule to compute source trustworthiness score used in Sums as $T^i(s) = \log |C_s| \frac{\sum_{c \in C_s} B^{i-1}(c)}{|C_s|}$. In *Investment* and *Pooled Investment*, sources "invest" their trustworthiness uniformly among claims and a non-linear function G was introduced to model the belief growth in each claim. Other fact-finders further enhanced the above basic framework by incorporating analysis on properties or dependencies within claims or sources. Galland et al. [38] took the notion of hardness of facts into consideration and proposed their algorithms: *Cosine, 2-Estimates, and 3-Estimates*. Dong et al. studied the source dependency and copying problem comprehensively and proposed several algorithms that give higher credibility to independent sources [41, 42, 97].

More recent works came up with several new fact-finding algorithms toward building more generalized framework and using more rigorous statistic models. Pasternack et al. [44] provided a generalized fact-finder framework to incorporate the background knowledge such as the confidence of the information extractor, attributes of information sources and similarity between claims. Instead of considering the source claim network as an unweighted bipartite graph, they proposed a generalized k-partite weighted graph where different types of background knowledge and contextual details can be encoded as weight links. Specifically, they defined the uncertainty expressed by the source in the claim, the attributes of sources and similarity between claims as different weights in their lifted model. They also rewrote several basic fact-finders (e.g., *Sums, Average Log, Investment,* and *TruthFinder*) to incorporate the background knowledge as the link weights in the computation of source trustworthiness and claim beliefs. New "layers" of groups and attributes can be added to the source and claim graph to model meta-groups and meta-attributes. The generalized fact-finders were shown to outperform the basic ones by exploring the background knowledge through experiments on several real-world datasets. Following the above work, Pasternack et al. [47] proposed a probabilistic model by using Latent Credibility Analysis (LCA) for information credibility analysis. In their model, they introduced hidden variables to model the truth of claims and related the estimation parameters to source reliability. The LCA model provides semantics to the credibility scores of sources and claims that are computed by the proposed algorithms. However, sources and claims are assumed to be independent to keep the credibility analysis mathematically rigorous. Such assumptions may not always hold in real-world applications.

Zhao et al. [46] presented a Bayesian approach to model different types of errors made by sources and merge multi-valued attribute types of entities in data integration systems. They assumed the possible true values of a fact are not unique and a source can claim multiple values of a fact at the same time. They built a Latent Truth Model (LTM) based on maximum a posterior (MAP), which in general needs the prior on both source reliability and claim truthfulness. In particular, the LTM explicitly models two aspects of source quality by considering both false positive and false negative errors made by a source. They solved the MAP estimation problem by using the collapsed Gibbs sampling method. An incremental approximation algorithm was also developed to efficiently handle streaming data. There exists some limitations of LTM that originate from several assumptions made by the model. For example, the model assumes all sources are independent and the majority of data coming from each source is not erroneous. These assumptions may not be necessarily true in various real-world applications (e.g., social sensing) where data collection is often open to all.

Qi et al. [43] proposed an integrated group reliability and true data value inference approach in collective intelligence applications to aggregate information from large crowds. The aggregation results in such applications are often negatively affected by the unreliable information sources with low quality data. To address this critical challenge, they developed a multi-source sensing model to jointly estimate source reliability and data correctness with explicit consideration of source dependency. High source dependency makes the collective intelligence systems vulnerable to overuse redundant and possibly incorrect information from dependent sources. The key insight of their model is to infer the source dependency by revealing latent group structures among dependent sources and analyze the source reliability at group levels. They studied two types of source reliability of their model: the general reliability that represents the overall performance of a group and the specific reliability on each individual object. The true data value is extracted from reliable groups to minimize the negative impacts of unreliable groups. They demonstrated the performance improvement of their model over other existing fact-finders through experiments on two real-world datasets.

Yu et al. [48] presented an unsupervised multi-dimensional truth finding framework to study credibility perceptions in the context of information extraction (IE). The proposed framework incorporates signals from multiple sources and multiple systems through knowledge graphs that are constructed from multiple evidences using multi-layer deep linguistic analysis. In particular, the proposed multi-dimensional truth-finding model (MTM) is constructed based on a tripartite graph where nodes in the graph represent sources, responses, and systems, respectively. The response in the model is defined as a claim and evidence pair, which is automatically generated from unstructured natural language texts by a Slot Filling system. The response is trustworthy if its claim is true and its evidence supports the claim. A trusted source is assumed to always support true claims by offering convincing evidence and a good system is assumed to extract trustworthy responses from trusted sources. They then computed the credibility scores of sources, responses, and systems by using a set of similar heuristics adapted from *TruthFinder* [36]. They also demonstrated a better accuracy and efficiency of their approach compared to baselines through case studies of Slot Filling Validation tasks.

Complementary to the above fact-finders that target to discover the truthfulness/correctness of claims, Sikdar et al. [98] defined credibility as the believability of claims, which can be different from truthfulness of claims in certain contexts. They developed machine learning based methods to find features or indicators (e.g., network location of sources, textual content of the claims) to assess the credibility of claims. These methods normally need to have sufficient training data that is representative of the current problem in order to work well. Such conditions may not hold in scenarios where no good features can be found for future predictions or the identified features are manipulated by others. To overcome this limitation, they recently conducted some interesting Twitter based case studies to demonstrate how data fusion techniques can be used to combine the credibility results from the machine learning based methods with the truthfulness analysis results from fact-finders to capture the trade off between discovering true versus credible information [99].

Toward an optimal fact-finding solution to address data reliability problem in social sensing, Wang et al. developed a maximum likelihood estimation (MLE) framework that jointly estimates both source reliability and claim correctness based on a set of general simplifying assumptions in the context of social sensing [100, 101]. The derived solutions are optimal in the sense that they are most consistent with the data observed without prior knowledge of source reliability and without independent ways to verify the correctness of claims. They also derived accuracy bounds by leveraging results from estimation theory and statistics to correctly assess the quality of the estimation results [102–104]. They further relaxed the assumptions they made in their basic model to address source dependency [105], claim dependency [106], and streaming data [107]. We will review this thread of research work in great details starting from the next chapter of the book. Before that, let us first review a Bayesian interpretation scheme for the basic fact-finders in information networks in the remaining sections of this chapter.

4.3 A BAYESIAN INTERPRETATION OF BASIC FACT-FINDING

Starting from this section, we will review a Bayesian interpretation of the basic fact-finding scheme that leads to a direct quantification of the accuracy of conclusions obtained from information network analysis [39]. When information sources are unreliable, information networks have been used in data mining literature to uncover facts from large numbers of complex relations between noisy variables. The approach relies on topology analysis of graphs, where nodes represent pieces of (possibly unreliable) information and links represent abstract relations. More specifically, let there be s sources, $S_1, \ldots, S_s$ who collectively assert c different pieces of information, $C_1, \ldots, C_c$. Each such piece of information is called a claim. All sources and claims are represented by a network, where these sources and claims are nodes, and nodes, and where an observation, $C_{i,j}$ (denoting that a source S_i makes claim C_j) is represented by a link between the corresponding source and claim nodes. It is assumed that a claim can either be true or false. An example is "John Smith is CEO of Company X" or "Building Y is on Fire." $Cred(S_i)$ is defined as the credibility of source S_i, and $Cred(C_j)$ as the credibility of claim C_j.

$\mathbf{C}_{cred}$ is defined as a $c \times 1$ vector that represents the claim credibility vector $[Cred(C_1) \ldots Cred(C_c)]^T$ and $\mathbf{S}_{cred}$ is a $s \times 1$ vector that represents the source credibility vector $[Cred(S_1) \ldots Cred(S_s)]^T$. CS is defined as a $c \times s$ array such that element $CS(j, i) = 1$ if source S_i makes claim C_j, and is zero otherwise.

$\mathbf{C}_{cred}^{est}$ is defined as a vector of *estimated* claim credibility, defined as $(1/\alpha)[CS]\mathbf{S}_{cred}$. One can pose the basic fact-finding problem as one of finding a least squares estimator (that minimizes the sum of squares of errors in source credibility estimates) for the following system:

$$\mathbf{C}_{cred}^{est} = \frac{1}{\alpha}[CS]\mathbf{S}_{cred} \tag{4.1}$$

$$\mathbf{S}_{cred} = \frac{1}{\beta}[CS]^T \mathbf{C}_{cred}^{est} + \mathbf{e} \tag{4.2}$$

where the notation X^T denotes the transpose of matrix X. It can further be shown that the condition for it to minimize the error is that α and β be chosen such that their product is an Eigenvalue of $[CS]^T[CS]$. The algorithm produces the credibility values $Cred(S_i)$ and $Cred(C_j)$ for every source S_i and for every claim C_j. These values are used for ranking. The question is, does the solution have an interpretation that allows quantifying the actual probability that a given source is truthful or that a given claim is true?

Let S_i^t denote the proposition that "Source S_i speaks the truth." Let C_j^t denote the proposition that "claim C_j is true." Also, let S_i^f and C_j^f denote the negation of the above propositions, respectively. The objective is to estimate the probabilities of these propositions. $S_i C_j$ means "Source S_i made claim C_j."

It is useful to define $Claims_i$ as the set of all claims made by source S_i, and $Sources_j$ as the set of all sources who claimed claim C_j. In the subsections below, we review the derivation of the posterior probability that a claim is true, followed by the derivation of the posterior probability that a source is truthful.

4.3.1 CLAIM CREDIBILITY

Consider some claim C_j, claimed by a set of sources $Sources_j$. Let i_k be the kth source in $Sources_j$, and let $|Sources_j| = K_j$. (For notational simplicity, the subscript j from K_j shall be occasionally omitted in the discussion below, where no ambiguity arises.) According to Bayes theorem:

$$P(C_j^t | S_{i_1} C_j, S_{i_2} C_j, \ldots, S_{i_K} C_j) = \frac{P(S_{i_1} C_j, S_{i_2} C_j, \ldots, S_{i_K} C_j | C_j^t)}{P(S_{i_1} C_j, S_{i_2} C_j, \ldots, S_{i_K} C_j)} P(C_j^t) \tag{4.3}$$

The above equation makes the implicit assumption that the probability that a source makes any given claim is sufficiently low that no appreciable change in posterior probability can be derived from the lack of a claim (i.e., lack of an edge between a source and a claim). Hence, only existence of claims is taken into account. Assuming further that sources are conditionally independent (i.e., given a claim, the odds that two sources claim it are independent), Equation (4.3) is rewritten as:

$$P(C_j^t|S_{i_1}C_j, S_{i_2}C_j, \ldots, S_{i_K}C_j) = \frac{P(S_{i_1}C_j|C_j^t) \ldots P(S_{i_K}C_j|C_j^t)}{P(S_{i_1}C_j, S_{i_2}C_j, \ldots, S_{i_K}C_j)} P(C_j^t) \tag{4.4}$$

It is further assumed that the change in posterior probability obtained from any single source or claim is small. This is typical when using evidence collected from many individually unreliable sources. Hence

$$\frac{P(S_{i_k}C_j|C_j^t)}{P(S_{i_k}C_j)} = 1 + \delta_{ikj}^t \tag{4.5}$$

where $|\delta_{ikj}^t| \ll 1$. Similarly

$$\frac{P(S_{i_k}C_j|C_j^f)}{P(S_{i_k}C_j)} = 1 + \delta_{ikj}^f \tag{4.6}$$

where $|\delta_{ikj}^f| \ll 1$. Under the above assumptions, the proof is provided in Appendix of Chapter 4 to show that the denominator of the right hand side in Equation (4.4) can be rewritten as follows:

$$P(S_{i_1}C_j, S_{i_2}C_j, \ldots, S_{i_K}C_j) \approx \prod_{k=1}^{K_j} P(S_{i_k}C_j) \tag{4.7}$$

Please see Appendix of Chapter 4 for a proof of Equation (4.7). Note that, the proof does *not* rely on an independence assumption of the marginals, $P(S_{i_k}C_j)$. Those marginals are, in fact, not independent but approximately so. The proof merely shows that, under the assumptions stated in Equations (4.5) and (4.6), the above approximation holds true. Substituting in Equation (4.4):

$$P(C_j^t|S_{i_1}C_j, S_{i_2}C_j, \ldots, S_{i_K}C_j) = \frac{P(S_{i_1}C_j|C_j^t) \ldots P(S_{i_K}C_j|C_j^t)}{P(S_{i_1}C_j) \ldots P(S_{i_K}C_j)} P(C_j^t) \tag{4.8}$$

which can be rewritten as:

$$P(C_j^t|S_{i_1}C_j, S_{i_2}C_j, \ldots, S_{i_K}C_j) = \frac{P(S_{i_1}C_j|C_j^t)}{P(S_{i_1}C_j)}$$

$$\times \ldots$$

$$\times \frac{P(S_{i_K}C_j|C_j^t)}{P(S_{i_K}C_j)}$$

$$\times P(C_j^t) \tag{4.9}$$

Substituting from Equation (4.5):

$$P(C_j^t|S_{i_1}C_j, S_{i_2}C_j, \ldots, S_{i_K}C_j) = P(C_j^t) \prod_{k=1}^{K_j}(1 + \delta_{ikj}^t)$$

$$= P(C_j^t)\left(1 + \sum_{k=1}^{K_j}\delta_{ikj}^t\right) \qquad (4.10)$$

The last line above is true because higher products of δ_{ikj}^t can be neglected, since it is assumed that $|\delta_{ikj}^t| \ll 1$. The above equation can be re-written as:

$$\frac{P(C_j^t|S_{i_1}C_j, S_{i_2}C_j, \ldots, S_{i_K}C_j) - P(C_j^t)}{P(C_j^t)} = \sum_{k=1}^{K_j}\delta_{ikj}^t \qquad (4.11)$$

where from Equation (4.5):

$$\delta_{ikj}^t = \frac{P(S_{i_k}C_j|C_j^t) - P(S_{i_k}C_j)}{P(S_{i_k}C_j)} \qquad (4.12)$$

4.3.2 SOURCE CREDIBILITY

Next, consider some source S_i, who makes the set of claims *Claims*$_i$. Let j_k be the kth claim in *Claims*$_i$, and let $|Claims_i| = L_i$. (For notational simplicity, the subscript i from L_i shall occasionally be omitted in the discussion below, where no ambiguity arises.) According to Bayes theorem:

$$P(S_i^t|S_iC_{j_1}, S_iC_{j_2}, \ldots, S_iC_{j_L}) = \frac{P(S_iC_{j_1}, S_iC_{j_2}, \ldots, S_iC_{j_L}|S_i^t)}{P(S_iC_{j_1}, S_iC_{j_2}, \ldots, S_iC_{j_L})} P(S_i^t) \qquad (4.13)$$

As before, assuming conditional independence:

$$P(S_i^t|S_iC_{j_1}, S_iC_{j_2}, \ldots, S_iC_{j_L}) = \frac{P(S_iC_{j_1}|S_i^t) \ldots P(S_iC_{j_L}|S_i^t)}{P(S_iC_{j_1}, S_iC_{j_2}, \ldots, S_iC_{j_L})} P(S_i^t) \qquad (4.14)$$

Once more the assumption that the change in posterior probability caused from any single claim is very small is invoked:

$$\frac{P(S_iC_{j_k}|S_i^t)}{P(S_iC_{j_k})} = 1 + \eta_{ijk}^t \qquad (4.15)$$

where $|\eta_{ijk}^t| \ll 1$. Similarly to the proof in Appendix of Chapter 4, this leads to:

$$P(S_i^t|S_iC_{j_1}, S_iC_{j_2}, \ldots, S_iC_{j_L}) = \frac{P(S_iC_{j_1}|S_i^t)}{P(S_iC_{j_1})}$$

$$\times \ldots$$

$$\times \frac{P(S_iC_{j_L}|S_i^t)}{P(S_iC_{j_L})}$$

$$\times P(S_i^t) \qquad (4.16)$$

The above can be re-written as follows:

$$P(S_i^t|S_iC_{j_1}, S_iC_{j_2}, \ldots, S_iC_{jL}) = P(S_i^t) \prod_{k=1}^{L_i}(1 + \eta_{ij_k}^t)$$

$$= P(S_i^t)\left(1 + \sum_{k=1}^{L_i} \eta_{ij_k}^t\right) \tag{4.17}$$

The above equation can be further re-written as:

$$\frac{P(S_i^t|S_iC_{j_1}, S_iC_{j_2}, \ldots, S_iC_{jL}) - P(S_i^t)}{P(S_i^t)} = \sum_{k=1}^{L_i} \eta_{ij_k}^t \tag{4.18}$$

where from Equation (4.15):

$$\eta_{ij_k}^t = \frac{P(S_iC_{j_k}|S_i^t) - P(S_iC_{j_k})}{P(S_iC_{j_k})} \tag{4.19}$$

4.4 THE ITERATIVE ALGORITHM

In the sections above, we reviewed the derivation of the expressions of posterior probability that a claim is true or that a source is truthful. These expressions were derived in terms of δ_{ikj}^t and $\eta_{ij_k}^t$. It remains to show how these quantities are related. Let us first consider the terms in Equation (4.12) that defines δ_{ikj}^t. The first is $P(S_iC_j|C_j^t)$, the probability that S_i claims claim C_j, given that C_j is true. (For notation simplicity, subscripts i and j shall be used to denote the source and the claim.) We have:

$$P(S_iC_j|C_j^t) = \frac{P(S_iC_j, C_j^t)}{P(C_j^t)} \tag{4.20}$$

where

$$P(S_iC_j, C_j^t) = P(S_i\ speaks)$$
$$= P(S_i\ claims\ C_j|S_i\ speaks)$$
$$= P(C_j^t|S_i\ speaks, S_i\ claims\ C_j) \tag{4.21}$$

In other words, the joint probability that link S_iC_j exists and C_j is true is the product of the probability that S_i speaks, denoted $P(S_i\ speaks)$, the probability that it claims C_j given that it speaks, denoted $P(S_i\ claims\ C_j|S_i\ speaks)$, and the probability that the claim is true, given that it is claimed by S_i, denoted $P(C_j^t|S_i\ speaks, S_i\ claims\ C_j)$. Here, $P(S_i\ speaks)$ depends on the rate at which S_i makes claims. Some sources may be more prolific than others. $P(S_i\ claims\ C_j|S_i\ speaks)$ is simply $1/c$, where c is the total number of claims. Finally, $P(C_j^t|S_i\ speaks, S_i\ claims\ C_j)$ is the probability that S_i is truthful. Since the ground truth is not known, that probability is estimated by the best information we have, which is $P(S_i^t|S_iC_{j_1}, S_iC_{j_2}, \ldots, S_iC_{jL})$. Thus:

$$P(S_iC_j, C_j^t) = \frac{P(S_i\ speaks)P(S_i^t|S_iC_{j_1}, S_iC_{j_2}, \ldots, S_iC_{jL})}{c} \tag{4.22}$$

Substituting in Equation (4.20) from Equation (4.22) and noting that $P(C_j^t)$ is simply the ratio of true claims, c_{true} to the total claims, c, we get:

$$P(S_i C_j | C_j^t) = \frac{P(S_i \ speaks) P(S_i^t | S_i C_{j_1}, S_i C_{j_2}, \ldots, S_i C_{j_L})}{c_{true}} \qquad (4.23)$$

Similarly,

$$P(S_i C_j) = \frac{P(S_i \ speaks)}{c} \qquad (4.24)$$

Substituting from Equations (4.23) and (4.24) into Equation (4.12) and re-arranging, we get:

$$\delta_{ikj}^t = \frac{P(S_{i_k} C_j | C_j^t) - P(S_{i_k} C_j)}{P(S_{i_k} C_j)}$$

$$= \frac{P(S_i^t | S_i C_{j_1}, S_i C_{j_2}, \ldots, S_i C_{j_L})}{c_{true}/c} - 1 \qquad (4.25)$$

If the fraction of all true claims to the total number of claims is taken as the prior probability that a source is truthful, $P(S_i^t)$ (which is a reasonable initial guess in the absence of further evidence), then the above equation can be re-written as:

$$\delta_{ikj}^t = \frac{P(S_i^t | S_i C_{j_1}, S_i C_{j_2}, \ldots, S_i C_{j_L})}{P(S_i^t)} - 1 \qquad (4.26)$$

Substituting for δ_{ikj}^t in Equation (4.11), we get:

$$\frac{P(C_j^t | S_{i_1} C_j, S_{i_2} C_j, \ldots, S_{i_K} C_j) - P(C_j^t)}{P(C_j^t)} = \sum_{i=1}^{K_j} \frac{P(S_i^t | S_i C_{j_1}, S_i C_{j_2}, \ldots, S_i C_{j_L}) - P(S_i^t)}{P(S_i^t)} \qquad (4.27)$$

The following can be similarly proven:

$$\eta_{ijk}^t = \frac{P(C_j^t | S_{i_1} C_j, S_{i_2} C_j, \ldots, S_{i_K} C_j)}{P(C_j^t)} - 1 \qquad (4.28)$$

and

$$\frac{P(S_i^t | S_i C_{j_1}, S_i C_{j_2}, \ldots, S_i C_{j_L}) - P(S_i^t)}{P(S_i^t)} = \sum_{j=1}^{L_i} \frac{P(C_j^t | S_{i_1} C_j, S_{i_2} C_j, \ldots, S_{i_K} C_j) - P(C_j^t)}{P(C_j^t)} \qquad (4.29)$$

Comparing the above equations to the iterative formulation of the basic fact-finder, described in this section, the sought interpretation of the credibility rank of sources $Rank(S_i)$ and credibility rank of claims $Rank(C_j)$ in iterative fact-finding is:

$$Rank(C_j) = \frac{P(C_j^t | S_{i_1} C_j, S_{i_2} C_j, \ldots, S_{i_K} C_j) - P(C_j^t)}{P(C_j^t)} \qquad (4.30)$$

$$Rank(S_i) = \frac{P(S_i^t | S_i C_{j_1}, S_i C_{j_2}, \ldots, S_i C_{j_L}) - P(S_i^t)}{P(S_i^t)} \qquad (4.31)$$

In other words, $Rank(C_j)$ is interpreted as the increase in the posterior probability that a claim is true, normalized by the prior. Similarly, $Rank(S_i)$ is interpreted as the increase in the posterior probability that a source is truthful, normalized by the prior. Substituting from Equations (4.30) and (4.31) into Equations (4.27) and (4.29), we then get:

$$Rank(C_j) = \sum_{k \in Sources_j} Rank(S_k)$$

$$Rank(S_i) = \sum_{k \in Claims_i} Rank(C_k) \qquad (4.32)$$

One should note that the credibility ranks are normalized in each iteration to keep the values in bound. The above equations make similar linear approximation as *Sums* (Hubs and Authorities) [35] as we reviewed in the previous section. However, we will review another set of work using a more principled approach (i.e., MLE) to avoid this approximation in the next chapter. Once the credibility ranks are computed such that they satisfy the above equations (and any other problem constraints), Equations (4.30) and (4.31), together with the assumption that prior probability that a claim is true is initialized to $p_a^t = c_{true}/c$, give us the main contribution of this effort, Namely*:

$$P(C_j^t|network) = p_a^t(Rank(C_j) + 1) \qquad (4.33)$$

Similarly, it is shown that if p_s^t is the prior probability that a randomly chosen source tells the truth, then:

$$P(S_i^t|network) = p_s^t(Rank(S_i) + 1) \qquad (4.34)$$

Hence, the above Bayesian analysis presents, for the first time, a basis for estimating the probability that *each individual source*, S_i, is truthful and that *each individual claim*, C_j, is true. These two vectors are computed based on two scalar constants: p_a^t and p_s^t, which represent estimated statistical averages over all claims and all sources, respectively.

4.5 EXAMPLES AND RESULTS

In this section, we review the experiments that were carried to verify the correctness and accuracy of the probability that a source is truthful or a claim is true estimated from the Bayesian interpretation of fact-finding in information networks. The Bayesian interpretation was compared to several state-of-the-art algorithms in fact-finder literature.

A simulator was built in Matlab 7.14.0 to simulate the source and claim information network. To test the results, the simulator generates a random number of sources

---

*The equations above are ambiguous with respect to a scale factor. To handle the ambiguity, the constraint that probabilities cannot exceed one is imposed.

and claims, and partition these claims into true and false ones. A random probability, P_i, is assigned to each source S_i representing the ground truth probability that the source speaks the truth. For each source S_i, L_i observations are generated. Each observation has a probability P_i of being true and a probability $1 - P_i$ of being false. A true observation links the source to a randomly chosen true claim (representing that the source made that claim). A false observation links the source to a randomly chosen false claim. This generates an information network.

Let P_i be uniformly distributed between 0.5 and 1 in the experiments.[†] An assignment of credibility values that satisfies Equation (4.32) is then found for the topology of the generated information network. Finally, the estimated probability that a claim is true or a source is truthful is computed from the resulting credibility values of claims and sources based on Equations (4.33) and (4.34). Since it is assumed that claims are either true or false, each claim is viewed as "true" or "false" based on whether the probability that it is true is above or below 50%. Then the computed results are compared against the ground truth to report the estimation accuracy.

For sources, the computed probability is simply compared to the ground truth probability that they tell the truth. For claims, we define two metrics to evaluate classification accuracy: false positives and false negatives. The false positives are defined as the ratio of the number of false claims that are classified as true over the total number of claims that are false. The false negatives are defined as the ratio of the number of true claims that are classified as false over the total number of claims that are true. Reported results are averaged over 100 random source correctness probability distributions.

The first experiment showed the effect of the number of sources on prediction accuracy. The number of true and false claims was fixed at 1000 respectively. The average number of observations per source was set to 100. The number of sources is varied from 20 to 100. The estimation accuracy for both sources and claims is shown in Figure 4.1. We note that both estimation accuracy of source probabilities to be truthful and the claim classification accuracy (i.e., false positives and false negatives) improves as the number of sources increases. This is intuitive: more sources provide more corroborating observations about the claims, which helps the Bayesian approach to get better estimations. The usefulness of the Bayesian interpretation increases for large networks.

The next experiment shows the effect of changing the claim mix on estimation accuracy. The ratio of the number of true claims to the total number of claims in the network was varied. Assuming that there is usually only one variant of the truth, whereas rumors have more versions, one might expect the set of true claims to be

[†]In practice, there is no incentive for a source to lie more than 50% of the time, since negating their statements would then give a more accurate truth. For such a malicious node to be effective, it must coordinate with a majority of nodes to swing the consensus to a false value, which is very difficult. Such a case is not studied in this work but is addressed by another line of work reviewed in a later chapter that discusses social networks and source dependency.

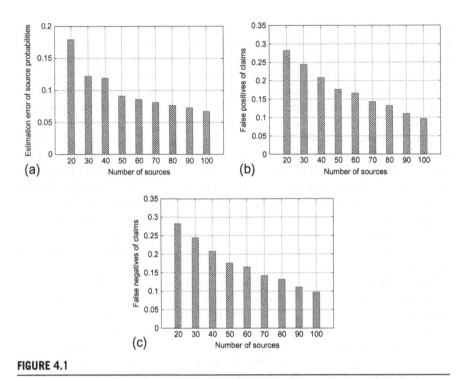

FIGURE 4.1

Estimation accuracy versus varying number of sources. (a) Source estimation accuracy.
(b) Claim classification false positives. (c) Claim classification false negatives.

smaller than the set of false ones. Hence, the total number of claims was fixed to be 2000 and change the ratio of true to total claims from 0.1 to 0.5. The c_{true}/c is set accordingly to the correct ratio used for the experiment. The number of sources in the network is set to 50 and the average observations per source is set to 100. The estimation accuracy for both sources and claims is shown in Figure 4.2. Observe that both the estimation error of source probabilities to be truthful and the error of claim classification increase as the ratio of true claims increases. This is because the true claim set becomes less densely claimed and more true and false claims are misclassified as each other as the number of true claims grows.

Finally, the Bayesian interpretation scheme was compared to three other fact-finder schemes: Sums (Hubs and Authorities) [35], Average-Log [37], and TruthFinder [36]. These algorithms were selected because, unlike other state-of-art fact-finders (e.g., 3-Estimates [38]), they do not require the knowledge about what mutual exclusion, if any, exists among the claims. In this experiment, the number of true and false claims is 1000 respectively, the number of observations per source is 150, and the number of sources is set to 50. The initial estimation offset on prior claim correctness was varied from 0.05 to 0.45. The initial claim beliefs of all fact-finders

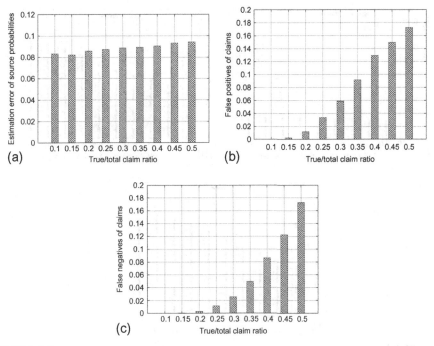

FIGURE 4.2

Estimation accuracy versus varying true/total claims. (a) Source estimation accuracy.
(b) Claim classification false positives. (c) Claim classification false negatives.

were set to the initial prior (i.e., 0.5) plus the offset used for the experiment. Each baseline fact-finder was ran for 20 iterations, and the 1000 highest-belief claims were selected as those predicted to be correct. The estimated probability of each source making a true claim was thus calculated as the proportion of predicted-correct claims asserted relative to the total number of claims asserted by source.

The compared results are shown in Figure 4.3. Observe that the prediction error of source correctness probability by the Bayesian interpretation scheme is significantly lower than all baseline fact-finder schemes. The reason is that Bayesian analysis estimates the source correctness probability more accurately based on Equation (4.34) derived in this chapter rather than using heuristic methods adopted by the baseline schemes that depends on the correct estimation on prior claim correctness. We also note that the prediction performance for claims in the Bayesian scheme is generally as good as the baselines. This is good since the other techniques excel at ranking, which (together with the hint on the number of correct claims) is sufficient to identify which ones these are. The results confirm the advantages of the Bayesian approach over previous ranking-based work at what the Bayesian analysis does best: estimation of probabilities of conclusions from observed evidence.

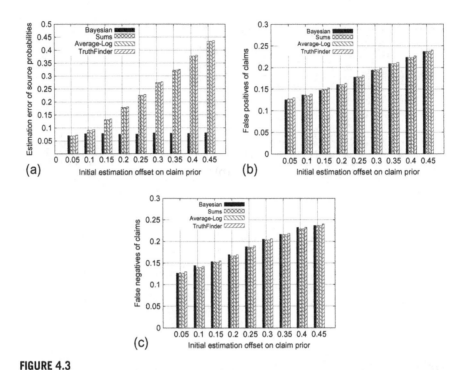

FIGURE 4.3

Estimation accuracy comparison with baseline fact-finders. (a) Source estimation accuracy. (b) Claim classification false positives. (c) Claim classification false negatives.

4.6 DISCUSSION

This chapter presented a Bayesian interpretation of the most basic fact-finding algorithm. The question was to understand why the algorithm is successful at ranking, and to use that understanding to translate the ranking into actual probabilities. Several simplifying assumptions were made that offer opportunities for future extensions.

No dependencies were assumed among different sources or different claims. In reality, sources could be influenced by other sources. Claims could fall into mutual exclusion sets, such as when one is the negation of the other. Taking such relations into account can further improve quality of fact-finding. The change in posterior probabilities due to any single edge in the source-claim network was assumed to be very small. In other words, it is assumed that $|\delta_{i,kj}^t| \ll 1$ and $|\eta_{ij_k}^t| \ll 1$. It is interesting to extend the scheme to situations where a mix of reliable and unreliable sources is used. In this case, claims from reliable sources can help improve the determination of credibility of other sources.

The probability that any one source makes any one claim was assumed to be low. Hence, the lack of an edge between a source and a claim did not offer useful information. There may be cases, however, when the absence of a link between a source and a claim is important. For example, when a source is expected to bear on an issue, a source that "withholds the truth" exhibits absence of a link that needs to be accounted for.

In this chapter, we reviewed a novel analysis technique for information networks that uses a Bayesian interpretation of the network to assess the credibility of facts and sources. Prior literature that uses information network analysis for fact-finding aims at computing the credibility *rank* of different facts and sources. This work, in contrast, proposes an analytically founded technique to convert rank to a probability that a fact is true or that a source is truthful. This chapter therefore lays out a foundation for quality of information assurances in iterative fact-finding, a common branch of techniques used in data mining literature for analysis of information networks. The fact-finding techniques addressed in this chapter are particularly useful in environments where a large number of sources are used whose reliability is not a priori known (as opposed collecting information from a small number of well-characterized sources). Such situations are common when, for instance, crowd-sourcing is used to obtain information, or when information is to be gleaned from informal sources such as Twitter messages. The reviewed Bayesian approach shows that accurate information may indeed be obtained regarding facts and sources even when we do not know the credibility of each source in advance, and where individual sources may generally be unreliable.

APPENDIX

Consider an assertion C_j made be several sources $S_{i_1}, \ldots, S_{i_K}$. Let $S_{i_k}C_j$ denote the fact that source S_{i_k} made assertion C_j. It is further assumed that Equations (4.5) and (4.6) hold. In other words:

$$\frac{P(S_{i_k}C_j|C_j^t)}{P(S_{i_k}C_j)} = 1 + \delta_{i_kj}^t$$

$$\frac{P(S_{i_k}C_j|C_j^f)}{P(S_{i_k}C_j)} = 1 + \delta_{i_kj}^f$$

where $|\delta_{i_kj}^t| \ll 1$ and $|\delta_{i_kj}^f| \ll 1$.

Under these assumptions, it can be proved that the joint probability $P(S_{i_1}C_j, S_{i_2}C_j, \ldots, S_{i_K}C_j)$, denoted for simplicity by $P(Sources_j)$, is equal to the product of marginal probabilities $P(S_{i_1}C_j), \ldots, P(S_{i_K}C_j)$.

First, note that, by definition:

$$P(Sources_j) = P(S_{i_1}C_j, S_{i_2}C_j, \ldots, S_{i_K}C_j)$$

$$= P(S_{i_1}C_j, S_{i_2}C_j, \ldots, S_{i_K}C_j|C_j^t)P(C_j^t)$$

$$+ P(S_{i_1}C_j, S_{i_2}C_j, \ldots, S_{i_K}C_j|C_j^f)P(C_j^f) \qquad (4.35)$$

Using the conditional independence assumption, we get:

$$P(Sources_j) = P(C_j^t) \prod_{k=1}^{K} P(S_{i_k} C_j | C_j^t)$$

$$+ P(C_j^f) \prod_{k=1}^{K} P(S_{i_k} C_j | C_j^f) \tag{4.36}$$

Using Equations (4.5) and (4.6), the above can be rewritten as:

$$P(Sources_j) = P(C_j^t) \prod_{k=1}^{K_j} (1 + \delta_{ikj}^t) \prod_{k=1}^{K_j} P(S_{i_k} C_j)$$

$$+ P(C_j^f) \prod_{k=1}^{K_j} (1 + \delta_{ikj}^f) \prod_{k=1}^{K_j} P(S_{i_k} C_j) \tag{4.37}$$

and since $|\delta_{ikj}^t| \ll 1$ and $|\delta_{ikj}^f| \ll 1$, any higher-order terms involving them can be ignored. Hence, $\prod_{k=1}^{K_j} (1 + \delta_{ikj}^t) = 1 + \sum_{k=1}^{K_j} \delta_{ikj}^t$, which results in:

$$P(Sources_j) = P(C_j^t) \left(1 + \sum_{k=1}^{K_j} \delta_{ikj}^t \right) \prod_{k=1}^{K} P(S_{i_k} C_j)$$

$$+ P(C_j^f) \left(1 + \sum_{k=1}^{K_j} \delta_{ikj}^f \right) \prod_{k=1}^{K} P(S_{i_k} C_j) \tag{4.38}$$

Distributing multiplication over addition in Equation (4.38), then using the fact that $P(C_j^t) + P(C_j^f) = 1$ and rearranging, we get:

$$P(Sources_j) = \prod_{k=1}^{K_j} P(S_{i_k} C_j)(1 + Terms_j) \tag{4.39}$$

where

$$Terms_j = P(C_j^t) \sum_{k=1}^{K_j} \delta_{ikj}^t + P(C_j^f) \sum_{k=1}^{K_j} \delta_{ikj}^f \tag{4.40}$$

Next, it remains to compute $Terms_j$.

Consider δ_{ikj}^t as defined in Equation (4.5). The equation can be rewritten as follows:

$$\delta_{ikj}^t = \frac{P(S_{i_k} C_j | C_j^t) - P(S_{i_k} C_j)}{P(S_{i_k} C_j)} \tag{4.41}$$

where by definition, $P(S_{i_k} C_j) = P(S_{i_k} C_j | C_j^t) P(C_j^t) + P(S_{i_k} C_j | C_j^f) P(C_j^f)$. Substituting in Equation (4.41), we get:

$$\delta^t_{i_k j} = \frac{P(S_{i_k} C_j | C^t_j)(1 - P(C^t_j)) - P(S_{i_k} C_j | C^f_j)P(C^f_j)}{P(S_{i_k} C_j | C^t_j)P(C^t_j) + P(S_{i_k} C_j | C^f_j)P(C^f_j)} \tag{4.42}$$

Using the fact that $1 - P(C^t_j) = P(C^f_j)$ in the numerator, and rearranging, we get:

$$\delta^t_{i_k j} = \frac{(P(S_{i_k} C_j | C^t_j) - P(S_{i_k} C_j | C^f_j))P(C^f_j)}{P(S_{i_k} C_j | C^t_j)P(C^t_j) + P(S_{i_k} C_j | C^f_j)P(C^f_j)} \tag{4.43}$$

We can similarly show that:

$$\begin{aligned} \delta^f_{i_k j} &= \frac{P(S_{i_k} C_j | C^f_j) - P(S_{i_k} C_j)}{P(S_{i_k} C_j)} \\ &= \frac{P(S_{i_k} C_j | C^f_j)(1 - P(C^f_j)) - P(S_{i_k} C_j | C^t_j)P(C^t_j)}{P(S_{i_k} C_j | C^t_j)P(C^t_j) + P(S_{i_k} C_j | C^f_j)P(C^f_j)} \\ &= \frac{(P(S_{i_k} C_j | C^f_j) - P(S_{i_k} C_j | C^t_j))P(C^t_j)}{P(S_{i_k} C_j | C^t_j)P(C^t_j) + P(S_{i_k} C_j | C^f_j)P(C^f_j)} \end{aligned} \tag{4.44}$$

Dividing Equation (4.43) by Equation (4.44), we get:

$$\frac{\delta^t_{i_k j}}{\delta^f_{i_k j}} = -\frac{P(C^f_j)}{P(C^t_j)} \tag{4.45}$$

Substituting for $\delta^t_{i_k j}$ from Equation (4.45) into Equation (4.40), we get $Terms_j = 0$. Substituting with this result in Equation (4.39), we get:

$$P(Sources_j) = \prod_{k=1}^{K_j} P(S_{i_k} C_j) \tag{4.46}$$

The above result completes the proof. We have shown that the joint probability $P(S_{i_1} C_j, S_{i_2} C_j, \ldots, S_{i_K} C_j)$, denoted for simplicity by $P(Sources_j)$, is well approximated by the product of marginal probabilities $P(S_{i_1} C_j), \ldots, P(S_{i_K} C_j)$. Note that, the proof did not assume independence of the marginals. Instead, it proved the result under the small $\delta_{i_k j}$ assumption.

Social sensing: A maximum likelihood estimation approach

5.1 THE SOCIAL SENSING PROBLEM

To formulate the reliable social sensing problem in a manner amenable to rigorous optimization, a social sensing application model was proposed by Wang et al. where a group of M sources, $S_1, \ldots, S_M$, make individual observations about a set of N claims $C_1, \ldots, C_N$ in their environment [100]. For example, a group of individuals interested in the appearance of their neighborhood might join a sensing campaign to report all locations of offensive graffiti. Alternatively, a group of drivers might join a campaign to report freeway locations in need of repair. Hence, each claim denotes the existence or lack thereof of an offending condition at a given location.* In this effort, only binary variables are considered, and it is assumed, without loss of generality, that their "normal" state is negative (e.g., no offending graffiti on walls, or no potholes on streets). Hence, sources report only when a positive value is encountered.

Each source generally observes only a subset of all variables (e.g., the conditions at locations they have been to). The goal here is to determine which observations are correct and which are not. As mentioned in the introduction, this work differs from a large volume of previous sensing literature in that no prior knowledge is assumed about source reliability and no prior knowledge is assumed for the correctness of individual observations. Also note that the reviewed work in this chapter assumes imperfect reliability of sources and claims made by sources are mostly true, which is reasonable in a large category of social sensing applications. However, if those assumptions do not hold, the algorithm reviewed later in the chapter could converge to other stationary solutions (e.g., all sources are perfectly reliable or unreliable).

Besides the notations defined in the previous chapter, let us introduce a few new notations that will be used in this chapter. Let the probability that source S_i makes an observation be s_i. Further, let the probability that source S_i is right be t_i and the probability that it is wrong be $1 - t_i$. Note that, this probability depends on the

---

*It is assumed that locations are discretized, and therefore finite. For example, they are given by street addresses or mile markers.

Association for Computing Machinery, Inc. being the copyright holder, grants permission to reprint text of the article, Dong Wang, Lance Kaplan, Hieu Le, and Tarek Abdelzaher. "On Truth Discovery in Social Sensing: A Maximum Likelihood Estimation Approach." Proceedings of *The 11th International Conference on Information Processing in Sensor Networks (IPSN 12)* Beijing, China April 2012.

source's reliability, which is not known a priori. Formally, t_i is defined as the odds of a claim to be true given that source S_i reports it:

$$t_i = P(C_j^t | S_i C_j) \tag{5.1}$$

Let a_i represent the (unknown) probability that source S_i reports a claim to be true when it is indeed true, and b_i represent the (unknown) probability that source S_i reports a claim to be true when it is in reality false. Formally, a_i and b_i are defined as follows:

$$a_i = P(S_i C_j | C_j^t)$$
$$b_i = P(S_i C_j | C_j^f) \tag{5.2}$$

From the definition of t_i, a_i, and b_i, their relationship can be determined by using the Bayesian theorem:

$$a_i = P(S_i C_j | C_j^t) = \frac{P(S_i C_j, C_j^t)}{P(C_j^t)} = \frac{P(C_j^t | S_i C_j) P(S_i C_j)}{P(C_j^t)}$$

$$b_i = P(S_i C_j | C_j^f) = \frac{P(S_i C_j, C_j^f)}{P(C_j^f)} = \frac{P(C_j^f | S_i C_j) P(S_i C_j)}{P(C_j^f)} \tag{5.3}$$

The only input to the algorithm is the social sensing topology represented by a matrix SC, where $S_i C_j = 1$ when source S_i reports that C_j is true, and $S_i C_j = 0$ otherwise. Let us call it the *observation matrix*.

The goal of the algorithm is to compute (i) the best estimate h_j on the correctness of each claim C_j and (ii) the best estimate e_i of the reliability of each source S_i. The sets of the estimates are denoted by vectors H and E, respectively. The goal is to find the H^* and E^* vectors that are most consistent with the observation matrix SC. Formally, this is given by:

$$\langle H^*, E^* \rangle = \underset{\langle H,E \rangle}{\arg\max}\, p(SC | H, E) \tag{5.4}$$

The background bias d will also be computed, which is the overall probability that a randomly chosen claim is true. For example, it may represent the probability that any street, in general, is in disrepair. It does not indicate, however, whether any particular claim about disrepair at a particular location is true or not. Hence, one can define the prior of a claim being true as $P(C_j^t) = d$. Note also that, the probability that a source makes an observation (i.e., s_i) is proportional to the number of claims observed by the source over the total number of claims observed by all sources, which can be easily computed from the observation matrix. Hence, one can define the prior $P(S_i C_j) = s_i$. Plugging these, together with t_i into the definition of a_i and b_i, we get:

$$a_i = \frac{t_i \times s_i}{d}$$
$$b_i = \frac{(1 - t_i) \times s_i}{1 - d} \tag{5.5}$$

So that

$$t_i = \frac{a_i \times d}{a_i \times d + b_i \times (1 - d)} \tag{5.6}$$

5.2 EXPECTATION MAXIMIZATION

In this section, we review the solution to the problem formulated in the previous section using the expectation maximization (EM) algorithm. As we discussed in Chapter 3, EM is a general algorithm for finding the maximum likelihood estimates (MLEs) of parameters in a statistic model, where the data are "incomplete" or the likelihood function involves latent variables [93]. In the following, we first briefly review the basic ideas and steps of EM that will be used in this chapter.

5.2.1 BACKGROUND

The EM algorithm is useful when the likelihood expression simplifies by the inclusion of a latent variable. Considering a latent variable Z, the likelihood function is given by:

$$L(\theta; X) = p(X|\theta) = \sum_{Z} p(X, Z|\theta) \tag{5.7}$$

where $p(X, Z|\theta)$ is $L(\theta|X, Z)$, which is uni-modal and easy to solve.

Once the formulation is complete, the EM algorithm finds the MLE by iteratively performing the following steps:

- E-step: Compute the expected log likelihood function where the expectation is taken with respect to the computed conditional distribution of the latent variables given the current settings and observed data.

$$Q(\theta|\theta^{(t)}) = E_{Z|X,\theta^{(t)}}[\log L(\theta; X, Z)] \tag{5.8}$$

- M-step: Find the parameters that maximize the Q function in the E-step to be used as the estimate of θ for the next iteration.

$$\theta^{(t+1)} = \arg\max_{\theta} Q(\theta|\theta^{(t)}) \tag{5.9}$$

5.2.2 MATHEMATICAL FORMULATION

The social sensing problem fits nicely into the EM model. First, a latent variable Z is introduced for each claim to indicate whether it is true or not. Specifically, a corresponding variable z_j is defined for the jth claim C_j such that: $z_j = 1$ when C_j is true and $z_j = 0$ otherwise. The observation matrix SC is denoted as the observed data X, and $\theta = (a_1, a_2, \ldots, a_M; b_1, b_2, \ldots, b_M; d)$ is defined as the parameter of the model that needs to be estimated. The goal is to obtain the MLE of θ for the model containing observed data X and latent variables Z.

The likelihood function $L(\theta; X, Z)$ is given by:

$$L(\theta; X, Z) = p(X, Z|\theta)$$

$$= \prod_{j=1}^{N} \left\{ \prod_{i=1}^{M} a_i^{S_iC_j} (1 - a_i)^{(1-S_iC_j)} \times d \times z_j \right.$$

$$\left. + \prod_{i=1}^{M} b_i^{S_iC_j} (1 - b_i)^{(1-S_iC_j)} \times (1 - d) \times (1 - z_j) \right\} \qquad (5.10)$$

where, as we mentioned before, a_i and b_i are the conditional probabilities that source S_i reports the claim C_j to be true given that C_j is true or false (i.e., defined in Equation (5.2)). $S_iC_j = 1$ when source S_i reports that C_j is true, and $S_iC_j = 0$ otherwise. d is the background bias that a randomly chosen claim is true. Additionally, it is assumed that sources and claims are independent respectively. The likelihood function above describes the likelihood to have current observation matrix X and hidden variable Z given the estimation parameter θ.

5.2.3 DERIVING THE E-STEP AND M-STEP

Given the above formulation, substitute the likelihood function defined in Equation (5.10) into the definition of Q function given by Equation (5.8) of EM. The Expectation step (E-step) becomes:

$$Q(\theta|\theta^{(t)}) = E_{Z|X,\theta^{(t)}}[\log L(\theta; X, Z)]$$

$$= \sum_{j=1}^{N} \left\{ p(z_j = 1|X_j, \theta^{(t)}) \right.$$

$$\times \left[\sum_{i=1}^{M} (S_iC_j \log a_i + (1 - S_iC_j) \log(1 - a_i) + \log d) \right] + p(z_j = 0|X_j, \theta^{(t)})$$

$$\left. \times \left[\sum_{i=1}^{M} (S_iC_j \log b_i + (1 - S_iC_j) \log(1 - b_i) + \log(1 - d)) \right] \right\} \qquad (5.11)$$

where X_j represents the jth column of the observed SC matrix (i.e., observations of the jth claim from all sources) and $p(z_j = 1|X_j, \theta^{(t)})$ is the conditional probability of the latent variable z_j to be true given the observation matrix related to the jth claim and current estimate of θ, which is given by:

$$p(z_j = 1|X_j, \theta^{(t)}) = \frac{p(z_j = 1; X_j, \theta^{(t)})}{p(X_j, \theta^{(t)})}$$

$$= \frac{p(X_j, \theta^{(t)}|z_j = 1)p(z_j = 1)}{p(X_j, \theta^{(t)}|z_j = 1)p(z_j = 1) + p(X_j, \theta^{(t)}|z_j = 0)p(z_j = 0)}$$

$$= \frac{A(t,j) \times d^{(t)}}{A(t,j) \times d^{(t)} + B(t,j) \times (1 - d^{(t)})} \qquad (5.12)$$

where $A(t,j)$ and $B(t,j)$ are defined as:

$$A(t,j) = p(X_j, \theta^{(t)} | z_j = 1)$$

$$= \prod_{i=1}^{M} a_i^{(t) S_i C_j} (1 - a_i^{(t)})^{(1 - S_i C_j)}$$

$$B(t,j) = p(X_j, \theta^{(t)} | z_j = 0)$$

$$= \prod_{i=1}^{M} b_i^{(t) S_i C_j} (1 - b_i^{(t)})^{(1 - S_i C_j)} \tag{5.13}$$

$A(t,j)$ and $B(t,j)$ represent the conditional probability regarding observations about the jth claim and current estimation of the parameter θ given the jth claim is true or false, respectively.

Next Equation (5.11) is simplified by noting that the conditional probability of $p(z_j = 1 | X_j, \theta^{(t)})$ given by Equation (5.12) is only a function of t and j. Thus, it is represented by $Z(t,j)$. Similarly, $p(z_j = 0 | X_j, \theta^{(t)})$ is simply:

$$p(z_j = 0 | X_j, \theta^{(t)}) = 1 - p(z_j = 1 | X_j, \theta^{(t)})$$

$$= \frac{B(t,j) \times (1 - d^{(t)})}{A(t,j) \times d^{(t)} + B(t,j) \times (1 - d^{(t)})}$$

$$= 1 - Z(t,j) \tag{5.14}$$

Substituting from Equations (5.12) and (5.14) into Equation (5.11), we get:

$$Q(\theta | \theta^{(t)}) = \sum_{j=1}^{N} \left\{ Z(t,j) \times \left[\sum_{i=1}^{M} (S_i C_j \log a_i + (1 - S_i C_j) \log(1 - a_i) + \log d) \right] \right.$$

$$\left. + (1 - Z(t,j)) \times \left[\sum_{i=1}^{M} (S_i C_j \log b_i + (1 - S_i C_j) \log(1 - b_i) + \log(1 - d)) \right] \right\} \tag{5.15}$$

The Maximization step (M-step) is given by Equation (5.9). θ^* (i.e., $(a_1^*, a_2^*, \ldots, a_M^*; b_1^*, b_2^*, \ldots, b_M^*; d^*))$ is chosen to maximize the $Q(\theta | \theta^{(t)})$ function in each iteration to be the $\theta^{(t+1)}$ of the next iteration.

To get θ^* that maximizes $Q(\theta | \theta^{(t)})$, the derivatives are set to 0: $\frac{\partial Q}{\partial a_i} = 0$, $\frac{\partial Q}{\partial b_i} = 0$, $\frac{\partial Q}{\partial d} = 0$ which yields:

$$\sum_{j=1}^{N} \left[Z(t,j) \left(S_i C_j \frac{1}{a_i^*} - (1 - S_i C_j) \frac{1}{1 - a_i^*} \right) \right] = 0$$

$$\sum_{j=1}^{N} \left[(1 - Z(t,j)) \left(S_i C_j \frac{1}{b_i^*} - (1 - S_i C_j) \frac{1}{1 - b_i^*} \right) \right] = 0$$

$$\sum_{j=1}^{N} \left[Z(t,j) M \frac{1}{d^*} - (1 - Z(t,j)) M \frac{1}{1 - d^*} \right] = 0 \tag{5.16}$$

Let us define SJ_i as the set of claims the source S_i actually observes in the observation matrix SC, and $\overline{SJ}_i$ as the set of claims source S_i does not observe. Thus, Equation (5.16) can be rewritten as:

$$\sum_{j \in SJ_i} Z(t,j)\frac{1}{a_i^*} - \sum_{j \in \overline{SJ}_i} Z(t,j)\frac{1}{1-a_i^*} = 0$$

$$\sum_{j \in SJ_i} (1 - Z(t,j))\frac{1}{b_i^*} - \sum_{j \in \overline{SJ}_i} (1 - Z(t,j))\frac{1}{1-b_i^*} = 0$$

$$\sum_{j=1}^{N} \left[Z(t,j)\frac{1}{d^*} - (1 - Z(t,j))\frac{1}{1-d^*} \right] = 0 \qquad (5.17)$$

Solving the above equations, the expressions of the optimal a_i^*, b_i^*, and d^* are:

$$a_i^{(t+1)} = a_i^* = \frac{\sum_{j \in SJ_i} Z(t,j)}{\sum_{j=1}^{N} Z(t,j)}$$

$$b_i^{(t+1)} = b_i^* = \frac{K_i - \sum_{j \in SJ_i} Z(t,j)}{N - \sum_{j=1}^{N} Z(t,j)}$$

$$d_i^{(t+1)} = d_i^* = \frac{\sum_{j=1}^{N} Z(t,j)}{N} \qquad (5.18)$$

where K_i is the number of claims espoused by source S_i and N is the total number of claims in the observation matrix.

Given the above, the E-step and M-step of EM optimization reduce to simply calculating Equations (5.12) and (5.18) iteratively until they converge. The convergence analysis has been done for EM scheme and it is beyond the scope of this chapter [108]. In practice, the algorithm runs until the difference of estimation parameter between consecutive iterations becomes insignificant. Since the claim is binary, the decision vector H^* can be computed from the converged value of $Z(t,j)$. Specially, h_j is true if $Z(t,j) \geq 0.5$ and false otherwise. At the same time, the estimation vector E^* of source reliability can also be computed from the converged values of $a_i^{(t)}$, $b_i^{(t)}$, and $d^{(t)}$ based on their relationship given by Equation (5.5). This completes the mathematical development. The resulting algorithm is summarized in the subsection below.

5.3 THE EM FACT-FINDING ALGORITHM

In summary of the EM scheme derived above, the input is the observation matrix SC from social sensing data, and the output is the MLE of source reliability and claim correctness (i.e., E^* and H^* vector defined in Equation (5.4)). In particular, given the observation matrix SC, the algorithm begins by initializing the parameter θ with random values between 0 and 1.[†] The algorithm then performs the E-steps

---

[†] In practice, the EM will converge faster if the rough estimate of the average reliability of sources is known to the algorithm.

ALGORITHM 1 EXPECTATION MAXIMIZATION ALGORITHM

1: Initialize θ with random values between 0 and 1
2: **while** $\theta^{(t)}$ does not converge **do**
3:      **for** $j = 1 : N$ **do**
4:          compute $Z(t, j)$ based on Equation (5.12)
5:      **end for**
6:      $\theta^{(t+1)} = \theta^{(t)}$
7:      **for** $i = 1 : M$ **do**
8:          compute $a_i^{(t+1)}, b_i^{(t+1)}, d^{(t+1)}$ based on Equation (5.18)
9:          update $a_i^{(t)}, b_i^{(t)}, d^{(t)}$ with $a_i^{(t+1)}, b_i^{(t+1)}, d^{(t+1)}$ in $\theta^{(t+1)}$
10:     **end for**
11:     $t = t + 1$
12: **end while**
13: Let Z_j^c = converged value of $Z(t, j)$
14: Let a_i^c = converged value of $a_i^{(t)}$; b_i^c = converged value of $b_i^{(t)}$; d^c = converged value of $d^{(t)}$
15: **for** $j = 1 : N$ **do**
16:     **if** $Z_j^c \geq 0.5$ **then**
17:         h_j^* is true
18:     **else**
19:         h_j^* is false
20:     **end if**
21: **end for**
22: **for** $i = 1 : M$ **do**
23:     calculate t_i^* from a_i^c, b_i^c, and d^c based on Equation (5.5)
24: **end for**
25: Return the computed the estimates of claims $C_j = h_j^*$ and source reliability t_i^*.

---

and M-steps iteratively until θ converges. Specifically, the conditional probability of a claim to be true (i.e., $Z(t, j)$) is computed from Equation (5.12) and the estimation parameter (i.e., $\theta^{(t+1)}$) is computed from Equation (5.18). After the estimated value of θ converges, the decision vector H^* (i.e., decide whether each claim C_j is true or not) is computed based on the converged value of $Z(t, j)$ (i.e., Z_j^c). The estimation vector E^* (i.e., the estimated t_i of each source) is computed from the converged values of $\theta^{(t)}$ (i.e., a_i^c, b_i^c, and d^c) based on Equation (5.5) as shown in the pseudocode of Algorithm 1.

One should note that a theoretical quantification of accuracy of MLE is well-known in the literature, and can be done using the Cramer-Rao lower bound (CRLB) on estimator variance [109]. The estimator reviewed in this chapter is shown to asymptotically approach CRLB when the number of observations becomes infinite [102]. This observation makes it possible to quantify estimation accuracy, or confidence in results generated from EM scheme, using the CRLB.

We now present a toy example to help readers better understand the EM algorithm reviewed in this section. In this toy example, 10 sources generate observations about 20 claims. The first 10 claims (i.e., Claim ID: 1-10) are true and the remaining are false. The sources include both reliable and unreliable ones, whose reliability

Table 5.1 The Source Reliability of the Toy Example

	Source ID									
	1	2	3	4	5	6	7	8	9	10
Source reliability	1	0.2	0.9	0.1	0.4	0.1	0.1	0.9	1	0.2

is shown in Table 5.1. The bipartite graph of the corresponding observation matrix *SC* representing "who said what" is shown in Figure 5.1, where a link between a source and a claim represents that the source reports the claim to be true. The results of using Voting and EM to classify the true claims from false ones in the toy example are shown in Table 5.2. For Voting, it is assumed that we have the prior knowledge on d (i.e., we know $d = 0.5$). Hence, voting takes the top half of the claims that receives the most number of "votes" as true and the remaining ones as false. For EM, a_i is initialized to s_i and b_i is initialized to $0.5 \times s_i$ based on the assumption that most of sources are reliable. We showed the probability of each claim to be true (i.e., $Z(t, j)$) computed in every iteration of the algorithm until the estimation converges. We observe that EM correctly classifies all true and false claims while voting only correctly classifies half of the claims and mis-classifies the other half. The mis-classified claims of Voting are highlighted in the table. The reason is that EM jointly estimates both source reliability and claim correctness under the MLE framework while Voting simply counts the "votes" from every source equally without considering the difference in their reliability.

5.4 EXAMPLES AND RESULTS

In this section, we review the experiments to evaluate the performance of the proposed EM scheme in terms of estimation accuracy of the probability that a source is right or a claim is true compared to other state-of-art solutions. The experiments begin by studying the algorithm performance for different abstract observation matrices (SC), then apply it to both an emulated participatory sensing scenario and a real world social sensing application. It is shown that the new algorithm outperforms the state of the art.

5.4.1 A SIMULATION STUDY

The simulator as described in the previous chapter was used in the simulation study. Remember that, as stated in the application model, sources do not report "lack of problems." Hence, they never report a variable to be false. Let t_i be uniformly distributed between 0.5 and 1 in the experiments. For initialization, the initial values of source reliability (i.e., t_i) in the evaluated schemes are set to the mean value of its definition range. The performance of EM scheme is compared to Bayesian interpretation [39] and three state-of-art fact-finder schemes from prior literature that can function using only the inputs offered in the reliable social sensing problem

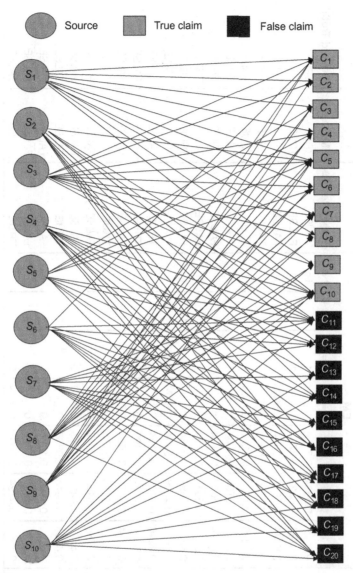

FIGURE 5.1

The bipartite graph of the toy example.

formulation [35–37]. Results show a significant performance improvement of EM over all heuristics compared.

The first experiment compares the estimation accuracy of EM and the baseline schemes by varying the number of sources in the system. The number of reported claims was fixed at 2000, of which 1000 variables were reported correctly and 1000

Table 5.2 The Comparison Between Voting and EM in the Toy Example

Claim ID	Voting Count	EM							Voting Results	EM Results	Ground Truth
		$t=1$	$t=2$	$t=3$	$t=4$	$t=5$	$t=6$	$t=7$			
1	5	0.5	0.5934	0.8754	1	1	1	1	TRUE	TRUE	TRUE
2	3	0.5784	0.6233	0.8793	1	1	1	1	**FALSE**	TRUE	TRUE
3	4	0.5394	0.5857	0.8504	0.9999	1	1	1	**FALSE**	TRUE	TRUE
4	5	0.5	0.5706	0.8905	1	1	1	1	TRUE	TRUE	TRUE
5	7	0.4216	0.4535	0.7053	0.9991	1	1	1	TRUE	TRUE	TRUE
6	5	0.5	0.5706	0.8905	1	1	1	1	TRUE	TRUE	TRUE
7	4	0.5394	0.6087	0.9134	1	1	1	1	**FALSE**	TRUE	TRUE
8	4	0.5394	0.6087	0.9134	1	1	1	1	**FALSE**	TRUE	TRUE
9	4	0.5394	0.6087	0.9134	1	1	1	1	**FALSE**	TRUE	TRUE
10	8	0.3837	0.4306	0.5234	0.8774	0.9996	1	1	TRUE	TRUE	TRUE
11	7	0.4216	0.3767	0.1194	0	0	0	0	**TRUE**	FALSE	FALSE
12	5	0.5	0.4524	0.1499	0	0	0	0	**TRUE**	FALSE	FALSE
13	4	0.5394	0.4452	0.156	0.0001	0	0	0	FALSE	FALSE	FALSE
14	5	0.5	0.4215	0.1375	0.0001	0	0	0	**TRUE**	FALSE	FALSE
15	3	0.5784	0.5465	0.2947	0.0007	0	0	0	FALSE	FALSE	FALSE
16	5	0.5	0.4215	0.1375	0.0001	0	0	0	FALSE	FALSE	FALSE
17	6	0.4606	0.3913	0.0866	0	0	0	0	**TRUE**	FALSE	FALSE
18	5	0.5	0.4295	0.1095	0	0	0	0	FALSE	FALSE	FALSE
19	5	0.5	0.4295	0.1095	0	0	0	0	FALSE	FALSE	FALSE
20	6	0.4606	0.4294	0.2003	0.0004	0	0	0	**TRUE**	FALSE	FALSE

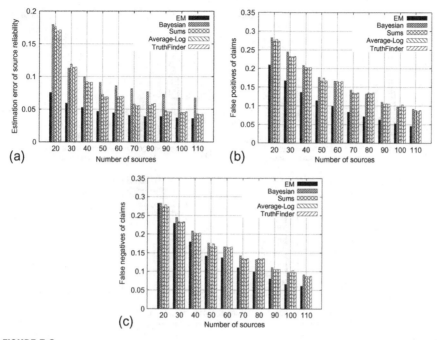

FIGURE 5.2

Estimation accuracy versus number of sources. (a) Source reliability estimation accuracy. (b) Claim classification: false positives. (c) Claim classification: false negatives.

were misreported. To favor the competition, the other baseline algorithms were given the correct value of bias d (in this case, $d = 0.5$). The average number of observations per source was set to 100. The number of sources was varied from 20 to 110. Reported results are averaged over 100 random source reliability distributions. Results are shown in Figure 5.2. Observe that EM has the smallest estimation error on source reliability and the least false positives among all schemes under comparison. For false negatives, EM performs similarly to other schemes when the number of sources is small and starts to gain improvements when the number of sources becomes large. This is because sources are assumed to espouse more true claims than false ones and more sources will provide better evidence for the algorithm to correctly classify claims. Note also that the performance gain of EM becomes large when the number of sources is small, illustrating that EM is more useful when the observation matrix is sparse.

The second experiment compares EM with baseline schemes when the average number of observations per source changes. As before, the number of correctly and incorrectly reported variables was fixed to 1000 respectively. Again, the competition favored by giving the baseline algorithms the correct value of background bias d (here, $d = 0.5$). The number of sources was set to 30. The average number of observations per source is varied from 100 to 1000. Results are averaged over 100

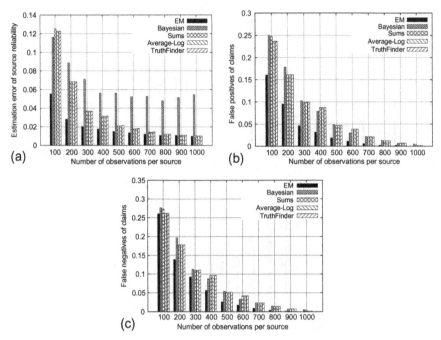

FIGURE 5.3

Estimation accuracy versus average number of observations per source. (a) Source
reliability estimation accuracy. (b) Claim classification: false positives. (c) Claim
classification: false negatives.

experiments. The results are shown in Figure 5.3. Observe that EM outperforms all
baselines in terms of both source reliability estimation accuracy and false positives as
the average number of observations per source changes. For false negatives, EM has
similar performance as other baselines when the average number of observations per
source is small and starts to gain advantage as the average number of observations per
source becomes large. This is because most observations are assumed to be true and
more observations will provide better evidence for the algorithm to correctly classify
claims. As before, the performance gain of EM is higher when the average number
of observations per source is low, verifying once more the high accuracy of EM for
sparser observation matrices.

The third experiment examines the effect of changing the claim mix on the
estimation accuracy of all schemes. The ratio of the number of correctly reported
variables to the total number of reported variables was varied from 0.1 to 0.6, while
fixing the total number of such variables to 2000. To favor the competition, the
background bias d is given correctly to the other algorithms (i.e., $d = varying\ ratio$).
The number of sources is fixed at 30 and the average number of observations per
source is set to 150. Results are averaged over 100 experiments. These results are
shown in Figure 5.4. We observe that EM has almost the same performance as other

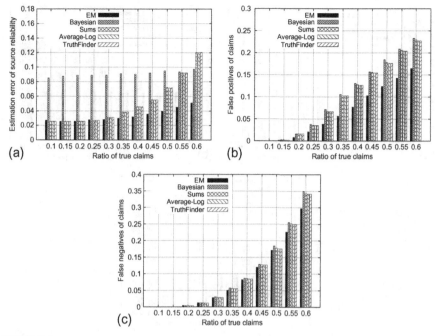

FIGURE 5.4

Estimation accuracy versus ratio of correctly reported claims. (a) Source reliability estimation accuracy. (b) Claim classification: false positives. (c) Claim classification: false negatives.

fact-finder baselines when the fraction of correctly reported variables is relatively small. The reason is that the small amount of true claims are densely observed and most of them can be easily differentiated from the false ones by both EM and baseline fact-finders. However, as the number of variables (correctly) reported as true grows, EM is shown to have a better performance in both source reliability and claim estimation. Additionally, we also observe that the Bayesian interpretation scheme predicts less accurately than other heuristics under some conditions. This is because the estimated posterior probability of a source to be reliable or a claim to be true in Bayesian interpretation is a linear transform of source and claim credibility values. Those values obtained from a single or sparse observation matrix may not be very accurate and must be refined [39].

The fourth experiment evaluates the performance of EM and other schemes when the offset of the initial estimation on the background bias d varies. The offset is defined as the difference between initial estimation on d and its ground-truth. The number of correctly and incorrectly reported variables was set to 1000 respectively (i.e., $d = 0.5$). The absolute value of the initial estimate offset on d was varied from 0 to 0.45. The reported results are averaged for both positive and negative offsets of the same absolute value. The number of sources is fixed at 50 and the average

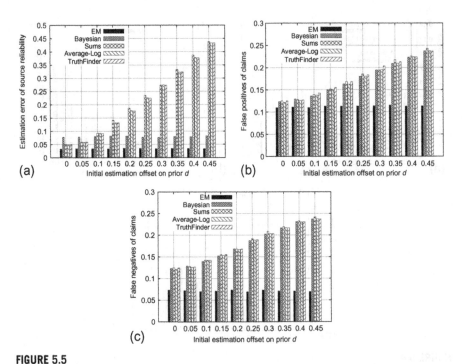

FIGURE 5.5

Estimation accuracy versus initial estimation offset on prior d. (a) Source reliability estimation accuracy. (b) Claim classification: false positives. (c) Claim classification: false negatives.

number of observations per source is set to 150. Reported results are averaged over 100 experiments. Figure 5.5 shows the results. We observe that the performance of EM scheme is stable as the offset of initial estimate on d increases. On the contrary, the performance of other baselines degrades significantly when the initial estimate offset on d becomes large. This is because the EM scheme incorporates the d as part of its estimation parameter and provides the MLE on it. However, other baselines depend largely on the correct initial estimation on d (e.g., from the past history) to find out the right number of correctly reported claims. These results verify the robustness of the EM scheme when the accurate estimate on the prior d is not available to obtain.

The fifth experiment shows the convergence property of the EM iterative algorithm in terms of the estimation error on source reliability, as well as the false positives and false negatives on claims. The number of correctly and incorrectly reported variables was fixed to 1000 respectively and the initial estimate offset on d was set to 0.3. The number of sources is fixed at 50 and the average number of observations per source is set to 250. Reported results are averaged over 100 experiments. Figure 5.6 shows the results. We observe that both the estimation error on source reliability and false positives/negatives on claim converge reasonably fast (e.g., less than 10 iterations) to stable values as the number of iterations of EM algorithm increases. It

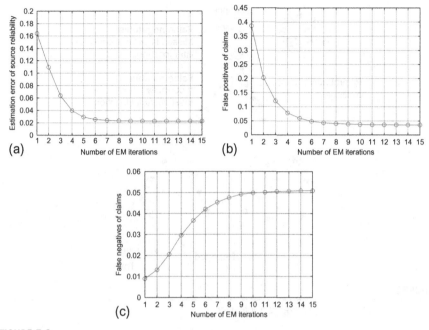

FIGURE 5.6

Convergence property of the EM algorithm. (a) Source reliability estimation accuracy.
(b) Claim classification: false positives. (c) Claim classification: false negatives.

verifies the efficiency of applying EM scheme to solve the MLE problem formulated. Note that the false negatives increase as the number of iteration increases. This is because the initial d was set to 0.8 which is larger than its true value (i.e., 0.5). Hence, the initial estimate of false negatives by the algorithm is smaller than its converged value (e.g., the algorithm could initially take true claims that very few sources reported as true and later classify them as false).

5.4.2 A GEOTAGGING CASE STUDY

In this subsection, we reviewed the application the EM scheme to a typical social sensing application: Geotagging locations of litter in a park or hiking area. In this application, litter may be found along the trails (usually proportionally to their popularity). Sources visiting the park geotag and report locations of litter. Their reports are not reliable however, erring both by missing some locations, as well as misrepresenting other objects as litter. The goal of the application is to find where litter is actually located in the park, while disregarding all false reports.

To evaluate the performance of different schemes, two metrics of interest were defined: (i) *false negatives* defined as the ratio of litter locations missed by a scheme to the total number of litter locations in the park, and (ii) *false positives* defined as the ratio of the number of incorrectly labeled locations by a scheme, to the total number of

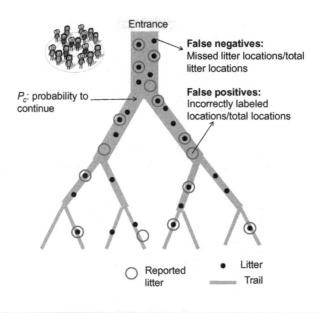

Entrance

False negatives:
Missed litter locations/total litter locations

P_c: probability to continue

False positives:
Incorrectly labeled locations/total locations

○ Reported litter   • Litter

                                ▬▬▬ Trail

FIGURE 5.7

A simplified trail map of geotagging application.

locations in the park. The EM scheme was compared to the Bayesian interpretation scheme and to voting, where locations are simply ranked by the number of times people report them.

A simplified trail map of a park represented by a binary tree was created and shown in Figure 5.7. The entrance of the park (e.g., where parking areas are usually located) is the root of the tree. Internal nodes of the tree represent forking of different trails. It is assumed trails are quantized into discretely labeled locations (e.g., numbered distance markers). In the emulation, at each forking location along the trails, sources have a certain probability P_c to continue walking and $1 - P_c$ to stop and return. Sources who decide to continue have equal probability to select the left or right path. The majority of sources are assumed to be reliable (i.e., when they geotag and report litter at a location, it is more likely than not that the litter exists at that location).

The first experiment studied the effect of the number of people visiting the park on the estimation accuracy of different schemes. A binary tree with a depth of 4 was chosen as the trail map of the park. Each segment of the trail (between two forking points) is quantized into 100 potential locations (leading to 1500 discrete locations in total on all trails). We define the pollution ratio of the park to be the ratio of the number of littered locations to the total number of locations in the park. The pollution ratio is fixed at 0.1 for the first experiment. The probability that people continue to walk past a fork in the path is set to be 95% and the percent of reliable sources is set to be 80%. The reliability of unreliable sources is uniformly distributed over $(0, 0.5)$. Reliable sources will report all pollution that they see. The number of sources visiting the park was varied from 5 to 50. The corresponding estimation results of different schemes

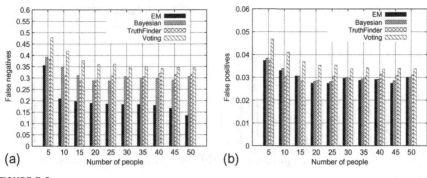

FIGURE 5.8

Litter geotagging accuracy versus number of people visiting the park. (a) False negatives (missed/total litter). (b) False positives (false/total locations).

are shown in Figure 5.8. Observe that both false negatives and false positives decrease as the number of sources increases for all schemes. This is intuitive: the chances of finding litter on different trails increase as the number of people visiting the park increases. Note that, the EM scheme outperforms others in terms of false negatives, which means EM can find more pieces of litter than other schemes under the same conditions. The improvement becomes significant (i.e., around 20%) when there is a sufficient number of people visiting the park. For the false positives, EM performs similarly to Bayesian interpretation and Truth Finder scheme and better than voting. Generally, voting performs the worst in accuracy because it simply counts the number of reports complaining about each location but ignores the reliability of individuals who make them.

The second experiment showed the effect of park pollution ratio (i.e., how littered the park is) on the estimation accuracy of different schemes. The number of individuals visiting the park is set to be 40. The pollution ratio of the park was varied from 0.05 to 0.15. The estimation results of different schemes are shown in Figure 5.9.

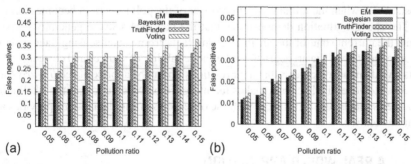

FIGURE 5.9

Litter geotagging accuracy versus pollution ratio of the park. (a) False negatives (missed/total litter). (b) False positives (false/total locations).

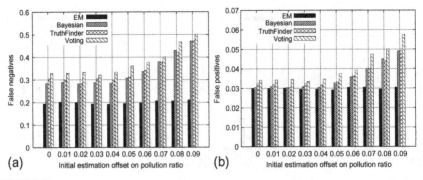

FIGURE 5.10

Litter geotagging accuracy versus initial estimation offset on pollution ratio of park. (a) False negatives (missed/total litter). (b) False positives (false/total locations).

Observe that both the false negatives and false positives of all schemes increase as the pollution ratio increases. The reason is that: litter is more frequently found and reported at trails that are near the entrance point. The amount of unreported litter at trails that are far from entrance increases more rapidly compared to the total amount of litter as the pollution ratio increases. Note that, the EM scheme continues to find more actual litter compared to other baselines. The performance of false positives is similar to other schemes.

The third experiment evaluated the effect of the initial estimation offset of the pollution ratio on the performance of different schemes. The pollution ratio is fixed at 0.1 and the number of individuals visiting the park is set to be 40. The absolute value of initial estimation offset of the pollution ratio was varied from 0 to 0.09. Results are averaged over both positive and negative offsets of the same absolute value. The estimation results of different schemes are shown in Figure 5.10. Observe that EM finds more actual litter locations and reports less falsely labeled locations than other baselines as the initial estimation offset of pollution ratio increases. Additionally, the performance of EM scheme is stable while the performance of other baselines drops substantially when the initial estimation offset of the pollution ratio becomes large.

The above evaluation demonstrates that the new EM scheme generally outperforms the current state of the art in inferring facts from social sensing data. This is because the state of the art heuristics infer the reliability of sources and correctness of facts based on the hypothesis that their relationship can be approximated *linearly* [36, 37, 39]. However, EM scheme makes its inference based on a maximum likelihood hypothesis that is most consistent with the observed sensing data, thus it provides an optimal solution.

5.4.3 A REAL WORLD APPLICATION

In this subsection, we reviewed the evaluation of the performance of the EM scheme through a real-world social sensing application, based on Twitter. The objective was to see whether the EM scheme would distill from Twitter feeds important events that may be newsworthy and reported by media. Specifically, the news coverage of Hurricane Irene was followed and 10 important events reported by media during that time were manually selected as ground truth. Independently from that collection, more than 600,000 tweets originating from New York City during Hurricane Irene were obtained using the Twitter API (by specifying keywords as "hurricane," "Irene,"

Table 5.3 Ground Truth Events and Related Tweets Found by EM in Hurricane Irene

#	Media	Tweet Found by EM
1	East Coast Braces For Hurricane Irene; Hurricane Irene is expected to follow a path up the East Coast	@JoshOchs A #hurricane here on the east coast
2	Hurricane Irene's effects begin being felt in NC, The storm, now a Category 2, still has the East Coast on edge.	Winds, rain pound North Carolina as Hurricane Irene closes in http://t.co/0gVOSZk
3	Hurricane Irene charged up the U.S. East Coast on Saturday toward New York, shutting down the city, and millions of Americans sought shelter from the huge storm.	Hurricane Irene rages up U.S. east coast http://t.co/u0XiXow
4	The Wall Street Journal has created a way for New Yorkers to interact with the location-based social media app Foursquare to find the nearest NYC hurricane evacuation center.	Mashable - Hurricane Irene: Find an NYC Evacuation Center on Foursquare … http://t.co/XMtpH99
5	Following slamming into the East Coast and knocking out electricity to more than a million people, Hurricane Irene is now taking purpose on largest metropolitan areas in the Northeast.	2M lose power as Hurricane Irene moves north - Two million homes and businesses were without power … http://t.co/fZWkEU3
6	Irene remains a Category 1, the lowest level of hurricane classification, as it churns toward New York over the next several hours, the U.S. National Hurricane Center said on Sunday.	Now its a level 1 hurricane. Let's hope it hits NY at Level 1
7	Blackouts reported, storm warnings issued as Irene nears Quebec, Atlantic Canada.	DTN Canada: Irene forecast to hit Atlantic Canada http://t.co/MjhmeJn
8	President Barack Obama declared New York a disaster area Wednesday, The New York Times reports, allowing the release of federal aid to the state's government and individuals.	Hurricane Irene: New York State Declared A Disaster Area By President Obama
9	Hurricane Irene's rampage up the East Coast has become the tenth billion-dollar weather event this year, breaking a record stretching back to 1980, climate experts said Wednesday.	Irene is 10th billion-dollar weather event of 2011.
10	WASHINGTON—On Sunday, September 4, the President will travel to Paterson, New Jersey, to view damage from Hurricane Irene.	White House: Obama to visit Paterson, NJ Sunday to view damage from Hurricane Irene

and "flood", and the location to be New York). These tweets were collected from August 26 until September 2nd, roughly when Irene struck the east coast. Retweets were removed from the collected data to keep sources as independent as possible.

An observation matrix was generated from these tweets by clustering them based on the Jaccard distance metric (a simple but commonly used distance metric for micro-blog data [110]). Each cluster was taken as a statement of claim about current conditions, hence representing a claim in the MLE model. Sources contributing to the cluster were connected to that variable forming the observation matrix. In the formed observation matrix, sources are the twitter users who provided tweets during the observation period, claims are represented by the clusters of tweets and the element S_iC_j is set to 1 if the tweets of source S_i belong to cluster C_j, or to 0 otherwise. The matrix was then fed to the EM scheme. The scheme ran on the collected data and picked the top (i.e., most credible) tweet in each hour. It was then checked if 10 "ground truth" events were reported among the top tweets. Table 5.3 compares the ground truth events to the corresponding top hourly tweets discovered by EM. The results show that indeed all events were reported correctly, demonstrating the value of EM scheme in distilling key information from large volumes of noisy data. Voting was observed to have similarly good performance in this case study. However, in other case studies, the EM scheme was shown to have a better coverage of events than the voting scheme [50].

5.5 DISCUSSION

This chapter reviewed a MLE approach to solve the reliable social sensing problem. Some simplifying assumptions are made to the model that offer opportunities for future work.

Sources are assumed to be independent from each other in the current EM scheme. However, sources can sometimes be dependent. That is, they copy observations from each other in real life (e.g., retweets of Twitter). Regarding possible solutions to this problem, one possibility is to remove duplicate observations from dependent sources and only keep the original ones. This can be achieved by applying copy detection schemes between sources [41, 42]. Another possible solution is to cluster dependent sources based on some *source-dependency* metric [40]. In other words, sources in the same cluster are closely related with each other but independent from sources in other clusters. Then EM scheme can be modified and be applied on top of the clustered sources. More importantly, we will review a direct extension of the MLE framework presented in this chapter in Chapter 2 that discusses social networks. The extended work nicely integrates source dependency information learned from social network into the MLE framework without sacrificing the rigor of the analytical model.

Observations from different sources on a given claim are assumed to be *corroborating* in this chapter. This happens in social sensing applications where people do not report "lack of problems." For example, a group of sources involved in a geotagging application to find litter of a park will only report locations where they observe litter and ignore the locations they do not find litter. However, sources can also make conflicting observations in other types of applications. For example, comments from different reviewers in an on-line review system on the same product often contradict with each other. Fortunately, the reviewed MLE model can be flexibly extended to handle conflicting observations. The idea is to extend the estimation vector to incorporate the conflicting states of a claim and rebuild the likelihood function based on the extended estimation vector. The general outline of the EM derivation still holds.

The EM scheme reviewed in this chapter is mainly designed to run on static data sets, where the computation overhead stays reasonable even when the dataset scales up (e.g., the Irene dataset). However, such computation may become less efficient for streaming data because we need to re-run the algorithm on the whole dataset from scratch every time the dataset gets updated. Instead, it will be more efficient for the algorithm to process only novel data by exploiting the previously results in an optimal (or suboptimal) way. One possibility is to develop a scheme that can compute the estimated parameters of interest recursively over time using incoming measurements and a mathematical process model. The challenge here is that the relationship between the estimation from the updated dataset and the complete dataset may not be linear. Hence, linear regression might not be generally plausible. Rather, recursive estimation schemes, such as the Recursive EM estimation, would be a better fit.

The reviewed EM scheme is an unsupervised scheme, where no data samples are assumed to be used to train the estimation model. What happens if we do have some training samples available? For example, we might have some prior knowledge on either source reliability or the correctness of claims from other independent ways of data verification. One possible way to incorporate such prior knowledge into the MLE model is to reset the known variables in each iteration of EM to their correct values, which may help the algorithm to converge much faster and also reduce the estimation error. Some techniques exist in machine learning community that try to incorporate the prior knowledge (e.g., source and claim similarity, common-sense reasoning, etc.) into the fact-finding framework by using linear programming [37] or k-partite graph generalization [44]. It would be interesting to investigate if it would be possible to borrow some of these techniques and leverage the training data to further improve the accuracy of the MLE estimation.

This chapter reviewed a MLE approach to solve the reliable social sensing problem. The approach can determine the correctness of reported observations given only the measurements sent without knowing the trustworthiness of sources. The optimal solution is obtained by solving an EM problem and can directly lead to an analytically founded quantification of the correctness of measurements as well as the reliability of sources. Evaluation results show that non-trivial estimation accuracy improvements can be achieved by the MLE approach compared to other state of the art solutions.

Confidence bounds in social sensing

6.1 THE RELIABILITY ASSURANCE PROBLEM

In this chapter, we introduce a reliability assurance problem in social sensing, where the estimation-theoretic approaches are used to quantify the accuracy of the maximum likelihood estimation (MLE) framework presented in the previous chapter [103, 104]. In particular, the goal is to demonstrate, in an analytically-founded manner, how to compute the confidence interval of each source's reliability. Formally, this is given by:

$$\left(\hat{t}_i^{MLE} - c_p^{lower}, \hat{t}_i^{MLE} + c_p^{upper} \right) \quad c\% \quad i = 1, 2, \ldots, M \tag{6.1}$$

where $\hat{t}_i^{MLE}$ is the MLE on the reliability of source S_i, $c\%$ is the confidence level of the estimation interval, c_p^{lower} and c_p^{upper} represent the lower and upper bound on the estimation deviation from the MLE $\hat{t}_i^{MLE}$, respectively. The goal is to find c_p^{lower} and c_p^{upper} for a given $c\%$ and an observation matrix SC. It turns out that the Cramer-Rao lower bounds (CRLBs) of the MLE on the source reliability need to be computed in order to obtain the c_p^{lower} and c_p^{upper}. Therefore, the goal of the reviewed work in this chapter is to: (i) derive the actual and asymptotic error bounds that characterize the accuracy of the MLE and compute its confidence interval; (ii) estimate the accuracy of claim classification without knowing the ground truth values of the variables; and (iii) derive the dependency of the accuracy of MLE on parameters of the problem space.

In this chapter, we show how to derive the confidence interval for source reliability through the computation of the CRLB for the estimation parameters (i.e., θ) and by leveraging the asymptotic normality of the MLE. We start with the review of the actual CRLB derivation and identify its scalability limitation. We then review the derivation of the asymptotic CRLB that works for the sensing topology with a large number of sources. We review the confidence interval on source reliability based on the derived CRLBs. Additionally, we also review the derivation of the expected number of misclassified claims (i.e., false claim classified as true and true claim classified as false).

IEEE being the copyright holder, grants permission to reprint text of the article, Dong Wang, Lance Kaplan, Tarek Abdelzaher and Charu C. Aggarwal. "On Scalability and Robustness Limitations of Real and Asymptotic Confidence Bounds in Social Sensing." Proceedings of *The 9th Annual IEEE Communications Society Conference on Sensor, Mesh and Ad Hoc Communications and Networks (SECON 12)*, Seoul, Korea, from June, 2012.
IEEE being the copyright holder, grants permission to reprint text of the article, Dong Wang, Lance Kaplan, Tarek Abdelzaher, and Charu Aggarwal, "On Credibility Estimation Tradeoffs in Assured Social Sensing," *IEEE Journal On Selected Areas in Communications (JSAC)*, Vol 31. No. 6, June 2013.

6.2 ACTUAL CRAMER-RAO LOWER BOUND

In this section, we first review the derivation of the actual CRLB that characterizes the estimation performance of the MLE of source reliability in social sensing. Similarly as the previous section, the reliability of sources is assumed to be imperfect and the majority of claims are assumed to be true. In estimation theory, the CRLB expresses a lower bound on the estimation variance of a minimum-variance unbiased estimator. In its simplest form, the bound states the variance of any unbiased estimator is at least as high as the inverse of the Fisher information [111]. The estimator that reaches this lower bound is said to be *efficient*. For notational convenience, the observation matrix SC is denoted as the observed data X and use $X_{ij} = S_i C_j$ for the following derivation.

The likelihood function (containing hidden variable Z) of the MLE we get from EM is expressed in Equation (5.10), where $Z = (z_j | j = 1, 2, \ldots, N)$ represent the hidden variables.

The EM scheme is used to handle the hidden variable and aims to find:

$$\hat{\theta} = \arg \max_{\theta} p(X|\theta) \tag{6.2}$$

where

$$p(X|\theta) = \prod_{j=1}^{N} \left\{ \prod_{i=1}^{M} a_i^{X_{ij}} (1 - a_i)^{(1-X_{ij})} \times d \right.$$
$$\left. + \prod_{i=1}^{M} b_i^{X_{ij}} (1 - b_i)^{(1-X_{ij})} \times (1 - d) \right\} \tag{6.3}$$

By definition of CRLB, it is given by

$$CRLB = J^{-1} \tag{6.4}$$

where

$$J = E[\nabla_\theta \ln p(X|\theta) \, \nabla_\theta^H \ln p(X|\theta)] \tag{6.5}$$

where J is the Fisher information of the estimation parameter, $\nabla_\theta = \left(\frac{\partial}{\partial a_1}, \ldots, \frac{\partial}{\partial a_M}, \frac{\partial}{\partial b_1}, \ldots, \frac{\partial}{\partial b_M} \right)^H$ and H denotes the conjugate transpose operation. In information theory, the Fisher information is a way of measuring the amount of information that an observable random variable X carries about an estimated parameter θ upon which the probability of X depends. The expectation in Equation (6.5) is taken over all values for X with respect to the probability function $p(X|\theta)$ for any given value of θ. Let $\mathcal{X}$ represent the set of all possible values of $X_{ij} \in \{0, 1\}$ for $i = 1, 2, \ldots, M$; $j = 1, 2, \ldots, N$. Note $|\mathcal{X}| = 2^{MN}$. Likewise, let $\mathcal{X}_j$ represent the set of all possible values of $X_{ij} \in \{0, 1\}$ for $i = 1, 2, \ldots, M$ and a given value of j. Note $|\mathcal{X}_j| = 2^M$. Taking the expectation, Equation (6.5) can be rewritten as follows:

$$J = \sum_{X \in \mathcal{X}} \nabla_\theta \ln p(X|\theta) \, \nabla_\theta^H \ln p(X|\theta) p(X|\theta) \tag{6.6}$$

Then, the Fisher information matrix can be represented as:

$$J = \begin{bmatrix} A & C \\ C^T & B \end{bmatrix}$$

where submatrices A, B, and C contain the elements related with the estimation parameter a_i, b_i, and their cross terms, respectively. The representative elements A_{kl}, B_{kl}, and C_{kl} of A, B, and C can be derived as follows:

$$
\begin{aligned}
A_{kl} &= E\left[\frac{\partial}{\partial a_k} \ln p(X|\theta) \frac{\partial}{\partial a_l} \ln p(X|\theta) \right] \\
&= E\left[\left(\sum_j \frac{(2X_{kj}-1)Z_j}{a_k^{X_{kj}}(1-a_k)^{(1-X_{kj})}} \sum_q \frac{(2X_{lq}-1)Z_q}{a_l^{X_{lq}}(1-a_l)^{(1-X_{lq})}} \right) \right] \\
&= \sum_j \sum_q E\left[\frac{(2X_{kj}-1)Z_j(2X_{lq}-1)Z_q}{a_k^{X_{kj}}(1-a_k)^{(1-X_{kj})}a_l^{X_{lq}}(1-a_l)^{(1-X_{lq})}} \right]
\end{aligned}
\tag{6.7}
$$

where

$$Z_j = p(z_j = 1|X) = \frac{A_j \times d}{A_j \times d + B_j \times (1-d)}$$

where

$$A_j = \prod_{i=1}^{M} a_i^{X_{ij}}(1-a_i)^{(1-X_{ij})} \quad B_j = \prod_{i=1}^{M} b_i^{X_{ij}}(1-b_i)^{(1-X_{ij})} \tag{6.8}$$

Z_j is the conditional probability of the claim C_j to be true given the observation matrix. After further simplification as shown in Appendix of Chapter 6, A_{kl} can be expressed as the summation of only the expectation terms where $j = q$:

$$
\begin{aligned}
A_{kl} &= \sum_j E\left[\frac{(2X_{kj}-1)(2X_{lj}-1)Z_j^2}{a_k^{X_{kj}}(1-a_k)^{(1-X_{kj})}a_l^{X_{lj}}(1-a_l)^{(1-X_{lj})}} \right] \\
&= \sum_{j=1}^{N} \sum_{X \in \mathcal{X}_j} \frac{(2X_{kj}-1)(2X_{lj}-1)\prod_{\substack{i=1 \\ i\neq k}}^{M} A_{ij} \prod_{\substack{i=1 \\ i\neq l}}^{M} A_{ij}d^2}{\prod_{i=1}^{M} A_{ij}d + \prod_{i=1}^{M} B_{ij}(1-d)}
\end{aligned}
\tag{6.9}
$$

where

$$A_{ij} = a_i^{X_{ij}}(1-a_i)^{(1-X_{ij})} \quad B_{ij} = b_i^{X_{ij}}(1-b_i)^{(1-X_{ij})} \tag{6.10}$$

Since the inner sum in (6.9) is invariant to the claim index j, $A_{k,l} = N\bar{A}_{k,l}$ where $\bar{A}_{kl}$ is:

$$\bar{A}_{kl} = \sum_{x \in \mathcal{X}_j} \frac{(2X_{kj}-1)(2X_{lj}-1)\prod_{\substack{i=1 \\ i\neq k}}^{M} A_{ij} \prod_{\substack{i=1 \\ i\neq l}}^{M} A_{ij}d^2}{\prod_{i=1}^{M} A_{ij}d + \prod_{i=1}^{M} B_{ij}(1-d)} \tag{6.11}$$

It should also be noted that the summation in Equation (6.11) is the same for all j.

By similar calculations, the inverse of the Fisher information matrix is obtained as follows:

$$J^{-1} = \frac{1}{N} \begin{bmatrix} \bar{A} & \bar{C} \\ \bar{C}^T & \bar{B} \end{bmatrix}^{-1}$$

where the *kl*th element of $\bar{B}, \bar{C}$ is defined as:

$$\bar{B}_{kl} = \sum_{x \in \mathcal{X}_j} \frac{(2X_{kj} - 1)(2X_{lj} - 1) \prod_{\substack{i=1 \\ i \neq k}}^{M} B_{ij} \prod_{\substack{i=1 \\ i \neq l}}^{M} B_{ij}(1 - d)^2}{\prod_{i=1}^{M} A_{ij}d + \prod_{i=1}^{M} B_{ij}(1 - d)} \tag{6.12}$$

$$\bar{C}_{kl} = \sum_{x \in \mathcal{X}_j} \frac{(2X_{kj} - 1)(2X_{lj} - 1) \prod_{\substack{i=1 \\ i \neq k}}^{M} A_{ij} \prod_{\substack{i=1 \\ i \neq l}}^{M} B_{ij}d(1 - d)}{\prod_{i=1}^{M} A_{ij}d + \prod_{i=1}^{M} B_{ij}(1 - d)} \tag{6.13}$$

Note that the sum of $\bar{A}_{kl}$, $\bar{B}_{kl}$, and $\bar{C}_{kl}$ are over the 2^M different permutations of X_{ij} for $i = 1, 2, \ldots, M$ at a given j. This is much smaller than the 2^{MN} permutations of $\mathcal{X}$.

This gives the actual CRLB. Note that more claims simply lead to better estimates for θ as the variance decreases as $\frac{1}{N}$. The decrease in variance for the estimates as a function of M is more complicated, which can only be computed numerically. Please note that the actual CRLB computation needs the true values of the estimation parameter. However in real applications, the true values are not known in advance, we substitute the unknown true values for MLEs as an approximation to estimate variances for determining the confidence bounds.

6.3 ASYMPTOTIC CRAMER-RAO LOWER BOUND

Observe that the complexity of the actual CRLB computation in the above subsection is exponential with respect to the number of sources (i.e., M) in the system. Therefore, it is inefficient (or infeasible) to compute the actual CRLB when the number of sources becomes large. In this subsection, we review the derivation of the asymptotic CRLB for efficient computation in the sensing topology with a large number of sources. The asymptotic CRLB is derived based on the assumption that the correctness of the hidden variable (i.e., z_j) can be correctly estimated from EM. This is a reasonable assumption when the number of sources is sufficient [100]. Under this assumption, the log-likelihood function of the MLE obtained from EM can be expressed as follows:

$$l_{em}(x; \theta) = \sum_{j=1}^{N} \left\{ z_j \times \left[\sum_{i=1}^{M} (X_{ij} \log a_i + (1 - X_{ij}) \log(1 - a_i) + \log d) \right] \right.$$

$$\left. + (1 - z_j) \times \left[\sum_{i=1}^{M} (X_{ij} \log b_i + (1 - X_{ij}) \log(1 - b_i) + \log(1 - d)) \right] \right\} \tag{6.14}$$

The Fisher information matrix at the MLE was computed from the log-likelihood function given by Equation (6.14). The converged estimates of a_i and b_i from the EM of the previous chapter were used as the MLE.

Plugging $l_{em}(x; \theta)$ given by Equation (6.14) into the Fisher information defined in Equation (6.5), the representative element of Fisher information matrix from N claims was shown as:

$$(J(\hat{\theta}_{MLE}))_{i,j} = \begin{cases} 0 & i \neq j \\ -E_X\left[\frac{\partial^2 l_{em}(x;a_i)}{\partial a_i^2}|_{a_i=a_i^0}\right] & i = j \in [1, M] \\ -E_X\left[\frac{\partial^2 l_{em}(x;b_i)}{\partial b_i^2}|_{b_i=b_i^0}\right] & i = j \in (M, 2M] \end{cases} \tag{6.15}$$

where a_i^0 and b_i^0 are the true values of a_i and b_i. In the following computation, we estimate them by substituting the known MLEs for the unknown parameter values.

Substituting the log-likelihood function in Equation (6.14) and MLE of θ into Equation (6.15), the asymptotic CRLB (i.e., the inverse of the Fisher information matrix) can be written as:

$$(J^{-1}(\hat{\theta}_{MLE}))_{i,j} = \begin{cases} 0 & i \neq j \\ \frac{\hat{a}_i^{MLE} \times (1-\hat{a}_i^{MLE})}{N \times d} & i = j \in [1, M] \\ \frac{\hat{b}_i^{MLE} \times (1-\hat{b}_i^{MLE})}{N \times (1-d)} & i = j \in (M, 2M] \end{cases} \tag{6.16}$$

Note that the asymptotic CRLB is independent of M under the assumption that M is sufficient, and it can be quickly computed from the MLE of the EM scheme.

6.4 CONFIDENCE INTERVAL DERIVATION

This subsection shows that the confidence interval of source reliability can be obtained by using the CRLB derived in previous sections and leveraging the asymptotic normality of the MLE.

The MLE posses a number of attractive asymptotic properties. One of them is called *asymptotic normality*, which basically states the MLE estimator is asymptotically distributed with Gaussian behavior as the data sample size goes up, in particular [112]:

$$(\hat{\theta}_{MLE} - \theta_0) \xrightarrow{d} N(0, J^{-1}(\hat{\theta}_{MLE})) \tag{6.17}$$

where J is the Fisher information matrix computed from all samples, θ_0 and $\hat{\theta}_{MLE}$ are the true value and the MLE of the parameter θ, respectively. The Fisher information at the MLE is used to estimate its true (but unknown) value [111]. Hence, the asymptotic normality property means that in a regular case of estimation and in the distribution limiting sense, the MLE $\hat{\theta}_{MLE}$ is unbiased and its covariance reaches the CRLB (i.e., an efficient estimator).

From the asymptotic normality of the MLE [100], the error of the corresponding estimation on θ follows a normal distribution with zero mean and the covariance matrix given by the CRLB derived in previous subsections. Let us denote the variance of estimation error on parameter a_i as $var(\hat{a}_i^{MLE})$. Recall the relation between source reliability (i.e., t_i) and estimation parameter a_i and b_i is t_i is given by Equation (5.6). For a sensing topology with small values of M and N, the estimation of t_i has a complex distribution and its estimation variance can be approximated [109]. The denominator of t_i is equivalent to s_i based on Equation (5.6).* Therefore, $(\hat{t}_i^{MLE} - t_i^0)$ also follows a normal distribution with zero mean and variance given by:

$$var(\hat{t}_i^{MLE}) = \left(\frac{d}{s_i}\right)^2 var(\hat{a}_i^{MLE}) \tag{6.18}$$

Hence, the confidence interval that can be obtained to quantify the estimation accuracy of the MLE on source reliability. The confidence interval of the reliability estimation of source S_i (i.e., $\hat{t}_i^{MLE}$) at confidence level p is given by the following:

$$(\hat{t}_i^{MLE} - c_p\sqrt{var(\hat{t}_i^{MLE})}, \hat{t}_i^{MLE} + c_p\sqrt{var(\hat{t}_i^{MLE})}) \tag{6.19}$$

where c_p is the standard score (z-score) of the confidence level p. For example, for the 95% confidence level, $c_p = 1.96$. Therefore, the derived confidence interval of the source reliability MLE can be computed by using the CRLB derived earlier.

We reviewed how to compute the CRLB and the confidence interval in source reliability from the MLE of the EM algorithm. However, one problem remains to be answered is how to estimate the accuracy of the claim classification (i.e., false positives and false negatives) without having the ground truth values of the claims at hand. In this subsection, we review a quick and effective method to answer the above question under the maximum likelihood hypothesis.

The results of the EM algorithm not only offered the MLE on the estimation parameters (i.e., θ) but also the probability of each claim to be true, which is given by [100]:

$$Z_j^* = p(z_j = 1|X_j, \theta^*) \tag{6.20}$$

where X_j is the observed data of the claim C_j and θ^* is the MLE of the parameter. Since the claim is binary, it is judged as true if $Z_j^* \geq 0.5$ and false otherwise. Based on the above definition, the false positives and false negatives of the claim classification can be estimated as follows:

$$FP = \sum_{j:Z_j^* \geq 0.5}^{N} \{Z_j^* \times 0 + (1 - Z_j^*) \times 1\}$$

$$= \sum_{j:Z_j^* \geq 0.5}^{N} (1 - Z_j^*) \tag{6.21}$$

---

*The value of s_i is known to be K_i/N no matter the output of the EM (see Equation (5.18)). Therefore, s_i can be treated as deterministic, i.e., no variance.

$$FN = \sum_{j:Z_j^* < 0.5}^{N} \{Z_j^* \times 1 + (1 - Z_j^*) \times 0\}$$

$$= \sum_{j:Z_j^* < 0.5}^{N} Z_j^* \qquad (6.22)$$

where *FP* and *FN* stand for false positives and false negatives, respectively. From above equations, the estimated false positives and false negatives of the claim classification can be computed under the maximum likelihood hypothesis. This enables us to estimate the accuracy of the claim classification without knowing the ground truth values a priori.

In this section, we reviewed a confidence interval derivation in source reliability and proposed an accuracy estimator on the claim classification. This allows social sensing applications to assess the quality of their estimation on source reliability as well as the accuracy of claim classification. In the following section, we will review the evaluation of the performance of the computed confidence bounds on source reliability and the estimated false positives and false negatives on the claim classification.

6.5 EXAMPLES AND RESULTS

In this section, we review the evaluation of the performance of the credibility estimation and confidence quantification approach through both extensive simulation studies and a real world social sensing application. The reported CRLB results are computed upon the estimated a's and b's instead of the ground truth. In practice, it provides a sense of the sensitivity (or significance) of the estimated values. The same simulator as described in the previous two chapters was used. The prior d discussed in Section 6.1 is set to be 0.5 unless otherwise specified and the initial value of d assumed by the EM algorithm is set to be uniformly distributed between 0.4 and 0.6.

6.5.1 EVALUATION OF CONFIDENCE INTERVAL

In this subsection, we review the evaluation of the accuracy of the confidence interval in source reliability derived in the previous section. Experiments were carried out over three different observation matrix scales: small, medium, and large. The simulation parameters are listed in Table 6.1. The total number of claims is the sum of both true and false ones. The average observations reported by each source is set to 100. For each observation matrix scale, the confidence interval in source reliability was computed based on Equation (6.19). The experiments were repeated 100 times for each observation matrix scale. Three representative confidence levels (i.e., 68%, 90%, and 95%) are used in the evaluation.

Figure 6.1 shows the normalized probability density function (PDF) of source reliability estimation error over three observation matrix scales. The experimental

Table 6.1 Parameters of Three Typical Observation
Matrix Scale

Observation Matrix Scale	Number of Sources	Number of True Claims	Number of False Claims
Small	100	500	500
Medium	1000	1000	1000
Large	10,000	5000	5000

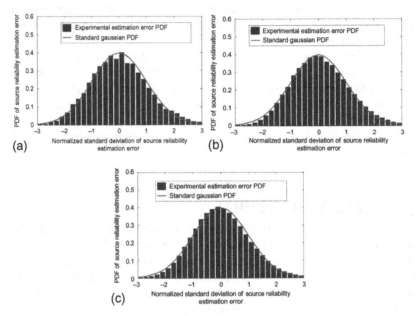

FIGURE 6.1

Normalized source reliability estimation error PDF. (a) Small observation matrix.
(b) Medium observation matrix. (c) Large observation matrix.

PDF was computed by leveraging the actual estimation error (i.e., compare to the
ground truth) and the confidence interval derived in Section 6.4. The experimental
PDF was compared with the standard Gaussian distribution to verify the asymptotic
normality property of estimation results. We observe the experimental PDF match
well with the theoretical Gaussian distribution over three observation matrix scales.

Figure 6.2 shows the comparison between the actual estimation confidence and
three different confidence levels that were set for the small observation matrix
scenario. The actual estimation confidence is computed as the percentage of sources
whose estimation error stay within the corresponding confidence bound for every
experiment. This percentage represents the probability that a randomly chosen source
keeps its reliability estimation error within the confidence bound. We observe that
the actual estimation confidence of using three different confidence bounds stays

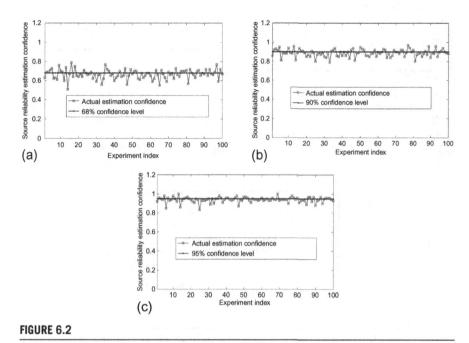

FIGURE 6.2

Source reliability estimation confidence for small observation matrix. (a) 68% confidence level. (b) 90% confidence level. (c) 95% confidence level.

close to the corresponding confidence levels that were used for the experiment. Moreover, at higher confidence levels, a lower fluctuation of the actual estimation confidence is observed. Similar results are observed for the medium and large observation matrices as well, which are shown in Figures 6.3 and 6.4, respectively. Additionally, we also note that the fluctuation of the actual estimation confidence decreases as the observation matrix scale increases. This is because the estimation variance characterized by CRLB is inversely proportional to the number of claims in the system, which will be further evaluated in the next subsection.

6.5.2 EVALUATION OF CRLB

In this subsection, we review the evaluation of the accuracy of derived CRLBs (both actual and asymptotic) in Sections 6.2 and 6.3 by comparing them to the actual estimation variance of the estimation parameter (i.e., a_i, b_i). The actual estimation variance is characterized by the average RMSE (square root of the mean squared error) of all sources.

Scalability study

The scalability of CRLB performance with respect to the sensing topology (i.e., M and N) was first evaluated. The first experiment evaluates the effect of the number of sources (i.e., M) in the system on the CRLB performance. It started with the

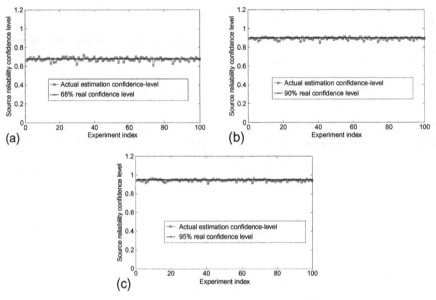

FIGURE 6.3

Source reliability estimation confidence for medium observation matrix. (a) 68% confidence level. (b) 90% confidence level. (c) 95% confidence level.

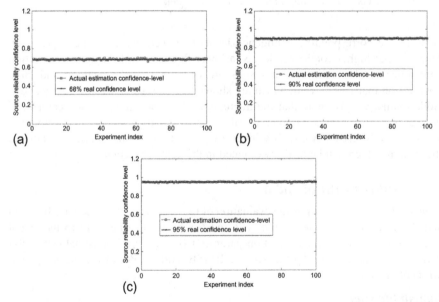

FIGURE 6.4

Source reliability estimation confidence for large observation matrix. (a) 68% confidence level. (b) 90% confidence level. (c) 95% confidence level.

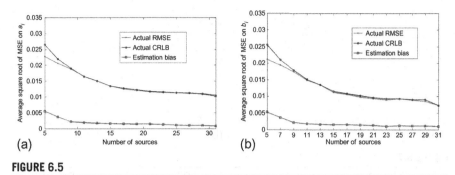

(a)   (b)

FIGURE 6.5

Actual CRLB of a_i and b_i versus varying M. (a) Actual CRLB of a_i. (b) Actual CRLB of b_i.

actual CRLB evaluation. The true and false claims were fixed to 1000 respectively, the average observations per source is set to 100. The number of sources from was varied 5 to 31. Reported results are averaged over 100 experiments and are shown in Figure 6.5. Observe that the actual CRLB tracks the variance of estimation parameters accurately even when the number of sources is small (e.g., $M \leq 20$) in the system. We also observe that the RMSE is smaller than the actual CRLB when there are too few sources. This is because the MLE is biased on those points due to the small dataset. As illustrated in Section 6.2, the computation of actual CRLB does not scale with the number of sources in the system. Hence, the accuracy of asymptotic CRLB was also evaluated when the number of sources becomes large. The experimental configuration was kept the same as above, but the number of sources was changed from 10 to 150. Results are shown in Figure 6.6. We observe that the asymptotic CRLB deviates from the actual estimation variance when the number of sources is small (e.g., $M \leq 20$). However, as the number of sources becomes sufficient in the network, the RMSE converges to the asymptotic CRLB quickly and the difference between the two becomes insignificant.

The second experiment compares the derived CRLBs (both actual and asymptotic) to the RMSE of estimation parameters when the number of claims (i.e., N) changes. As shown in Sections 6.2 and 6.3, both the actual and asymptotic CRLB decrease

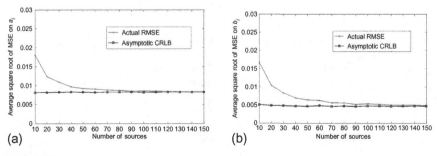

(a)   (b)

FIGURE 6.6

Asymptotic CRLB of a_i and b_i versus varying M. (a) Asymptotic CRLB of a_i. (b) Asymptotic CRLB of b_i.

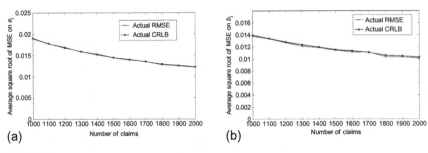

FIGURE 6.7

Actual CRLB of a_i and b_i versus Varying N. (a) Actual CRLB of a_i. (b) Actual CRLB of b_i.

as $\frac{1}{N}$. As before, the accuracy of actual CRLB was first evaluated. The number of sources was fixed as 20, the average number of observations per source is set to 100. The number of true and false claims were kept the same. The number of claims varies from 1000 to 2000. Reported results are averaged over 100 experiments and are shown in Figure 6.7. We observe that the actual CRLB is able to track the RMSE on estimation parameter correctly and they both decrease approximately as $\frac{1}{N}$ when the number of claim increases. Similarly, the experiment was carried out to evaluate the accuracy of asymptotic CRLB. The experimental configuration was kept the same as above, but the number of sources was set to be 100. Results are shown in Figure 6.8. We observe that the asymptotic CRLB also follows closely on the RMSE of the estimation parameter and they reduce approximately as $\frac{1}{N}$ when the number of claim increases.

Trustworthiness and assertiveness study
In the trustworthiness study, the estimation performance of CRLB was evaluated when the ratio of trusted sources in the system changes. The trusted sources are the sources who always make correct observations (i.e., their reliability is 1) and the ratio of trusted sources is the ratio of the number of trusted sources over the total number of sources in the system. The reliability of non-trusted sources is uniformly distributed in the range of (0, 1). The true and false claims were fixed to 1000 respectively, the

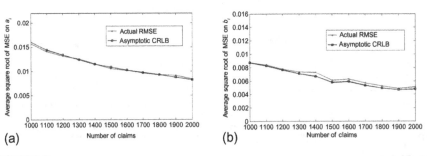

FIGURE 6.8

Asymptotic CRLB of a_i and b_i versus varying N. (a) Asymptotic CRLB of a_i. (b) Asymptotic CRLB of b_i.

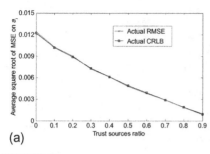 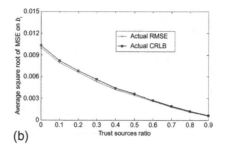

(a)   (b)

FIGURE 6.9

Actual CRLB of a_i and b_i versus trusted sources ratio. (a) Actual CRLB of a_i. (b) Actual CRLB of b_i.

number of sources is set to 20 and each source reports 100 observations on average. The trusted source ratio was varied from 0 to 0.9. Reported results are averaged over 100 experiments and shown in Figure 6.9. Observe that the actual CRLB tracks the estimation variance tightly when the trusted source ratio changes. We also note that both the actual CRLB and the estimation variance of estimation parameters improve as the trusted source ratio increases. The reason is: the estimation error decreases as the ratio of sources with $t_i = 1$ increases. This is also reflected by the fact that $b_i = 0$ for trusted sources and the asymptotic variance goes to zero as one can see in (6.16). Similarly, experiments were carried out to evaluate the accuracy of the asymptotic CRLB. The experiment configuration was kept the same as above, but the number of sources was set to be 100. Results are shown in Figure 6.10. We observe that the asymptotic CRLB also follows the estimation variance of the estimation parameters correctly and they improve as the trusted source ratio increases.

In the assertiveness study, the estimation performance of CRLB was evaluated when the assertiveness ratio of sources changes. The assertiveness ratio is defined as the ratio of the input data size (in terms of the number of observations) normalized by a pre-defined data size. This ratio reflects the sparsity of the sensing topology when the algorithm starts to run. The true and false claims were fixed to 1000 respectively. The number of sources is set to 20. The input data size that is used for the

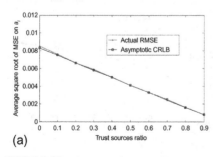 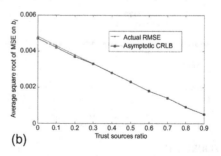

(a)   (b)

FIGURE 6.10

Asymptotic CRLB of a_i and b_i versus trusted sources ratio. (a) Asymptotic CRLB of a_i. (b) Asymptotic CRLB of b_i.

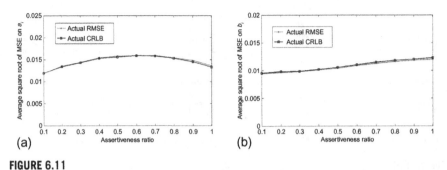

FIGURE 6.11

Actual CRLB of a_i and b_i versus assertiveness ratio. (a) Actual CRLB of a_i. (b) Actual CRLB of b_i.

assertiveness ratio normalization (i.e., having assertiveness ratio of 1) is set to 1000 observations per source. The assertiveness ratio was varied from 0.1 to 1. Reported results are averaged over 100 experiments and shown in Figure 6.11. We observe that the actual CRLB tracks the RMSE of the estimation parameters correctly as the assertiveness ratio changes. We also note that the estimation variance of parameter a_i first increases and then decreases while the estimation variance of parameter b_i increases as the assertiveness ratio increases. The reason is: two factors affect the variance of the estimation parameters in different directions when the assertiveness ratio changes. One factor is the probability that a source reports a claim (i.e., s_i), defined in Section 6.1. This factor increases as the assertiveness ratio increases, which will enlarge the estimation variance of a_i and b_i based on (5.5). The other factor is the estimation variance of the source reliability (i.e., t_i), which decreases as the assertiveness ratio increases. Hence, the estimation variance of a_i is first dominated by the first factor and then by the second one while the estimation variance of b_i is dominated by the first factor in the evaluation range as the assertiveness ratio increases. Similar experiments were then carried out to evaluate the accuracy of the asymptotic CRLB. The experiment configuration was kept the same as above, but the number of sources was set to be 100. Results are shown in Figure 6.12. We observe

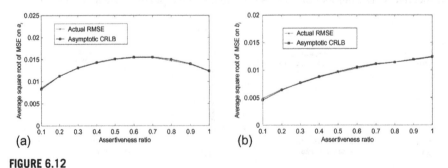

FIGURE 6.12

Asymptotic CRLB of a_i and b_i versus assertiveness ratio. (a) Asymptotic CRLB of a_i. (b) Asymptotic CRLB of b_i.

that the asymptotic CRLB also follows the variance of the estimation parameters tightly and their trends are similar as those of actual CRLB.

Robustness study

In the robustness study, the robustness (or sensitivity) of the estimation performance and the derived CRLBs were evaluated when the number of sources changes under different source reliability distributions. The key characteristic that determines the resilience of a network is the network topology. The social sensing topology is characterized by the link connections between sources and two sets of claims (i.e., true and false). The link connection skew is mainly determined by the source reliability distribution. Two representative network topologies were considered: scale-free and exponential topologies in the evaluation. For scale-free topology, sources have diverse reliability and the probability for sources to have different reliability is similar. For exponential topology, sources have similar reliability and nodes with higher reliability are exponentially less probable. The experiments were done by source removal (i.e., sources are randomly selected and removed from the system). This represents the scenario where random sources decide to quit the sensing application or their sensing devices fail. However, it is equivalent to reversing the steps and investigating the addition of sources.

In the first experiment, the estimation performance and the derived CRLBs were evaluated under the scale-free network topology. To generate the scale-free network topology, source reliability follows a uniform distribution on its definition range. The actual CRLB compared to the RMSE on the estimation parameter. Both the number of true and false claims were fixed to 1000. The average number of observations per source was set to 100. The experiments started with 25 sources and gradually removed sources from the system. Figure 6.13 shows the actual CRLB and RMSE of the estimation parameter. Observe that the estimation accuracy (i.e., RMSE) degrades gracefully and the actual CRLB tracks the RMSE reasonably well as the number of removed sources increases. Also note that the actual CRLB deviates slightly from the RMSE when majority of sources are removed from the system. Then similar

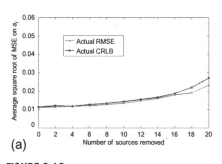
(a)

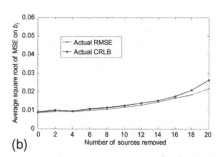
(b)

FIGURE 6.13

Actual CRLB of a_i and b_i versus source removal of scale-free topology. (a) Actual CRLB of a_i. (b) Actual CRLB of b_i.

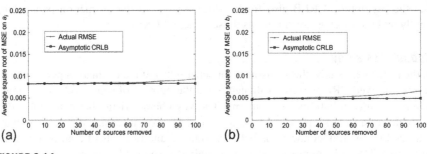

FIGURE 6.14

Asymptotic CRLB of a_i and b_i versus source removal of scale-free topology. (a) Asymptotic CRLB of a_i. (b) Asymptotic CRLB of b_i.

experiments were repeated for the asymptotic CRLB as well. The experiments started with 150 sources and gradually removed the sources from the system. Results are shown in Figure 6.14. The results for asymptotic CRLB are similar to actual CRLB.

In the second experiment, the estimation performance and the derived CRLBs were evaluated under the exponential network topology. To generate the exponential network topology, the source reliability follows a normal distribution (with the mean value as the mean of its definition range and a reasonably small variance). Similar as before, the actual CRLB compared to the RMSE on the estimation parameter. The standard deviation of the normal distribution of source reliability was set to 0.02, other settings were kept the same as the first experiment. Figure 6.15 shows the actual CRLB and RMSE of the estimation parameter. Observe that RMSE increases gradually as the number of removed sources grows and the actual CRLB tracks the RMSE well. Similar experiments were repeated for the asymptotic CRLB as well. The experimental settings were kept the same as the first experiment. Results are shown in Figure 6.16. Similar results of the actual CRLB are observed for the asymptotic CRLB.

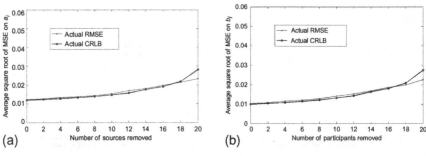

FIGURE 6.15

Actual CRLB of a_i and b_i versus source removal of exponential topology. (a) Actual CRLB of a_i. (b) Actual CRLB of b_i.

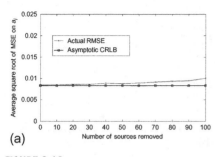 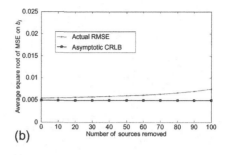

(a)   **(b)**

FIGURE 6.16

Asymptotic CRLB of a_i and b_i versus source removal of exponential topology.
(a) Asymptotic CRLB of a_i. (b) Asymptotic CRLB of b_i.

For both the scale-free and exponential topology of social sensing, the above results show that the estimation performance is relatively robust (or insensitive) to changes in the number of sources in the network. Both actual and asymptotic CRLBs are able to track the estimation performance as long as a limited number of sources stay in the system.

6.5.3 EVALUATION OF ESTIMATED FALSE POSITIVES/NEGATIVES ON CLAIM CLASSIFICATION

In this subsection, the estimated false positives/negatives on claim classification were evaluated by comparing them to the actual false positives/negatives (i.e., the ones that are computed from the ground truth). Similar experiments in the previous subsection were carried out to evaluate its performance through scalability, trustworthiness, assertiveness, and robustness studies.

Scalability study

The scalability of the estimated false positives/negatives with respect to the sensing topology were first evaluated. The first experiment evaluated the performance when the number of sources (i.e., M) in the system changes. The number of true and false claims were fixed to 1000 respectively, the average number of observations per source was set to 200. The number of sources was varied from 10 to 150. Reported results were averaged over 100 experiments and are shown in Figure 6.17. Observe that both estimated false positives and false negatives track the actual values accurately as the number of sources changes. We also note that the false positives/negatives decrease as the number of sources increases. The second experiment compared the estimated false positives/negatives to the actual values when the number of claims (i.e., N) changes. The number of sources was fixed as 50, the average number of observations per source was set to 200. The number of true and false claims as kept the same. The number of claims was varied from 1000 to 2000. Reported results are averaged over 100 experiments and shown in Figure 6.18. Observe that the estimated false positives/negatives are able to track the actual values correctly when the number

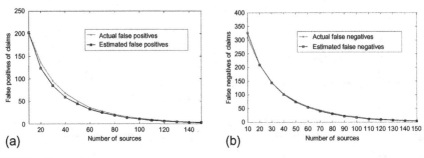

FIGURE 6.17

Estimation of claim classification accuracy versus varying M. (a) False positives. (b) False negatives.

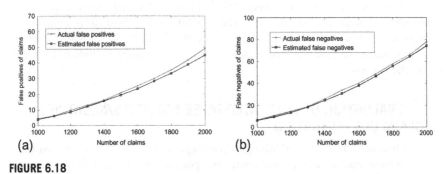

FIGURE 6.18

Estimation of claim classification accuracy versus varying N. (a) False positives. (b) False negatives.

of claims changes. We also note that the estimation performance degrades as the number of claims increases. The reason is: the sensing topology becomes sparser as the number of claims increases while the number of sources and observations per source stay the same.

Trustworthiness and assertiveness study

In the trustworthiness study, the estimated false positives/negatives were evaluated when the ratio of trusted sources changes in the system. In the experiment, the number of sources was set to be 50. The number of true and false claims were set to be 1000 respectively and the observations per source is set to be 200. The trusted source ratio was varied from 0 to 0.9. The reliability of non-trusted sources is uniformly distributed in the range of $(0, 1)$. The reported results are averaged over 100 experiments and shown in Figure 6.19. Observe that the estimated false positives/negatives track the actual values correctly and both of them decrease as the trusted source ratio increases. The reason is: trusted sources always provide correct observations, which helps the algorithm to estimate the truthfulness of claims more accurately.

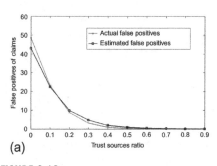 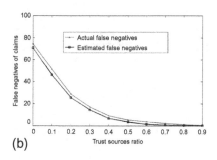

FIGURE 6.19

Estimation of claim classification accuracy versus trusted sources ratio. (a) False positives. (b) False negatives.

In the assertiveness study, the estimated false positives/negatives were evaluated when the assertiveness ratio changes in the system. In the experiment, the number of sources was fixed to be 50. The number of true and false claims were set to be 1000 respectively. The data size that is used for the assertiveness ratio normalization was set to 1000 observations per source. The assertiveness ratio was varied from 0.1 to 1. The reported results are averaged over 100 experiments and shown in Figure 6.20. Observe that the estimated false positives/negatives track the actual values correctly and both of them decrease as the assertiveness ratio increases. The reason is: the sensing topology becomes more densely connected and offers a better chance for the algorithm to correctly judge the truthfulness of the claims as the assertiveness ratio increases.

Robustness study

In the robustness study, similarly as before, the estimated false positives/negatives were evaluated when the number of sources changes under different source reliability

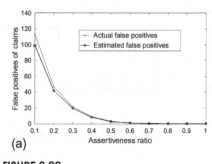 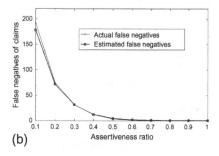

FIGURE 6.20

Estimation of claim classification accuracy versus assertiveness ratio. (a) False positives. (b) False negatives.

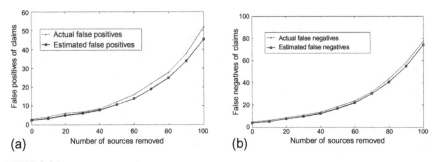

FIGURE 6.21

Estimation of claim classification accuracy versus source removal of scale-free topology.
(a) False positives. (b) False negatives.

distribution.[†] The first experiment evaluated the estimation performance of the scale-free network topology. The number of true and false claims were fixed to 1000. The average number of observations per source was set to 200. The experiment started with 150 sources and gradually removed sources from the system. Reported results are averaged over 100 experiments and shown in Figure 6.21. Observe that the estimation performance degrades and the estimated false positives/negatives track the actual values reasonably well as the number of removed sources increases. Also note that the estimated values deviate slightly from the actual values when majority of the sources are removed from the system. In the second experiment, the estimation performance was evaluated under the exponential network topology. The source reliability distribution was changed to be normal distribution and other settings were kept the same as the first experiment. Reported results are averaged over 100 experiments and shown in Figure 6.22. We observe the estimated false positives/negatives track the actual values well when a reasonable number of sources

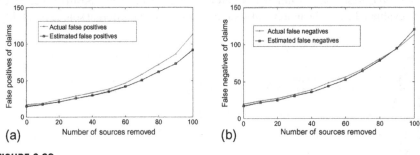

FIGURE 6.22

Estimation of claim classification accuracy versus source removal of exponential topology.
(a) False positives. (b) False negatives.

[†]The source reliability distribution parameters for scale-free and exponential topology generation are set the same as the previous subsection.

stay in the system. However, we also note that the estimation performance degrades compared to the results of scale-free topology. The reason is: sources are more likely to have similar reliability in the exponential topology. Such similarity makes it a more challenging scenario for the reviewed algorithm to accurately pinpoint the source reliability and identity the correctness of claims. For both scale-free and exponential topology, the above results show that the estimated false positives/negatives are able to track the actual values as long as limited number of sources stay in the system. The estimation performance on claim classification is relatively robust to changes in the number of sources in the network.

6.5.4 A REAL WORLD CASE STUDY

In this section, we review the evaluation of the performance of the credibility estimation and confidence quantification approach through a real-world social sensing application. The goal of this application is to identify the correct locations of traffic lights and stop signs in the twin city of Urbana-Champaign by leveraging GPS devices on a set of vehicles traveling regularly in town. (The identified traffic light and stop sign locations were then used along with other information to compute fuel and delay estimates on city routes for a recent green navigation service [113]). The dataset from a smartphone-based vehicular sensing testbed, called SmartRoad [114] was used. Their test application, on the phone, recorded GPS traces, where every GPS reading is composed of an instantaneous latitude-longitude location, speed, time, and bearing of the vehicle. The application then computed simple features that constitute (intentionally unreliable) indicators that the vehicle is waiting at stop sign or a traffic light. Specifically, if a vehicle stops at a location for 15-90 s, the application concludes that it is stopped at a traffic light at that location. Similarly if it stops for 2-10 s, it concludes that it is at a stop sign. These conclusions were reported as claims from the corresponding source. The claim would be that a stop sign (or a traffic light, as applicable) exists at the current location and bearing. Clearly, these generated claims are unreliable, due to the simple-minded nature of the "sensor" and the complexity of road conditions and driver's behaviors. For example, a car can stop anywhere on the road due to a traffic jam or a crossing pedestrian, not necessarily at the location of traffic lights or stop signs. Also, cars do not stop at traffic lights when they are green. Finally, different drivers have different attitudes toward stop signs. Some are more careless and may pass stop signs without stopping or do a "rolling stop," whereas others reliably stop at each sign.

The general lack of reliability of claims and sources (and the differences in driver behavior) constituted a good test for the fact-finding algorithm described in this paper. Hence, the credibility estimation approach was applied to the collected claim data with the hope to find the correct locations of traffic lights and stop signs, and to identify the reliability of sources. For evaluation purposes, they also independently manually collected ground truth locations of traffic lights and stop signs.

In the experiment, 34 people were invited to participate in the application and 1,048,572 GPS readings (around 300 h of driving) were collected. A total of 4865

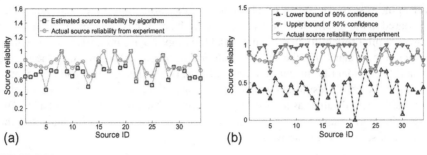

FIGURE 6.23

Estimation of source reliability in the case of traffic lights. (a) Source reliability prediction.
(b) Source reliability bound.

claims were generated by the phones, of which 3303 were for stop signs and 1562
were for traffic lights, collectively identifying 369 distinct locations. The observation
matrix was generated by taking the sources as sources and their stop sign/traffic light
reports as claims. The reviewed credibility estimation approach was applied to the
data collected and its accuracy was evaluated at inferring which reports were correct.

Figures 6.23 and 6.24 show the results for the case of traffic lights identification.
Figure 6.23 shows the results of source reliability. In Figure 9.1, the source reliability
estimated by the credibility estimation algorithm was compared with the actual source
reliability (i.e., the percentage of claims from that source that were actually correct)
computed from ground truth. We observed that estimated values track actual results
well for most of the sources. Figure 6.23(b) shows the 90% confidence bounds on
source reliability estimation. We observe that actual source reliability stays mostly
within the 90% confidence bound. Only 3 sources out of 34 (about 10%) have their
reliability slightly outside the bound, which is what a 90% confidence interval means.
Hence, the experiment verifies the accuracy and tightness of the confidence bounds
derived in Section 6.4. The 68% and 95% confidence bounds were also examined
and we observed that they capture the 70.6% and 94.1% of sources whose reliability

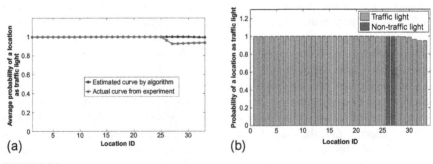

FIGURE 6.24

Estimation of claim correctness in the case of traffic lights. (a) Claim correctness prediction.
(b) Claim classification.

estimations stay within bounds, respectively. This again verifies accuracy of those confidence intervals. Figure 6.24 shows the results of claim classification on traffic lights. All locations were sorted, where the system identified traffic lights (i.e., concluded that the corresponding claims were true), by the probability of correctness, also returned by the system. It is expected that traffic light locations identified with a higher probability will tend to be real lights, whereas those identified with a lower probability will include progressively more false positives.

Figure 6.24(a) shows the sorted locations on the x-axis, and computes for each n, the average probability that the first n locations are traffic lights. The estimated probability was compared to the actual ground truth probability. We observe that the estimation follows quite well the actual experimental ground truth. It verifies the accuracy of the probability values computed and used for claim classification. Additionally, Figure 6.24(b) shows for each traffic light, in the same sorted order, the actual location status (i.e., whether a traffic light is in fact present at the location or not). We observe that most of the traffic light locations identified by the reviewed scheme are correct, although false positives arise as we go down in location ranking. The blue curve (dark gray in print versions) did have a slightly dip when false positives appear even though it is not very obvious in the figure.

The above experiments were repeated for stop sign identification and observed similar trends as in the case of traffic lights. However, the identification of stop signs is found to be more challenging than that of traffic lights. The reasons are: (i) the corroborated data for stop signs is sparser because the chances of different cars to stop at the same stop sign are much lower than that for traffic lights; (ii) cars have quite a few short wait behaviors at non-stop sign locations such as exists from parking lots, left turns, and pedestrian crossings; (iii) cars' bearings are usually not well aligned with the directions of stop signs, which is especially true when the car wants to make a turn after the stop sign. Therefore, for the evaluation of stop signs, only sources whose reliability was more than 50% were picked. Figure 6.25 shows the estimation results of source reliability. We observe that the actual source reliability is estimated accurately and bounded correctly by the 90% confidence bounds. Figure 6.26 shows

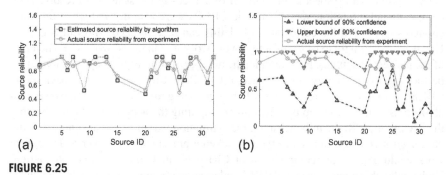

(a)   (b)

FIGURE 6.25

Estimation of source reliability in the case of stop signs. (a) Source reliability prediction. (b) Source reliability bound.

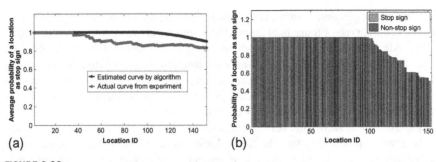

FIGURE 6.26

Estimation of claim correctness in the case of stop signs. (a) Claim correctness prediction. (b) Claim classification.

the results of claim classification at stop signs. We observe that the actual probability of correctness curve stays close to but slightly lower than the estimated one. The reasons of such deviation can be explained by the short wait behaviors mentioned above at non-stop sign locations in real world scenarios. In a sense, given the wait-based features, the reviewed algorithms actually did a better job at identifying actual *stop* locations of vehicles than would be predicted by looking at stop signs only. For example, it also found exits from parking lots and locations of pedestrian crossings. Note that, the aforementioned false positives gradually appear at locations that are ranked lower by the algorithm.

6.6 DISCUSSION

This chapter reviews the derivation and evaluation of confidence intervals in source reliability and estimated classification accuracy of claims in social sensing. Some limitations exist in the reviewed work that offer opportunities for future work.

As we discussed in this chapter, the computation of actual CRLBs of the MLE is exponential with respect to the number of sources in the system. To resolve such computational limitation, the asymptotic CRLBs were also derived when there are enough sources and the correctness of claims can be estimated with full accuracy. However, there might exist a gap between the working ranges of two CRLBs in terms of the number of sources. For example, the number of sources in an application might be too large to efficiently compute actual CRLBs but too small for the asymptotic CRLBs to converge. Therefore, it would be interesting to develop new approximation algorithms to fill in the gap by efficiently computing the actual CRLBs or adjusting the asymptotic CRLBs to better track the estimation variance. We also note that the parameter d is also estimated in the EM scheme presented in Chapter 5. The future work could expand the computation of CRLB by including d in the calculation. Technically, this makes the actual CRLB calculation slightly more complicated, but it should have no effect on the asymptotic CRLB as the z_j for each claim was assumed to be known in that case.

This chapter reviews recently developed confidence bounds on source reliability estimation error as well as estimated classification accuracy of claims in social sensing applications. The reviewed work allow the applications to not only assess the reliability of sources and claims, given neither in advance, but also estimate the accuracy of such assessment. The confidence bounds are computed based on the CRLB of the MLE of source reliability. The accuracy of claim classification is estimated by computing the probability that each claim is correct. The derived accuracy results are shown to predict actual errors very well. The results reviewed in this chapter are important because they allow social sensing applications to assess the reliability of un-vetted sources (like human sources) to a desired confidence level and estimate the accuracy of claim classification under the maximum likelihood hypothesis, in the absence of independent means to verify the data and in the absence of prior knowledge of reliability of sources. This is attained via a well-founded analytic problem formulation and a solution that leverages well-known results in estimation theory.

APPENDIX

The expectation term in Equation (6.7) can be further simplified:

$$
E\left[\frac{(2X_{kj}-1)Z_j(2X_{lq}-1)Z_q}{a_k^{X_{kj}}(1-a_k)^{(1-X_{kj})}a_l^{X_{lq}}(1-a_l)^{(1-X_{lq})}}\right]
$$

$$
= \sum_{x\in\mathcal{X}}\frac{(2X_{kj}-1)Z_j(2X_{lq}-1)Z_q}{a_k^{X_{kj}}(1-a_k)^{(1-X_{kj})}a_l^{X_{lq}}(1-a_l)^{(1-X_{lq})}}p(X|\theta)
$$

$$
= \sum_{x\in\mathcal{X}}\frac{(2X_{kj}-1)(2X_{lq}-1)Z_jZ_q}{a_k^{X_{kj}}(1-a_k)^{(1-X_{kj})}a_l^{X_{lq}}(1-a_l)^{(1-X_{lq})}}
$$

$$
\times\left(\prod_{j'=1}^{N}\left\{\prod_{i=1}^{M}a_i^{X_{ij'}}(1-a_i)^{(1-X_{ij'})}\times d\right.\right.
$$

$$
\left.\left.+\prod_{i=1}^{M}b_i^{X_{ij'}}(1-b_i)^{(1-X_{ij'})}\times(1-d)\right\}\right) \tag{6.23}
$$

When $j\neq q$, plugging the expressions of Z_j and Z_q, the expectation term in Equation (6.7) is shown to be zero:

$$
E\left[\frac{(2X_{kj}-1)Z_j(2X_{lq}-1)Z_q}{a_k^{X_{kj}}(1-a_k)^{(1-X_{kj})}a_l^{X_{lq}}(1-a_l)^{(1-X_{lq})}}\right]
$$

$$
= \sum_{x\in\mathcal{X}}(2X_{kj}-1)(2X_{lq}-1)
$$

$$\times \left(\prod_{\substack{i=1 \\ i\neq k}}^{M} a_i^{X_{ij}}(1-a_i)^{(1-X_{ij})} \times d \prod_{\substack{i=1 \\ i\neq l}}^{M} a_i^{X_{iq}}(1-a_i)^{(1-X_{iq})} \times d \right)$$

$$\times \left(\prod_{\substack{j'=1 \\ j'\neq j \text{ or } q}}^{N} \left\{ \prod_{i=1}^{M} a_i^{X_{ij'}}(1-a_i)^{(1-X_{ij'})} \times d + \prod_{i=1}^{M} b_i^{X_{ij'}}(1-b_i)^{(1-X_{ij'})} \times (1-d) \right\} \right)$$

$$= \sum_{x\in \mathcal{X}_j \times \mathcal{X}_q} (2X_{kj}-1)(2X_{lq}-1)$$

$$\times \left(\prod_{\substack{i=1 \\ i\neq k}}^{M} a_i^{X_{ij}}(1-a_i)^{(1-X_{ij})} \times d \prod_{\substack{i=1 \\ i\neq l}}^{M} a_i^{X_{iq}}(1-a_i)^{(1-X_{iq})} \times d \right)$$

$$= \left(\prod_{\substack{i=1 \\ i\neq k}}^{M} a_i^{X_{ij}}(1-a_i)^{(1-X_{ij})} \times d \prod_{\substack{i=1 \\ i\neq l}}^{M} a_i^{X_{iq}}(1-a_i)^{(1-X_{iq})} \times d \right)$$

$$\times \sum_{X_{kj}=0}^{1} \sum_{X_{lq}=0}^{1} (2X_{kj}-1)(2X_{lq}-1) = 0 \quad j\neq q \tag{6.24}$$

Resolving conflicting observations and non-binary claims

In this chapter, we redefine some terminology in order to discuss conflicting observations and non-binary claims. Let us first define the variables that sources actually observe and report in social sensing applications as *measured variables*. These measured variables could have multiple values and only one of them represents the actual state of the variable. We then define the collection of all observations asserting the *same value* of a measured variable as a *claim*. Let us use a simple example as shown in Figure 7.1 to illustrate the terms we defined. In this example, measured variable C_1 has two possible values (i.e., $X_1 = 1$ and $X_1 = 0$). Claim "$X_1 = 1$" represents all observations reported by sources asserting the value of C_1 is 1. In the case only the positive state of a measured variable is reported (as we reviewed in previous chapters), we can just use the claim to represent the measured variable since there is no ambiguity.

7.1 HANDLING CONFLICTING BINARY OBSERVATIONS

In this section, we review the extension of the maximum likelihood estimation (MLE) model to handle conflicting binary observations (e.g., positive or negative assertion) from different sources on the same measured variable [101]. An important assumption made in the original MLE model is that observations from different sources on a given measured variable are *corroborating* (i.e., no conflicting observations exist). However, this is not always true in reality. For example, comments from different reviewers in an on-line review system often contradict with each other, making it difficult for readers to make a decision. This section addresses the challenge of having *conflicting observations* in quality of information (QoI) quantification of social sensing. An extended expectation maximization (EM) scheme is developed to provide MLE on source reliability and measured variable correctness while taking care of conflicting observations from different sources on the same measured variable.

Association for Computing Machinery, Inc. being the copyright holder, grants permission to reprint text of the article, Dong Wang, Lance Kaplan, Tarek Abdelzaher, "Maximum Likelihood Analysis of Conflicting Observations in Social Sensing," *ACM Transactions on Sensor Networks (ToSN)*, Vol. 10, No. 2, Article 30, January, 2014.

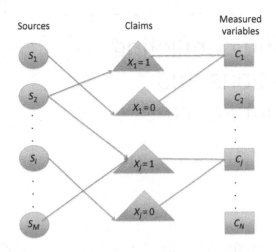

FIGURE 7.1

Concept of claims and measured variables.

7.1.1 EXTENDED MODEL

In the extended model to handle conflicting binary observations, it is assumed that observations are either *positive* or *negative* assertion of the corresponding measured variable. As we mentioned before, the measured variable is assumed to be binary. Let the probability that source S_i makes a positive observation be s_i^T, probability that source S_i makes a negative observation be s_i^F. Furthermore, t_i still denotes the odds that source S_i is right, but it is redefined as the probability that the source's observation *matches* the ground truth of the measured variable and $1 - t_i$ denotes the probability that it is wrong. Note that, this probability depends on the source's reliability, which is not known a priori. Formally, t_i is redefined in the context of conflicting observations as two metrics:

$$t_i^T = P(C_j^t|S_iC_j^t)$$

$$t_i^F = P(C_j^f|S_iC_j^f) \tag{7.1}$$

where $S_iC_j^t$ denotes source S_i reports the measured variable C_j to be true (i.e., S_i makes positive observation on C_j) and $S_iC_j^f$ denotes source S_i reports the measured variable C_j to be false (i.e., S_i makes negative observation on C_j). C_j^t and C_j^f denote the measured variable C_j is indeed true or false as we mentioned before.

a_i^T and a_i^F are defined as the (unknown) probability that source S_i reports a variable to be true or false when it is indeed true, respectively. Formally, a_i^T and a_i^F are defined as follows:

$$a_i^T = P(S_i C_j^t | C_j^t)$$

$$a_i^F = P(S_i C_j^f | C_j^t) \qquad (7.2)$$

b_i^T and b_i^F are defined as the (unknown) probability that source S_i reports a variable to be true or false when it is in reality false. Formally, b_i^T and b_i^F are defined as follows:

$$b_i^T = P(S_i C_j^t | C_j^f)$$

$$b_i^F = P(S_i C_j^f | C_j^f) \qquad (7.3)$$

The observation matrix SC to handle conflicting observations should be redefined as well: $S_i C_j = 1$ when source S_i reports that C_j is true, $S_i C_j = -1$ when source S_i reports that C_j is false and $S_i C_j = 0$ when source S_i does not observe C_j. This observation matrix is called the *conflicting observation matrix*. As we mentioned before, d represents the overall prior probability that a randomly chosen measured variable is true. Additionally, we denote $P(C_j^t) = d$ and $P(S_i C_j^t) = s_i^T$, $P(S_i C_j^f) = s_i^F$. Plugging these, together with t_i into the definition of a_i^T, a_i^F, b_i^T, and b_i^F, the relations between the terms defined above can be obtained by using the Bayesian theorem:

$$a_i^T = \frac{t_i^T \times s_i^T}{d} \qquad a_i^F = \frac{(1 - t_i^F) \times s_i^F}{d}$$

$$b_i^T = \frac{(1 - t_i^T) \times s_i^T}{1 - d} \qquad b_i^F = \frac{t_i^F \times s_i^F}{1 - d} \qquad (7.4)$$

The goal of the extended model for conflicting observations is similar as the regular model in Section 5.1. That is to find the MLE of the source reliability and the correctness of the measured variables given conflicting observations on the same measured variable.

7.1.2 RE-DERIVE THE E-STEP AND M-STEP

Fortunately, it turns out that the MLE approach in Chapter 5 can be extended to solve the optimization problem with conflicting observations. The estimation parameter now becomes: $\theta = (a_1^T, a_2^T, \ldots, a_M^T;\ a_1^F, a_2^F, \ldots, a_M^F;\ b_1^T, b_2^T, \ldots, b_M^T;\ b_1^F, b_2^F, \ldots, b_M^F; d)$. Corresponding changes need to be made to the likelihood function and the E-step and M-step of the EM scheme need to be re-derived accordingly to incorporate this new estimation parameter. The converged results of the extended approach offers the MLE of θ for the model that is most consistent with the conflicting observation matrix. From there, similar procedures as discussed in Section 5.2 can be adapted to compute the H^* and E^* in Equation (5.4).

The likelihood function $L(\theta; X, Z)$ is given by:

$$L(\theta; X, Z) = p(X, Z|\theta)$$

$$= \prod_{j=1}^{N}\left\{\prod_{i=1}^{M}\left[a_i^{T S_i C_j^T} \times a_i^{F S_i C_j^F} \times \left(1 - a_i^T - a_i^F\right)^{\left(1 - S_i C_j^T - S_i C_j^F\right)}\right] \times d \times z_j\right.$$

$$\left. + \prod_{i=1}^{M}\left[b_i^{T S_i C_j^T} \times b_i^{F S_i C_j^F} \times \left(1 - b_i^T - b_i^F\right)^{\left(1 - S_i C_j^T - S_i C_j^F\right)}\right] \times (1 - d) \times (1 - z_j)\right\}$$

(7.5)

where $S_i C_j^T = 1$ when source S_i claims the measured variable C_j to be true and $S_i C_j^T = 0$ otherwise. Similarly, $S_i C_j^F = 1$ when source S_i claims the measured variable C_j to be false and $S_i C_j^F = 0$ otherwise.

Given the above formulation, the E-Step can be derived as follows:

$$Q(\theta|\theta^{(t)}) = \sum_{j=1}^{N}\left\{Z(t,j) \times \left[\sum_{i=1}^{M}\left(S_i C_j^T \log a_i^T + S_i C_j^F \log a_i^F\right.\right.\right.$$

$$+ \left(1 - S_i C_j^T - S_i C_j^F\right)\log\left(1 - a_i^T - a_i^F\right) + \log d\Big)\Big]$$

$$+ (1 - Z(t,j)) \times \left[\sum_{i=1}^{M}\left(S_i C_j^T \log b_i^T + S_i C_j^F \log b_i^F\right.\right.$$

$$+ \left(1 - S_i C_j^T - S_i C_j^F\right)\log\left(1 - b_i^T - b_i^F\right) + \log(1 - d)\Big)\Big]\right\}$$

(7.6)

where $Z(t,j)$ is given by:

$$Z(t,j) = p\left(z_j = 1|X_j, \theta^{(t)}\right) = \frac{A(t,j) \times d^{(t)}}{A(t,j) \times d + B(t,j) \times (1 - d^{(t)})}$$

(7.7)

where $A(t,j)$ and $B(t,j)$ are defined as:

$$A(t,j) = p\left(X_j, \theta^{(t)}|z_j = 1\right)$$

$$= \prod_{i=1}^{M}\left\{a_i^{T(t)S_i C_j^T} \times a_i^{F(t)S_i C_j^F} \times \left(1 - a_i^{T(t)} - a_i^{F(t)}\right)^{\left(1 - S_i C_j^T - S_i C_j^F\right)}\right\}$$

$$B(t,j) = p\left(X_j, \theta^{(t)}|z_j = 0\right)$$

$$= \prod_{i=1}^{M}\left\{b_i^{T(t)S_i C_j^T} \times b_i^{F(t)S_i C_j^F} \times \left(1 - b_i^{T(t)} - b_i^{F(t)}\right)^{\left(1 - S_i C_j^T - S_i C_j^F\right)}\right\}$$

(7.8)

The Maximization step (M-step) is given by Equation (5.9). θ^* (i.e., $(a_1^{T*}, \ldots, a_M^{T*}; a_1^{F*}, \ldots, a_M^{F*}; b_1^{T*}, \ldots, b_M^{T*}; b_1^{F*}, \ldots, b_M^{F*}; d^*)$) is chosen to maximize the $Q(\theta|\theta^{(t)})$ function in each iteration to be the $\theta^{(t+1)}$ of the next iteration.

To get θ^* that maximizes $Q(\theta|\theta^{(t)})$, the derivatives are set to zero: $\frac{\partial Q}{\partial a_i^T} = 0$, $\frac{\partial Q}{\partial a_i^F} = 0$, $\frac{\partial Q}{\partial b_i^T} = 0$, $\frac{\partial Q}{\partial b_i^F} = 0$, and $\frac{\partial Q}{\partial d} = 0$. Solving the above equations, the expressions of the optimal a_i^{T*}, a_i^{F*}, b_i^{T*}, b_i^{F*}, and d^* are:

$$a_i^{T\,(t+1)} = a_i^{T*} = \frac{\sum_{j \in SJ_i^T} Z(t,j)}{\sum_{j=1}^N Z(t,j)}$$

$$a_i^{F\,(t+1)} = a_i^{F*} = \frac{\sum_{j \in SJ_i^F} Z(t,j)}{\sum_{j=1}^N Z(t,j)} \tag{7.9}$$

$$b_i^{T\,(t+1)} = b_i^{T*} = \frac{K_i^T - \sum_{j \in SJ_i^T} Z(t,j)}{N - \sum_{j=1}^N Z(t,j)}$$

$$b_i^{F\,(t+1)} = b_i^{F*} = \frac{K_i^F - \sum_{j \in SJ_i^F} Z(t,j)}{N - \sum_{j=1}^N Z(t,j)} \tag{7.10}$$

$$d^{(t+1)} = d^* = \frac{\sum_{j=1}^N Z(t,j)}{N} \tag{7.11}$$

where K_i^T and K_i^F are the number of true and false observations made by source S_i, respectively, and N is the total number of claims in the conflicting observation matrix. SJ_i^T and SJ_i^F are the sets of claims the source S_i actually observes as true and false, respectively, in the conflicting observation matrix (i.e., SC). $Z(t,j)$ is defined in (7.7). For details of deriving the above solution, please refer to Appendix of Chapter 7. This completes the mathematical development. The EM algorithm to handle conflicting observations is summarized in the next subsection.

7.1.3 THE BINARY CONFLICT EM ALGORITHM

We refer to the EM scheme reviewed above that handles conflicting observations as the Conflict EM algorithm. The input to the conflict EM algorithm is the conflicting observation matrix (i.e., SC) and the output is the MLE of source reliability and corresponding judgment on the correctness of claims in the context of conflicting observations. The E-step and M-step of the conflict EM algorithm reduce to simply calculating (7.7) and (7.9)–(7.11) iteratively until they converge. The convergence analysis has been done for EM scheme and it is beyond the scope of this book [108]. In practice, the algorithm can run until the difference of estimation parameter between consecutive iterations becomes insignificant. Since the claim is binary, C_j is true if $Z(t,j) \geq 0.5$ and false otherwise. At the same time, the MLE on source reliability can be computed from the converged values of $\theta^{(t)}$ based on (7.4). The resulting algorithm is shown in Algorithm 2.

Similarly as we did before, we present here a toy example to help readers better understand the extended EM algorithm to handle conflicting observations. In this toy example, 10 sources generate conflicting observations about 20 measured variables. The first 10 measured variable (i.e., Variable ID: 1-10) are true and the remaining

---

ALGORITHM 2 EXPECTATION MAXIMIZATION ALGORITHM FOR CONFLICTING OBSERVATIONS

1: Initialize θ with random values between 0 and 1
2: **while** $\theta^{(t)}$ does not converge **do**
3:     **for** $j = 1 : N$ **do**
4:         compute $Z(t,j)$ based on Equation (7.7)
5:     **end for**
6:     $\theta^{(t+1)} = \theta^{(t)}$
7:     **for** $i = 1 : M$ **do**
8:         compute $a_i^{T(t+1)}, a_i^{F(t+1)}, b_i^{T(t+1)}, b_i^{F(t+1)}, d^{(t+1)}$ based on Equation (7.9), (7.10), and (7.11)
9:         update $a_i^{T(t)}, a_i^{F(t)}, b_i^{T(t)}, b_i^{F(t)}, d^{(t+1)}$ with $a_i^{T(t+1)}, a_i^{F(t+1)}, b_i^{T(t+1)}, b_i^{F(t+1)}, d^{(t)}$ in $\theta^{(t+1)}$
10:     **end for**
11:     $t = t + 1$
12: **end while**
13: Let Z_j^c = converged value of $Z(t,j)$
14: Let $a_i^{T^c}$ = converged value of $a_i^{T(t)}$;
    $b_i^{F^c}$ = converged value of $b_i^{F(t)}$;
    d^c = converged value of $d^{(t)}$
15: **for** $j = 1 : N$ **do**
16:     **if** $Z_j^c \geq 0.5$ **then**
17:         h_j^* is true
18:     **else**
19:         h_j^* is false
20:     **end if**
21: **end for**
22: **for** $i = 1 : M$ **do**
23:     calculate t_i^{T*}, t_i^{F*} from $a_i^{T^c}, a_i^{F^c}, b_i^{T^c}, b_i^{F^c}, d^c$ based on Equation (7.4).
24: **end for**
25: Return the computed optimal estimates of measured variables $C_j = h_j^*$ and source reliability t_i^{T*}, t_i^{F*}.

---

are false. The sources include both reliable and unreliable ones, whose reliability is shown in Table 7.1. The bipartite graph of the *conflicting observation matrix SC* is shown in Figure 7.2, where the solid and dash line in the graph indicate the corresponding source reports the measured variable to be true and false, respectively, and 0 indicates the source does not report the measured variable. The results of using Voting, Regular EM (i.e., the basic EM approach to handle corroborating

Table 7.1 The Source Reliability of the Toy Example

	Source ID									
	1	2	3	4	5	6	7	8	9	10
Source reliability	0.9	0.4	0.9	0.9	1	0.3	0.3	1	0.2	0.9

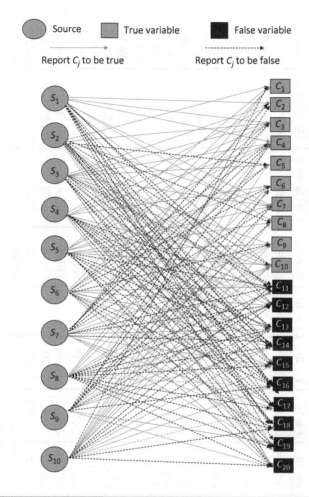

FIGURE 7.2

The conflicting bipartite graph of the toy example.

observations only), and Conflict EM (i.e., the extended EM approach to handle conflicting observations) to classify the true and false measured variables in the toy example are shown in Table 7.2. For the Regular EM, it takes conflicting observations of the same measured variable as two independent observations and pick the one with higher probability to believe after the algorithm terminates. For Voting, the measured variable is judged as true if the number of positive observations (i.e., sources claim the variable to be true) is larger or equal to the negative ones and false otherwise. For both Regular and Conflict EM, we showed the probability of each measured variable to be true (i.e., $Z(t, j)$) computed in first few iterations as well as the last iteration of the algorithm when the estimation converges. We observe that ConflictEM correctly classifies all true and false measured variables while Voting and Regular

Table 7.2 The Comparison Between Voting, Regular EM and Conflict EM in the Toy Example

Variable ID	Voting Count	Regular EM			Conflict EM			Voting Results	Regular EM Results	Conflict EM Results	Ground Truth
		$t=1$	$t=2$	$t=10$	$t=1$	$t=2$	$t=10$				
1	2	0.7682	0.4361	0.0033	0.8496	0.9771	1	TRUE	**FALSE**	TRUE	TRUE
2	1	0.5604	0.9298	0.9901	0.6004	0.9953	1	TRUE	TRUE	TRUE	TRUE
3	6	0.9831	0.9995	1	0.9863	0.999	1	TRUE	TRUE	TRUE	TRUE
4	3	0.9573	0.9997	1	0.8707	0.9999	1	TRUE	TRUE	TRUE	TRUE
5	0	0.5604	0.5552	0.1212	0.5854	0.9767	1	TRUE	**FALSE**	TRUE	TRUE
6	2	0.7682	0.9872	1	0.781	0.9996	1	TRUE	TRUE	TRUE	TRUE
7	3	0.896	0.9915	0.9994	0.8944	0.9998	1	TRUE	TRUE	TRUE	TRUE
8	1	0.5604	0.8968	0.9927	0.6792	0.9994	1	TRUE	TRUE	TRUE	TRUE
9	4	0.896	0.9888	1	0.9472	0.9998	1	TRUE	TRUE	TRUE	TRUE
10	6	0.9831	0.9996	1	0.9807	0.9998	1	TRUE	TRUE	TRUE	TRUE
11	-4	0.5604	0.0777	0	0.0588	0.0001	0	FALSE	FALSE	FALSE	FALSE
12	-2	0.5604	0.3643	0.0042	0.1823	0.0348	0	FALSE	FALSE	FALSE	FALSE
13	0	0.896	0.3172	0.0005	0.5	0.0013	0	**TRUE**	FALSE	FALSE	FALSE
14	-4	0.329	0.0435	0.0001	0.0588	0.0012	0	FALSE	FALSE	FALSE	FALSE
15	0	0.5604	0.3855	0.0074	0.4427	0.0499	0	**TRUE**	FALSE	FALSE	FALSE
16	-7	0.1587	0.1413	0.0277	0.0082	0.0016	0	FALSE	FALSE	FALSE	FALSE
17	-4	0.329	0.0472	0.0001	0.0588	0.0002	0	FALSE	FALSE	FALSE	FALSE
18	-6	0.1587	0.0449	0.0006	0.0172	0.0002	0	FALSE	FALSE	FALSE	FALSE
19	0	0.7682	0.069	0	0.4715	0.0018	0	**TRUE**	FALSE	FALSE	FALSE
20	-1	0.7682	0.3161	0.0007	0.3462	0.001	0	FALSE	FALSE	FALSE	FALSE

EM mis-classify 3 and 2 measured variables, respectively. The mis-classified claims are highlighted in the table. The better performance of Conflict EM is achieved by explicitly considering the conflicting observations on the same variable in its estimation framework.

7.2 HANDLING NON-BINARY CLAIMS

Recall the value of the measured variable (claim) is assumed to be *binary* in the original MLE model. Though this covers a wide range of social sensing applications where the status of the measured variable is either "true" or "false." For example, a building is either on fire or not. Jeffery is either the CEO of company X or not. However, there are also some other application scenarios that the values of measured variables may not necessarily be binary. For example, the types of parking lots in a district can be "parking meters," "permit only," or "private." In this effort, we review generalization of the MLE model to incorporate the *non-binary* values of measured variables.

The generalized model for non-binary measured variables is the same as the original model except there can be more than two values reported by different sources about the same measured variable. Hence, the measured variable in this section is assumed to have K ($K \geq 2$) mutually exclusive possible values and only one of them represents the true value of the measured variable. In the model to handle conflicting observations, it is assumed that observations from sources assert one of the K values of the corresponding measured variable, thus can be potentially conflicting. Let S_i represent the ith source and C_j represent the jth measured variable. Each source generally observes only a subset of all measured variables (e.g., the conditions at locations they visited). Let $S_i C_j = k$ denote source S_i reports the measured variable C_j to be of value k for $k = 0, \ldots, K$. Note that $S_i C_j = 0$ means that source S_i does not report an observation for measured variable C_j. Let probability that source S_i reports the measured variable to be of value k be s_i^k (i.e., $s_i^k = P(S_i C_j = k)$ for $k = 0, \ldots, K$). Let $s_i^{\bar{k}}$ represent the probability that S_i reports a measured variable to be of value other than k (i.e., $s_i^{\bar{k}} = \sum_{k' \neq 0, k} s_i^{k'}$).

In the case of non-binary claims, t_i^k denotes the probability that source S_i is right when the measured variable is of value k (i.e., probability that the source's observation *matches* the ground truth of the measured variable) and $1 - t_i^k$ denotes the probability that it is wrong under the same condition. Note that, this probability depends on the source's reliability, which is not known a priori.

Let us also define $a_{k,i}^T$ and $a_{k,i}^F$ as the (unknown) probability that source S_i reports a measured variable to be of value k and value other than k when the measured variable is indeed of value k, respectively. Formally, $a_{k,i}^T$ and $a_{k,i}^F$ are defined as follows:

$$a_{k,i}^T = P(S_i C_j = k | C_j = k)$$

$$a^F_{k,i} = \sum_{k' \neq 0,k}^{K} P(S_i C_j = k' | C_j = k) \tag{7.12}$$

where $C_j = k$ denotes the measured variable C_j is indeed of value k for $k = 1, \ldots, K$. It is assumed that source S_i can report one (and only one) of the K mutually exclusive values for measured variable C_j (i.e., a source is not self-contradictory on its assertion for a measured variable). Since a source may not assert a measured variable ($k = 0$), $a^T_{k,i} + a^F_{k,i} \leq 1$.

Let us define the observation matrix SC to handle conflicting observations: $S_i C_j = k$ when source S_i reports that C_j is of value k, $S_i C_j = 0$ when no sources reports C_j. Let us call this observation matrix the *conflicting observation matrix*. Let d_k represent the overall prior probability that an arbitrary measured variable is of value k.

Plugging these, together with the definitions of t_i and $a^T_{k,i}$, the relations between them can be obtained by using the Bayesian theorem:

$$a^T_{k,i} = \frac{t^k_i \times s^k_i}{d_k} \tag{7.13}$$

7.2.1 GENERALIZED E AND M STEPS FOR NON-BINARY MEASURED VARIABLES

In this subsection, we review the solution of the problem formulated in the previous subsection for non-binary measured variables using a generalized version of the EM algorithm. Similarly as before, we have a latent variable Z for each measured variable to indicate the value of the measured variable. However the definition of Z is generalized for non-binary measured variables: we have a corresponding variable z_j for the jth measured variable C_j such that: $z_j = k$ when C_j is of value k. The observation matrix SC is again denoted as the observed data X, and $\theta = (\theta_1, \theta_2, \ldots, \theta_K)$ are the parameters of the model that we want to estimate, where $\theta_k = \left(a^T_{k,1}, a^F_{k,1}, a^T_{k,2}, a^F_{k,2}, \ldots, a^T_{k,M}, a^F_{k,M}, d_k \right)$. The goal is to get the MLE of θ for the model containing observed data X and latent variables Z.

Given the estimation parameter and hidden variables defined above, the likelihood function $L(\theta; X, Z)$ for conflicting observations is:

$$L(\theta; X, Z) = p(X, Z|\theta) = \prod_{j=1}^{N} \left\{ \sum_{k=1}^{K} \left[\prod_{i=1}^{M} a^{T \, S_i C^k_j}_{k,i} \times a^{F \, S_i C^{\bar{k}}_j}_{k,i} \right. \right.$$
$$\left. \left. \times \left(1 - a^T_{k,i} - a^F_{k,i} \right)^{\left(1 - S_i C^k_j - S_i C^{\bar{k}}_j \right)} \times d_k \times z^k_j \right] \right\} \tag{7.14}$$

where $S_i C^k_j = 1$ when source S_i asserts the measured variable C_j to be of value k (i.e., $S_i C_j = k$) and 0 otherwise, $S_i C^{\bar{k}}_j = 1$ when source S_i asserts the measured variable C_j to be of value other than k (i.e., $S_i C_j \neq k$ or 0) and 0 otherwise, and $z^1_j, z^2_j, \ldots, z^K_j$

is a set of indicator variables for measured variable C_j where $z_j^k = 1$ when C_j is of value k and $z_j^k = 0$ otherwise. Additionally, the values of S_iC_j are statistically independent over the M sources and N measured variables. The likelihood function above describes the likelihood to have current observation matrix X and hidden variable Z given the estimation parameter θ.

Given the above formulation, the E-Step can be derived as

$$Q(\theta|\theta^{(t)}) = \sum_{j=1}^{N} \left\{ \sum_{k=1}^{K} Z_k(t,j) \times \left[\sum_{i=1}^{M} \left(S_iC_j^k \log a_{k,i}^T + S_iC_j^{\bar{k}} \log a_{k,i}^F \right) \right. \right.$$

$$\left. \left. + \left(1 - S_iC_j^k - S_iC_j^{\bar{k}} \right) \log \left(1 - a_{k,i}^T - a_{k,i}^F \right) + \log d_k \right) \right] \right\} \qquad (7.15)$$

where $Z_k(t,j)$ is given by:

$$Z_k(t,j) = p(z_j = k|X_j, \theta^{(t)}) = \frac{A_k(t,j) \times d_k^{(t)}}{\sum_{k=1}^{K} A_k(t,j) \times d_k^{(t)}} \qquad (7.16)$$

where $A_k(t,j)$ is defined as:

$$A_k(t,j) = p(X_j, \theta^{(t)}|z_j = k)$$

$$= \prod_{i=1}^{M} \left\{ a_{k,i}^{T\ (t)S_iC_j^k} \times a_{k,i}^{F\ (t)S_iC_j^{\bar{k}}} \right.$$

$$\left. \times (1 - a_{k,i}^{T\ (t)} - a_{k,i}^{F\ (t)})^{(1-S_iC_j^k - S_iC_j^{\bar{k}})} \right\} \qquad (7.17)$$

where $Z_k(t,j)$ is the conditional probability of the measured variable C_j to have value k given the observation matrix related to the jth measured variable and current estimate of θ. X_j represents the jth column of the observed SC matrix (i.e., observations of the jth measured variable from all sources). $A_k(t,j)$ represents the conditional probability regarding observations about the jth measured variable and current estimation of the parameter θ given the jth measured variable is of value k.

The M-step is given by (5.9). θ^* $\left(\text{i.e.,} \left(a_{k,1}^T{}^*, \ldots, a_{k,M}^T{}^*; a_{k,1}^F{}^*, \ldots, a_{k,M}^F{}^*; d^* \right) \right.$ $k = 1, 2, \ldots, K)$ is chosen to maximize the $Q(\theta|\theta^{(t)})$ function in each iteration to be the $\theta^{(t+1)}$ of the next iteration.

To get θ^* that maximizes $Q(\theta|\theta^{(t)})$, the derivatives are set to zero: $\frac{\partial Q}{\partial a_{k,i}^T} = 0$, $\frac{\partial Q}{\partial a_{k,i}^F} = 0$, and $\frac{\partial Q}{\partial d_k} = 0$.

Solving the above equations, expressions of the optimal $a_{k,i}^T{}^*$, $a_{k,i}^F{}^*$, and d_k^* are:

$$a_{k,i}^T{}^{(t+1)} = a_{k,i}^T{}^* = \frac{\sum_{j \in SJ_i^k} Z_k(t,j)}{\sum_{j=1}^{N} Z_k(t,j)}$$

$$a_{k,i}^F{}^{(t+1)} = a_{k,i}^F{}^* = \frac{\sum_{j \in SJ_i^{\bar{k}}} Z_k(t,j)}{\sum_{j=1}^{N} Z_k(t,j)}$$

$$d_k^{(t+1)} = d_k^* = \frac{\sum_{j=1}^{N} Z_k(t,j)}{N} \qquad (7.18)$$

where N is the total number of measured variables in the conflicting observation matrix. SJ_i^k are the sets of measured variables the source S_i actually observes to have value k and $SJ_i^{\bar{k}}$ are the ones S_i observes to have value other than k in the conflicting observation matrix (i.e., SC). $Z_k(t,j)$ is defined in (7.16). For details of deriving the above solution, please refer to Appendix of Chapter 7. Note that the case where the value of the measured variable is binary (i.e., $K = 2$) can be considered as a special case of the algorithm derived in this section, which is equivalent to the conflicting EM derived in the prior section.

This completes the mathematical development. The EM algorithm to handle non-binary measured variables is summarized in the next subsection.

7.2.2 THE GENERALIZED EM ALGORITHM FOR NON-BINARY MEASURED VARIABLES

We refer to the EM scheme reviewed above to handle non-binary measured variables as the general EM algorithm. The input to the general EM algorithm is the general observation matrix (i.e., SC) and the output is the MLE of source reliability and corresponding judgment on the correctness of measured variables in the context of non-binary values. The E-step and M-step of the general EM algorithm reduce to simply calculating (7.16) and (7.18) iteratively until they converge. The convergence analysis has been done for EM scheme and it is beyond the scope of this book [108]. In practice, the algorithm can run until the difference of estimation parameter between consecutive iterations becomes insignificant. Then the value of measured variable C_j is decided as the one that has the highest $Z_k(t,j)$ value for $k = 1, 2, \ldots, K$. In the special case where the measured variable is binary, C_j is true if $Z_k(t,j) \geq 0.5$ and false otherwise. At the same time, the MLE on source reliability can be computed from the converged values of $\theta^{(t)}$ based on (7.13). The resulting algorithm is shown in Algorithm 3.

7.3 PERFORMANCE EVALUATION

In this section, we review the experiments that were carried out to evaluate the performance of the generalized EM models reviewed in this chapter in terms of estimation accuracy of the probability that a participant is right or a claim is true compared to the regular EM scheme described in Chapter 5 and other state-of-art solutions for conflicting observations. Those baselines include Sums [35], Average-Log [37], TruthFinder [36], and the simple voting scheme. It is shown that the extended EM algorithms outperforms the regular EM algorithm and the state of the art baselines.

7.3.1 A REAL WORLD APPLICATION

In this subsection, we review the evaluation of the performance of the extended EM scheme for conflicting observations through a real world application, finding free

---

ALGORITHM 3 GENERALIZED EXPECTATION MAXIMIZATION ALGORITHM FOR NON-BINARY MEASURED VARIABLES

1: Initialize θ with random values between 0 and 1
2: **while** $\theta^{(t)}$ does not converge **do**
3:    **for** $j = 1 : N$ **do**
4:       **for** $k = 1 : K$ **do**
5:          compute $Z_k(t, j)$ based on (7.16)
6:       **end for**
7:    **end for**
8:    $\theta^{(t+1)} = \theta^{(t)}$
9:    **for** $k = 1 : K$ **do**
10:       **for** $i = 1 : M$ **do**
11:          compute $a_{k,i}^{T\ (t+1)}, a_{k,i}^{F\ (t+1)}$ and $d_k^{(t+1)}$ based on (7.18)
12:          update $a_{k,i}^{T\ (t)}, a_{k,i}^{F\ (t)}, d_k^{(t)}$ with $a_{k,i}^{T\ (t+1)}, a_{k,i}^{F\ (t+1)}$ and $d_k^{(t+1)}$ in $\theta^{(t+1)}$
13:       **end for**
14:    **end for**
15:    $t = t + 1$
16: **end while**
17: Let $Z_{k,j}^c$ = converged value of $Z_k(t, j)$
18: Let θ^c = converged value of $\theta^{(t)}$
19: **for** $j = 1 : N$ **do**
20:    $max = 0; k^* = 0$
21:    **for** $k = 1 : K$ **do**
22:       **if** $Z_{k,j}^c \geq max$ **then**
23:          $max = Z_{k,j}^c$ and $k^* = k$
24:       **end if**
25:    **end for**
26:    measured variable C_j is of value k^*
27: **end for**
28: **for** $i = 1 : M$ **do**
29:    calculate t_i^{k*} from θ^c based on (7.13).
30: **end for**
31: Return the computed maximum likelihood estimation on source reliability t_i^* and corresponding judgment on the correctness of measured variable C_j.

---

parking lots on UIUC campus. "Free parking lots" refer to the parking lots that is free of charge after 5pm on weekday as well as weekends. The goal was to see if the reviewed scheme to handle conflicting observations can find the free parking lots most accurately compared to other state-of-art baselines. Specifically, 106 parking lots were selected around the campus and asked volunteers to mark them as either "Free" or "Not Free." Participants mark those parking lots they have been to or are familiar with. It is noted that there are actually various types of parking lots on campus: enforced parking lots with time limits, parking meters, permit parking, street parking, etc. Different parking lots have different regulations for free parking. Moreover, instructions and permit signs sometimes read similar and are easy to miss. Hence, people are prone to generate both false positives and false negatives in their

Table 7.3 Accuracy of Finding Free Parking
Lots on Campus

Schemes	False Positives	False Negatives
EM-Conflict	6.67%	10.87%
EM-Regular	11.67%	17.39%
Average-Log	16.67%	19.57%
Truth-Finder	18.33%	15.22%
Voting	21.67%	23.91%

reports. For evaluation purpose, the ground truth were manually collected on those selected parking lots.

In the experiment, 30 participants were invited to offer their marks on the 106 parking lots (46 of which are indeed free). There were 901 marks collected from participants in total. The observation matrix was then generated by taking the participants as sources and different parking lots as measured variables. The free parking lots map to the true measured variables while the non-free ones map to the false measured variables. The corresponding element $S_i C_j$ is set according to the marks each participant placed on those parking lots. The extended EM scheme discussed in Section 7.1 that handles conflicting observations and other state-of-art baselines (including the regular EM scheme adapted for conflicting claims as we explained in Section 7.1) as well as the simple voting scheme were applied to the data we collected. The false positives and false negatives of different schemes in identifying the free parking lots among all places selected were compared. The result is shown in Table 7.3. We observe that the extended EM scheme to handle conflicting observations (i.e., EM-Conflict) achieved the least false positives and false negatives among all schemes under comparison. The reason is the extended EM scheme modeled the conflicting observations explicitly and used the MLE approach to find the value of each measured variable that is most consistent with the observations.

7.3.2 A SIMULATION STUDY FOR CONFLICTING OBSERVATIONS

In this subsection, we further reviewed evaluation of the performance of the extended EM scheme for conflicting observations compared to the regular EM scheme and several state-of-art techniques in literature through extensive simulation studies. The simulation we reviewed in the previous chapters was modified. The simulator generates a random number of sources and measured variables. A random probability P_i is assigned to each source S_i representing his/her reliability (i.e., the ground truth probability that they report correct observations). For each source S_i, L_i observations are generated. Each observation from source S_i has a probability t_i of being matched to the correctness of the measured variable (i.e., reporting a variable to be the same as its ground truth) and a probability $1 - t_i$ of being mismatched. Note that, for simplicity, t_i is assumed to be independent of the claimed value in the simulation experiments, and therefore, $t_i^1 = t_i^2 = \cdots = t_i^K$. Thus, t_i can be thought as the average of $\dfrac{a_k^T \times d_k}{\left(a_k^T \times d_k + a_k^F \times (1-d_k)\right)}$ over all k. Also note that sources can report conflicting observations for the same measured variable in this scenario. For simplicity, measured variables were assumed to be binary.

The conflict EM scheme reviewed in this chapter and the regular EM scheme reviewed in Chapter 5 were applied to the sensing topology with conflicting observations and it is shown that the conflict EM scheme outperformed the regular EM scheme and other state-of-art baselines. Note that for the regular EM scheme, it was adapted in a similar way as fact-finders to handle the conflicting observations of the same measured variable [37]. Reported results are averaged over 100 experiments.

In the first experiment, the estimation accuracy of the conflict EM scheme and baselines (including regular EM scheme) was evaluated while varying the number of sources in the network. The number of reported measured variables was fixed at 2000, of which 1000 measured variables were reported correctly and 1000 were misreported. The average number of observations per source was set to 200. The number of sources was varied from 20 to 110. Results are shown in Figure 7.3. Observe that the conflict EM scheme has both smaller estimation error on source

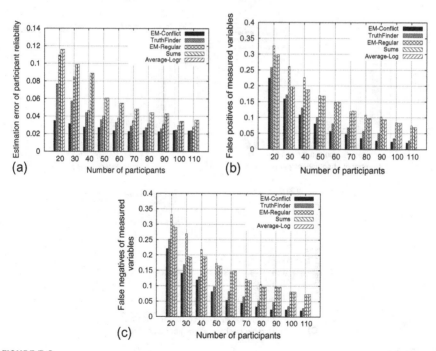

FIGURE 7.3

Estimation accuracy versus number of participants for conflicting observations.
(a) Source reliability estimation accuracy. (b) Measured variable estimation: false positives.
(c) Measured variable estimation: false negatives.

reliability and less false positives/negatives on measured variables among all schemes under comparison. Note also that the performance gain of the conflict EM scheme is large when the number of sources is small.

The second experiment compares the conflict EM scheme with baselines when the average number of observations per source changes. As before, the number of correctly and incorrectly reported measured variables were fixed to be 1000 respectively. The number of sources was fixed at 50. The average number of observations per source was varied from 100 to 1000. The results are shown in Figure 7.4. Observe that the EM scheme outperforms the regular EM scheme and other baselines in terms of both source reliability estimation accuracy and false positives/negatives of measured variables as the average number of observations per source changes. The performance gain of the conflict EM scheme is higher when the average number of observations per source is low.

The third experiment examines the effect of changing the percentage of correct measured variables on the estimation accuracy of all schemes. The ratio of the number of correctly reported measured variables to the total number of measured variables was varied from 0.1 to 0.6, while fixing the total number of such measured variables to 2000. The number of sources was fixed to 50 and the average number of observations

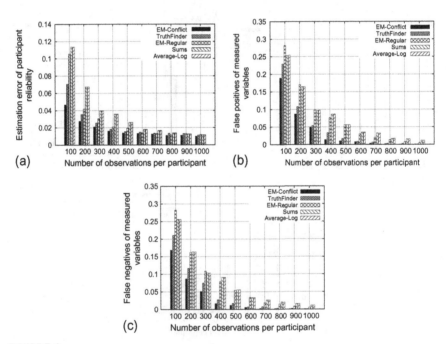

FIGURE 7.4

Estimation accuracy versus average number of observations per participant for conflicting observations. (a) Source reliability estimation accuracy. (b) Measured variable estimation: false positives. (c) Measured variable estimation: false negatives.

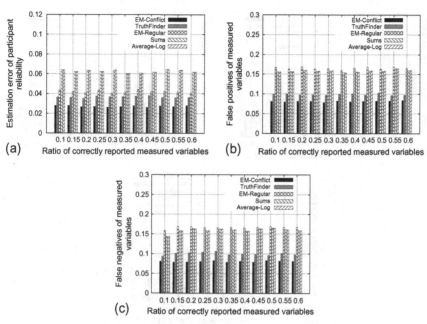

FIGURE 7.5

Estimation accuracy versus ratio of correctly reported measured variables for conflicting observations. (a) Source reliability estimation accuracy. (b) Measured variable estimation: false positives. (c) Measured variable estimation: false negatives.

reported by a source was set to 200. Reported results are shown in Figure 7.5. We observe that the conflict EM scheme has less error in both source reliability estimation and false positives/negatives on measured variables under different mix of correct and false measured variables.

Finally, the fourth experiment was to evaluate the performance of the conflict EM scheme and other schemes when the offset of the initial estimation on the background bias d varies. The offset is defined as the difference between the initial estimation on d and its ground-truth. The number of correctly and incorrectly reported measured variables were fixed to 1000 respectively (i.e., $d = 0.5$). The absolute value of the initial estimate offset on d was varied from 0 to 0.45. The number of sources was fixed at 50 and the average number of observations per source was set to 200. Results are averaged over both positive and negative offsets of the same absolute value. Figure 7.6 shows the results. We observe that the performance of the conflict EM scheme is better than other baselines in terms of both source reliability estimation and false positives/negatives on measured variables when the initial estimate offset on d changes. We also observe the performance of all schemes are relatively stable when offset on d increases. The reason is the schemes for conflicting observations mainly depend on the mutual exclusive property of the reports (rather than correct estimation on prior d) to decide the correctness of measured variables.

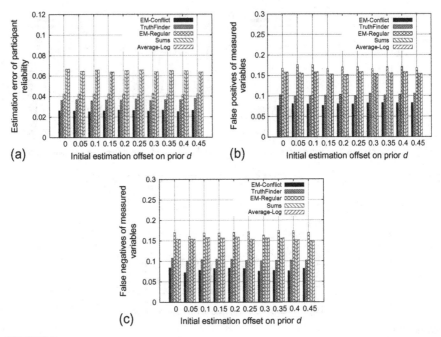

FIGURE 7.6

Estimation accuracy versus initial estimation offset on prior d for conflicting observations.
(a) Source reliability estimation accuracy. (b) Measured variable estimation: false positives.
(c) Measured variable estimation: false negatives.

7.3.3 A SIMULATION STUDY FOR NON-BINARY CLAIMS

In this section, we review similar experiments that were carried out to evaluate the performance of the generalized model and extended EM approach derived in section 7.2 to the sensing topology with non-binary claims. It is shown that the generalized EM scheme outperform all state-of-art baselines. In the context of non-binary claims, each observation of participant S_i has a probability t_i of being matched to the real value of the measured variable (i.e., reporting a variable to be the same as its ground truth) and a probability $1 - t_i$ of being mismatched. Note that participants can report every possible value of the measured variable in this scenario. For simplicity, we review the case where the measured variable can have three different values a, b, c. The remaining simulation configurations are kept the same as before. Reported results are averaged over 100 experiments.

The first experiment was to show the performance comparison between the generalized EM scheme for non-binary claims and other baselines by varying the number of participants in the network. The number of reported measured variables was fixed at 1500. The number of the a, b, and c valued measured variables is 500 each. The average number of observations per participant was set to 200. The number of participants was varied from 30 to 120. Results are shown in Figure 7.7. Observe

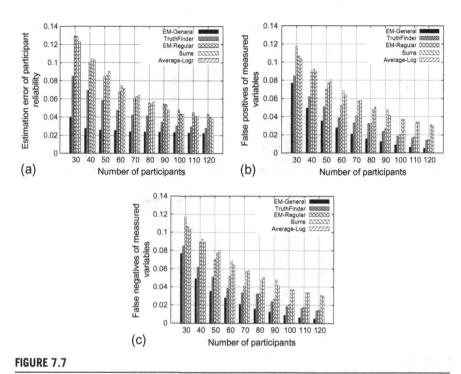

FIGURE 7.7

Estimation accuracy versus number of participants for non-binary claims. (a) Participant reliability estimation accuracy. (b) Measured variable estimation: false positives. (c) Measured variable estimation: false negatives.

that the generalized EM has both smaller estimation error on participant reliability and less false positives/negatives on measured variables among all schemes under comparison. Note also that the performance gain of the generalized EM is large when the number of participants is small.

The second experiment was to compare the generalized EM scheme for non-binary claims with other baselines while varying the average number of observations per participant. The number of participants was fixed at 50. The average number of observations per participant was varied from 100 to 1000. The results are shown in Figure 7.8. Observe that the generalized EM outperforms all baselines in terms of both participant reliability estimation accuracy and false positives/negatives of measured variables as the average number of observations per participant changes. As before, the performance gain of the generalized EM is higher when the average number of observations per participant is low.

Finally, the third experiment was to evaluate the performance of the generalized EM scheme for non-binary claims compared to baselines when the ratio of the measured variable with one value (e.g., a in this study) changes. The number of participants was fixed to 50 and the average number of observations reported by a participant was set to 200. The total number of measured variable was kept as

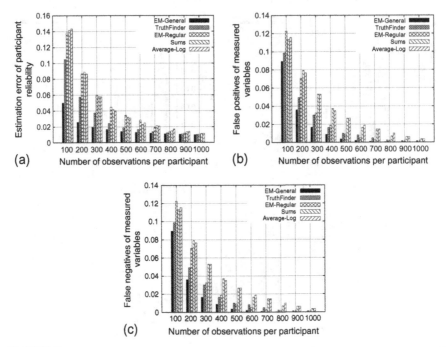

FIGURE 7.8

Estimation accuracy versus average number of observations per participant for non-binary claims. (a) Participant reliability estimation accuracy. (b) Measured variable estimation: false positives. (c) Measured variable estimation: false negatives.

1500 and the ratio of *a* valued measured variables varied from 0.1 to 0.6. Reported results are shown in Figure 7.9. We observe that the generalized EM has less error in both participant reliability estimation and false positives/negatives on measured variables under different ratio of value *a* measured variables. Moreover, the estimation performance of the generalized EM scheme is also more stable compared to other baselines when the ratio of *a* valued measured variable changes.

7.4 DISCUSSION

In this chapter, we reviewed the extensions of the basic MLE model to handle more general cases in social sensing applications where reported observations from different participants can be conflicting and claims can be non-binary. Several future research directions exist by further addressing some assumptions that were made on the reviewed generalized MLE models.

First, values of the measured variable are assumed to be discrete and the true value is unique. What happens if there are degrees of truth on the measured variable? For example, the true value of a measured variable may not simply be true or false but

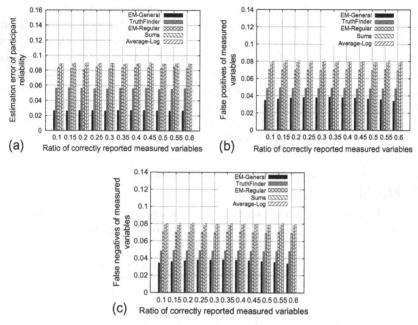

FIGURE 7.9

Estimation accuracy versus ratio of value *a* measured variables for non-binary claims. (a) Participant reliability estimation accuracy. (b) Measured variable estimation: false positives. (c) Measured variable estimation: false negatives.

could stay within a continuous spectrum between the two. In such case, we may not be able to use the current discrete indication vectors to represent all possible values of the measured variable. Instead, some continuous variables could be used to reconstruct the likelihood function and reflect the actual degrees of truth on the measured variable. Closed form solutions are possible to be derived for the continuous variable scenarios. In statistics, some filtering algorithms (e.g., Kalman filter, particle filter, etc.) are designed to remove the noise from continuous variables [115, 116]. Their models usually make different assumptions on the underlying distribution of variable state space and the sample size. For example, Kalman filter assumes the measurements have a Gaussian distribution and the underlying system is linear. These assumptions may not necessarily hold for the data collected from social sensing applications. However, it would be interesting to see if it is possible to adapt some of the filtering techniques and further extend the MLE model to better handle continuous measured variables.

Second, the observations participants make on measured variables are assumed to be affirmative (i.e., either completely positive or negative). What happens if there are degrees of support on the observations reported by participants on the measured variables? For example, a participant may report a measurement with a certain degree of confidence. In the reviewed models, it is assumed that a source either reports an observation or not, the degrees of support on the reported observations are not considered. One possible way to incorporate such degrees of support on observations into the MLE model is to associate links with different weights in the bipartite graph of the sensing topology. Some prior work applied similar ideas to incorporate the prior knowledge into their fact-finding framework [44]. However, the challenge for the current model is that it needs to keep the probability semantics of the estimation parameters defined when link weights are added into the graph. Another possibility is to model the degrees of support on the observations separately and relate them to the estimation parameters defined for the MLE model.

APPENDIX

The following derivation demonstrates the details to obtain the results in (7.9)–(7.11). The derivation that maximizes the $Q(\theta|\theta^{(t)})$ in the M-step in Section 7.1 yields:

$$\sum_{j=1}^{N} Z(t,j) \left[\frac{S_i C_j^T}{a_i^{T*}} - \frac{(1 - S_i C_j^T - S_i C_j^F)}{1 - a_i^{T*} - a_i^{F*}} \right] = 0$$

$$\sum_{j=1}^{N} Z(t,j) \left[\frac{S_i C_j^F}{a_i^{F*}} - \frac{(1 - S_i C_j^T - S_i C_j^F)}{1 - a_i^{T*} - a_i^{F*}} \right] = 0 \qquad (7.19)$$

$$\sum_{j=1}^{N} (1 - Z(t,j)) \left[\frac{S_i C_j^T}{b_i^{T*}} - \frac{(1 - S_i C_j^T - S_i C_j^F)}{1 - b_i^{T*} - b_i^{F*}} \right] = 0$$

$$\sum_{j=1}^{N} (1 - Z(t,j)) \left[\frac{S_i C_j^F}{b_i^{F*}} - \frac{(1 - S_i C_j^T - S_i C_j^F)}{1 - b_i^{T*} - b_i^{F*}} \right] = 0 \qquad (7.20)$$

$$\sum_{j=1}^{N} \left[Z(t,j) \sum_{i=1}^{M} \frac{1}{d^*} - (1 - Z(t,j)) \sum_{i=1}^{M} \frac{1}{1 - d^*} \right] = 0 \qquad (7.21)$$

As we mentioned earlier, SJ_i^T and SJ_i^F represent the sets of claims the participant S_i actually reports as true and false, respectively, in the conflicting observation matrix (i.e., SC). $\overline{SJ}_i$ is defined as the set of claims participant S_i does not report in the conflicting observation matrix. Thus, (7.19) and (7.20) can be rewritten as:

$$\sum_{j \in SJ_i^T} Z(t,j) \frac{1}{a_i^{T*}} - \sum_{j \in \overline{SJ}_i} Z(t,j) \frac{1}{1 - a_i^{T*} - a_i^{F*}} = 0$$

$$\sum_{j \in SJ_i^F} Z(t,j) \frac{1}{a_i^{F*}} - \sum_{j \in \overline{SJ}_i} Z(t,j) \frac{1}{1 - a_i^{T*} - a_i^{F*}} = 0 \qquad (7.22)$$

$$\sum_{j\in SJ_i^T}(1-Z(t,j))\frac{1}{b_i^{T*}}-\sum_{j\in \overline{SJ}_i}(1-Z(t,j))\frac{1}{1-b_i^{T*}-b_i^{F*}}=0$$

$$\sum_{j\in SJ_i^F}(1-Z(t,j))\frac{1}{a_i^{F*}}-\sum_{j\in \overline{SJ}_i}(1-Z(t,j))\frac{1}{1-b_i^{T*}-b_i^{F*}}=0 \qquad (7.23)$$

Solving the above equations, the expressions of the optimal a_i^{T*}, a_i^{F*}, b_i^{T*}, b_i^{F*}, and d^* are shown in (7.9)–(7.11).

The following derivation demonstrates the details to obtain the results in (7.18). The derivation that maximizes the $Q(\theta|\theta^{(t)})$ in the M-step in Section 7.2 yields:

$$\sum_{j=1}^{N}Z_k(t,j)\left[\frac{S_iC_j^k}{a_{k,i}^{T*}}-\frac{(1-S_iC_j^k-S_iC_j^{\bar{k}})}{1-a_{k,i}^{T*}-a_{k,i}^{F*}}\right]=0$$

$$\sum_{j=1}^{N}Z_k(t,j)\left[\frac{S_iC_j^{\bar{k}}}{a_{k,i}^{F*}}-\frac{(1-S_iC_j^k-S_iC_j^{\bar{k}})}{1-a_{k,i}^{T*}-a_{k,i}^{F*}}\right]=0 \quad k=1,2,\ldots,K \qquad (7.24)$$

$$\sum_{j=1}^{N}\left[Z_k(t,j)\frac{1}{d_k^*}-\left(1-\sum_{k=1}^{K-1}Z_k(t,j)\right)\frac{1}{1-\sum_{i=1}^{K-1}d_i^*}\right]=0 \quad k=1,2,\ldots,K-1 \qquad (7.25)$$

As we defined earlier, SJ_i^k and $SJ_i^{\bar{k}}$ represent the sets of claims the participant S_i actually reports as value k and value other than k, respectively, in the conflicting observation matrix (i.e., SC). $\overline{SJ}_i$ is defined as the set of claims participant S_i does not report in the conflicting observation matrix. Thus, (7.24) can be rewritten as:

$$\sum_{j\in SJ_i^k}Z_k(t,j)\frac{1}{a_{k,i}^{T*}}-\sum_{j\in \overline{SJ}_i}Z_k(t,j)\frac{1}{1-a_i^{T*}-a_{k,i}^{F*}}=0$$

$$\sum_{j\in SJ_i^{\bar{k}}}Z_k(t,j)\frac{1}{a_{k,i}^{F*}}-\sum_{j\in \overline{SJ}_i}Z_k(t,j)\frac{1}{1-a_{k,i}^{T*}-a_{k,i}^{F*}}=0 \qquad (7.26)$$

Solving the above equations, we can obtain the expressions of the optimal $a_{k,i}^{T*}$, $a_{k,i}^{F*}$, and d_k^* as shown in (7.18).

Understanding the social network

8.1 INFORMATION PROPAGATION CASCADES

With the advent of online social networks, humans are able to volunteer free observations about the physical world at scale, as well as communicate and share their observations with each other in a prompt and efficient way. As individuals choose to propagate information, their observations spread through the underlying social networks that connect them. We call such information spread on social networks *information propagation cascades* as the propagated information will eventually reach a larger population in a similar way as epidemic cascades (ECs) [117]. Information cascades happen naturally within social networks (e.g., Twitter) where individuals are given the option to forward messages or follow behaviors of other people in the network. The properties of information propagation cascades have been well studied in different types of online social networks such as Twitter [118], Facebook [119], Flickr [120], Digg [121], and YouTube [122].

In this chapter, we review the work that address two important problems: (i) How will the information propagation cascades on social network affect the performance of the social sensing model discussed in the previous chapters? (ii) How to further generalize the basic maximum likelihood estimation (MLE) model to consider the information propagation properties? Twitter is a good platform to study the information propagation cascades, especially during the process of natural disasters and emergency events where a lot of warnings, news, and rumors are generated and propagated on Twitter [123]. In particular, Twitter allows users to send short messages through various devices and broadcasts messages to a large population. In particular, Twitter has the option that allows users to follow each other. When a user posts a tweet, that tweet is immediately visible to all of his/her followers. Twitter also has the function called Retweet, which allows users to easily forward tweets from other users. Follower-followee relationship and the Retweet function make it easy and fast for the information propagation cascades to occur on Twitter.

The reader must be cautioned that social networks carry a lot of extraneous information as well, such as subjective opinions (e.g., "It is an inspiring day!") and personal emotions (e.g., "I am depressed"). These are not the topic of this chapter. Instead, we are interested in objective claims in social sensing that describe external

IEEE being the copyright holder, grants permission to reprint text of the article, Dong Wang, Tanvir Amin, Shen Li, Tarek Abdelzaher, Lance Kaplan, Siyu Gu, Chenji Pan, Hengchang Liu, Charu Aggrawal, Raghu Ganti, XinLei Wang, Prasant Mohapatra, Boleslaw Szymanski, Hieu Le, "Using Humans as Sensors: An Estimation Theoretic Perspective," Proceedings of *The 13th IEEE International Conference on Information Processing in Sensor Networks (IPSN 14)*, Berlin, Germany, April, 2014.

physical state. In the aftermath of important events, many microblog entries offer physical descriptions of the event (e.g., "Shooting erupts on Liberty Square!"). Such reporting is an act of sensing of the physical environment that is external to the human observers. In this case, the physical environment has a unique state, leading to a unique ground truth, according to which these descriptions are either true or false (e.g., either there was shooting on Liberty Square or not). It is this category of claims about the physical environment that this chapter is concerned with. The reviewed work has developed tools to collect such claims from online social media in large-scale disaster and unrest events [124].

8.2 A BINARY MODEL OF HUMAN SENSING

In this section, we review a model that takes humans as sources of (i) *unknown reliability*, generating (ii) *binary observations* of (iii) *uncertain provenance* [105]. Of these three features, the first is perhaps the most intuitive. Unlike physical sensors whose characteristics, calibration, and failure modes are known, we do not, in general, know the reliability of human observers and hence cannot assume it in the problem formulation. In the following subsections, we explain the remaining two model features; namely, binary observations and uncertain provenance.

8.2.1 A BINARY SENSOR MODEL

From a sensor modeling perspective, an obvious difference between physical sensors and human observations is one of functional specialization versus breadth. Humans, are much broader in what they can observe, albeit less accurate. Table 8.1 gives examples of actual observations made on Twitter.

Such observations can be thought of as measurements of different *binary variables*. They are binary because the observation reported can either be true or false. In a system featuring a collaboration of sensors and humans, it is therefore meaningful to collect from humans these binary states. On the other hand, sensors provide continuous values that can be used to infer some state of the work (e.g., the room is occupied since the room temperature is 72.2 degrees). This has been the practice in participatory sensing, where participants were asked to make *binary* observations,

Table 8.1 Examples of Twitter Observations

Crash blocking lanes on I-5S @ McBean Pkwy in Santa Clarita
BREAKING NEWS: Shots fired in Watertown; source says Boston Marathon terror bomb suspect has been pinned down
The police chief of Afghanistan's southern Kandahar province has died in a suicide attack on his headquarters.
Yonkers mayor has lifted his gas rationing order. Fill it up!

such as "there is garbage here"; whereas sensors, such as GPS, would provide the corresponding continuous variable (e.g., location).

With the above in mind, the reviewed work focuses on a binary observation model, common to geotagging applications. Generalizing from participatory sensing, each human reports an arbitrary number of observations, which refer to as *claims*, that can be individually either true or false. Different individuals have different reliability, expressed as the probability of producing true claims. In this model, the physical world is just a collection of mention-worthy facts. For example, "Main Street is flooded," "The BP gas station on University Ave. is out of gas," or "Police are shooting people on Market Square." Human observers report some of the facts they observe (e.g., on Twitter). The problem of reliable sensing is to infer which of the reported human observations match ground truth in the physical world.

8.2.2 UNCERTAIN PROVENANCE

A feature that lends novelty to the human sensor model, is the notion of *uncertain data provenance*. Namely, it is not unusual for a person to report observations they received from others as if they were his/her own. Such rumor spreading behavior has no analogy in correctly functioning physical sensors. We call this problem one of uncertain data provenance because when Bob tweets that "Main Street is flooded," even if we authenticate Bob as the actual source of the tweet, we do not know if Bob truly observed the event first-hand or heard it from another source such as Sally. From a sensing perspective, this means that errors in "measurements" across "sensors" may be non-independent, as one erroneous observation may be propagated by other sources without being verified.

8.2.3 A WORD ON SIMPLICITY

In the interest of initial progress, the model discussed in this chapter is purposely simple to promote applicability in many different contextual situations. The reader will legitimately find several key ways this simplified model can be extended. One can think of the method presented in this chapter as offering a performance baseline against which such future potential enhancements can be benchmarked. Clearly, the performance of the baseline sheds light on the utility of such enhancements. To emphasize its simplicity, we call the reviewed baseline model the *binary model of human sensing* and show in evaluation review section that the resulting ground truth reconstruction algorithm does very well.

8.3 INFERRING THE SOCIAL NETWORK

In this section, we discuss possible methods that can be used to infer the social network with a focus on Twitter. In order to have a holistic view of the entire system, we put such discussion in the context of the solution architecture. To enable reconstruction of ground truth information from data reported by human sources, a solution needs to (i) collect data from the "humans as a sensor network," (ii) structure the data for analysis, (iii) understand how sources are related, and (iv) use this collective information to estimate the probability of correctness of individual observations. These steps are described in the following subsections, respectively. The reviewed solution focused on Twitter as the underlying "humans as a sensor network."

8.3.1 DATA COLLECTION

The solution performs data collection using Apollo, a data distillation tool built for social sensing applications [125]. In principle, Apollo can collect data from different participatory sensing front end, such as a online social media and smartphone applications. In the reviewed work, Apollo was used to collect data from Twitter. Tweets are collected through a long-standing query via the exported Twitter API to match given query terms (keywords) and an indicated geographic region on a map. These overall query can either be a conjunction or disjunction of the keyword and location terms. In essence, Apollo acts as the "base station" for a participatory sensing network, where the query defines the scope of information collected from participants.

8.3.2 COMPUTING THE SOURCE-CLAIM GRAPH

Next, the solution determines the internal consistency in reported observations. For this reason, observations are clustered based on a *distance function*. This function, distance (t_1, t_2), takes two reported observations, t_1 and t_2, as input and returns a measure of similarity between them, represented by a logical distance. The more dissimilar the observations, the larger the distance. In the case of data collection from Twitter, the solution regarded individual tweets as individual observations, and borrowed from natural language processing literature a simple cosine similarity function [110] that returns a measure of similarity based on the number of matching tokens in the two inputs. The distance function nicely separates natural language processing concerns from sensing concerns.

As distances are computed, the set of input observations is transformed to a graph where vertices are individual observations and links represent similarity among them. Then the graph is clustered, causing similar observations to be clustered together. Note that clustering is an important step that significantly improves the scalability and quality of the process. In a real-world human sensing application, sources will typically report slightly different observations, even when they measure the same variable or observe the same event. This results in a large number of (slightly different) individual claims and a large, poorly-connected, source-claim network, which has at least two negative consequences. First, it impairs scalability of the human sensing (and increases its convergence time). Second, it lowers the quality of outputs because similar claims are treated separately and cannot get the credibility boost they would have enjoyed had they been considered together. Clustering of similar claims alleviates the above problems. It results in smaller well-connected source-claim networks in which joint estimation of source and claim correctness converges rapidly and the outcome becomes more accurate. One limitation of the reviewed work is that it has not applied more advanced natural language processing techniques in the clustering function (e.g., it does not account for sentiment analysis). This is partly because of the difficulty of applying those NLP techniques in short text messages (e.g., tweets) that are lack of context information. In the future, the authors plan to explore the possibility of using some deep NLP or semantic analysis techniques to further improve the performance of the clustering component.

The output of the clustering algorithm is a graph of individual sources and claim clusters (we call consolidated claims). In such graph, each source, S_i, is connected to all claims they made (i.e., clusters they contributed to), and each claim, C_j, is connected to all sources who espoused it (i.e., all sources of tweets in the corresponding cluster). We say that $S_i C_j = 1$ if source S_i makes claim C_j. Each claim can either be true or false. The claim is true if it is consistent with ground truth in the physical world. Otherwise, it is false. The source-claim graph constitutes an input to our analysis algorithm.

8.3.3 INFERRING THE SOCIAL NETWORK

Next, the solution infers the social network to account for uncertain data provenance. Sources may have reported either their own observations or observations they heard from others. It is assumed there exists a latent social network represented by an information dissemination graph, SD, that estimates how information might propagate from one person to another. A recent Sigmetrics paper [117] describes an algorithm to infer the latent contagion network underlying ECs, given the time when each node got infected. For the current work, an EC social graph was constructed using the iterative greedy strategy described in the Sigmetrics paper, where each distinct observation is modeled as a cascade and the time of contagion of a source describes when the source mentioned this observation. The resulting graph is called the EC network. Specific to Twitter, three other ways were also used to estimate potential information dissemination among sources. The first is to construct this graph based on the follower-followee relationship. A directed link (S_i, S_k) exists in the social graph from source S_i to source S_k if S_k is a follower of S_i. This graph is called the FF network. The second option is to construct the social network from the retweeting (RT) behavior of twitter users. In this case, a directed link (S_i, S_k) exists in the social graph if source S_k retweets some tweets from source S_i. This graph is called the RT network. The third option combines the above two, forming a network where a directed link (S_i, S_k) exists when either S_k follows S_i or S_k retweets what S_i said. The third type of social network is called the RT+FF network. Though arbitrary network can be formed, as of now, we constrain the analysis to a two-level forest (clusters) in the following sections, but will consider arbitrary networks in the future.

8.3.4 SOLVING THE ESTIMATION PROBLEM

With inputs computed, the next stage is to perform the analysis that estimates correctness of claims. For each claim, C_j, Apollo determines if it is true or false. Apollo uses a sliding window approach for analyzing received tweets. Let the total number of claims computed from tweets received in the last window be N. A trivial solution would be to count the number of sources, S_i, that made each claim. In other words, for each C_j, where $1 \leq j \leq N$, count all S_i, where $S_iC_j = 1$. The idea being that claims with more support are more believable. This solution is called *voting*, in an analogy with counting the number of votes. Unfortunately, it is suboptimal for two reasons. First, different sources have different degrees of reliability. Hence, their "votes" do not have the same weight. Second, sources may not be independent. When a source simply repeats what they heard from others, their "vote" does not add to the credibility of the claim.

Since the only information available to the model (other than the reported observations themselves) is the source claim graph, SC, and the social dissemination graph, SD, computed from the two steps above, the question becomes: Given graphs SC and SD what is the likelihood that claim C_j is true, for each j? Formally, it is given by:

$$\forall j, 1 \leq j \leq N : P(C_j = 1 | SC, SD) \tag{8.1}$$

where $P(C_j = 1 | SC, SD)$ is the conditional probability that C_j is true given SC and SD. With the aforementioned probability computed, Apollo forward to the user those tweets that meet a specified (user configurable) probability of correctness. This feed is the solution to the reliable sensing problem.

8.4 A SOCIAL-AWARE ALGORITHM

It remains to show how to cast the problem of computing the probability of correctness of claims as a MLE problem when sources have *unknown reliability* and data has *uncertain provenance*. This section presents a social-aware algorithm that solves this problem. Let m be the total number of sources in the system from which we have data. Let us describe each source (i.e., "sensor"), S_i, $1 \leq i \leq m$, by two parameters; the likelihoods of true positives, $a_i = P(S_iC_j = 1 | C_j = 1)$ and the likelihoods of false positives, $b_i = P(S_iC_j = 1 | C_j = 0)$, neither of which are known in advance. d is denoted as the unknown expected ratio of correct claims in the system, $d = P(C_j = 1)$. The vector θ is defined to be the vector of the above unknowns:

$$\theta = [a_1, \ldots, a_m, b_1, \ldots, b_m, d] \tag{8.2}$$

A MLE finds the values of the unknowns that maximize the probability of observations, SC, given the social network SD. Hence, the goal is to find θ that maximizes $P(SC|SD, \theta)$. The probability $P(SC|SD, \theta)$ depends on which claims are true and which are false. Let us therefore introduce the vector Z where element $z_j = 1$ if C_j is true and zero otherwise. Using the total probability theorem, the expression to maximize, namely $P(SC|SD, \theta)$, can be rewritten as follows:

$$P(SC|SD,\theta) = \sum_z P(SC,z|SD,\theta) \tag{8.3}$$

This problem can be solved by using the expectation maximization (EM) algorithm [93, 126]. The current work explicitly models the source dependency and uncertain data provenance in the MLE and presents an enhanced EM algorithm to address these challenges. The EM scheme starts with some initial guess for θ, say θ_0 and iteratively updates it using the formula:

$$\theta_{n+1} = \text{argmax}_\theta\{E_{z|SC,\theta_n}\{ln\,P(SC,z|SD,\theta)\}\} \tag{8.4}$$

The above breaks down into three quantities that need to be derived:

- The log likelihood function, $\ln P(SC,z|SD,\theta)$
- The expectation step, $Q_\theta = E_{z|SC,\theta_n}\{\ln P(SC,z|SD,\theta)\}$
- The maximization step, $\theta_{n+1} = \arg \max_\theta\{Q_\theta\}$

Note that, the latter two steps are computed iteratively until the algorithm converges. The above functions are derived below.

8.4.1 DERIVING THE LIKELIHOOD

The key contribution of the social-aware EM scheme lies in incorporating the role of uncertain provenance into the MLE algorithm. To compute the log likelihood, the function $P(SC,z|SD,\theta)$ needs to be computed first. The source claim graph SC can be divided into subsets, SC_j, one per claim C_j. The subset describes which sources espoused the claim and which did not. Since claims are independent, we have:

$$P(SC,z|SD,\theta) = \prod_{j=1}^{N} P(SC_j,z_j|SD,\theta) \tag{8.5}$$

which can in turn be re-written as:

$$P(SC,z|\theta) = \prod_{j=1}^{N} P(SC_j|SD,\theta,z_j)P(z_j) \tag{8.6}$$

where $P(SC_j|SD,\theta,z_j)$ is the joint probability of all observations involving claim C_j. Unfortunately, in general, the sources that make these observations may not be independent since they may be connected in the social network leading to a possibility that one expressed the observation of another. Let $p_{ik} = P(S_iC_j|S_kC_j)$ be the probability that source S_i makes claim C_j given that his parent S_k (in the social dissemination network) makes that claim. p_{ik} is referred to as *repeat ratio* and can be approximately computed from graph SC, for pairs of nodes connected in graph SD, as follows:

$$p_{ik} = \frac{\text{number of times } S_i \text{ and } S_k \text{ make same claim}}{\text{number of claims } S_k \text{ makes}} \tag{8.7}$$

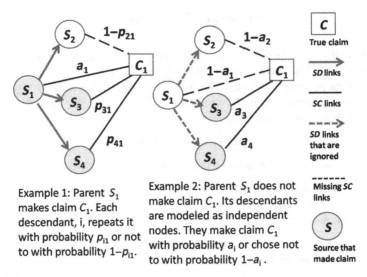

Example 1: Parent S_1 makes claim C_1. Each descendant, i, repeats it with probability p_{i1} or not to with probability $1-p_{i1}$.

Example 2: Parent S_1 does not make claim C_1. Its descendants are modeled as independent nodes. They make claim C_1 with probability a_i or chose not to with probability $1-a_i$.

FIGURE 8.1

Simple illustrative examples for proof.

Hence, the joint probability that a parent S_p and its children S_i make the same claim is given by $P(S_pC_j) \prod_i P(S_iC_j|S_pC_j)$ which is $P(S_pC_j) \prod_i p_{ip}$. This probability accounts for the odds of one source repeating claims by another. Note that the model assumes that a child will not independent make the same claim as a parent. For illustration, let us now consider the special case of social network topology SD, where the network is given by a forest of two-level trees.* Hence, when considering claim C_j, sources can be divided into a set M_j of independent subgraphs, where a link exists in subgraph $g \in M_j$ between a parent and child only if they are connected in the social network and the *parent claimed* C_j. The link implies source dependency as far as the claim in question is concerned. The intuition is that if the parent does not make the claim, then the children act as if they are independent sources. If the parent makes the claim, then each child repeats it with a given repeat probability. The assumed repeat probability determines the degree to which the algorithm accounts for redundant claims from dependent sources. The higher it is, the less credence is given to the dependent source. Two scenarios are illustrated by the two simple examples in Figure 8.1, showing the situation where source S_1, who has children S_2, S_3, and S_4, makes claim C_1 and when it does not make it, respectively. Note the differences in the computed probabilities of its children making claim C_1. In general, let S_g denote the parent of subgraph g and c_g denote the set of its children, if any. Equation (8.6) can then be rewritten as follows:

$$P(SC, z|SD, \theta) = \prod_{j=1}^{N} P(z_j) \times \left\{ \prod_{g \in M_j} P(S_gC_j|\theta, z_j) \prod_{i \in c_g} P(S_iC_j|S_gC_j) \right\} \quad (8.8)$$

*The authors are working on generalizing the topology to a directed acyclic graph (DAG).

where

$$
P(z_j) = \begin{cases} d & z_j = 1 \\ (1-d) & z_j = 0 \end{cases}
$$

$$
P(S_g C_j | \theta, z_j) = \begin{cases} a_g & z_j = 1, S_g C_j = 1 \\ (1-a_g) & z_j = 1, S_g C_j = 0 \\ b_g & z_j = 0, S_g C_j = 1 \\ (1-b_g) & z_j = 0, S_g C_j = 0 \end{cases}
$$

$$
P(S_i C_j | S_g C_j) = \begin{cases} p_{ig} & S_g C_j = 1, S_i C_j = 1 \\ 1 - p_{ig} & S_g C_j = 1, S_i C_j = 0 \\ a_i & S_g C_j = 0, S_i C_j = 1, z_j = 1 \\ (1-a_i) & S_g C_j = 0, S_i C_j = 0, z_j = 1 \\ b_i & S_g C_j = 0, S_i C_j = 1, z_j = 0 \\ (1-b_i) & S_g C_j = 0, S_i C_j = 0, z_j = 0 \end{cases} \qquad (8.9)
$$

8.4.2 DERIVING THE E-STEP AND M-STEP

Given the above formulation, substitute the likelihood function defined in Equation (8.8) into the definition of Q function of EM. The Expectation step (E-step) becomes:

$$
\begin{aligned}
Q(\theta|\theta^{(n)}) = \sum_{j=1}^{N} & \Bigg\{ Z(n,j) \times \Bigg[\Bigg\{ \sum_{g \in M_j} \big(\log P(S_g C_j | \theta, z_j) \\
& + \sum_{i \in c_g} \log P(S_i C_j | S_g C_j) \big) \Bigg\} + \log d \Bigg] \\
& + (1 - Z(n,j)) \times \Bigg[\Bigg\{ \sum_{g \in M_j} \big(\log P(S_g C_j | \theta, z_j) \\
& + \sum_{i \in c_g} \log P(S_i C_j | S_g C_j) \big) \Bigg\} + \log(1-d) \Bigg] \Bigg\}
\end{aligned} \qquad (8.10)
$$

where $Z(n,j)$ is the conditional probability of claim C_j to be true given the observed source claim subgraph SC_j and current estimation on θ. It is given by:

$$
\begin{aligned}
Z(n,j) = p(z_j = 1 | SC_j, \theta^{(n)}) &= \frac{p(z_j = 1; SC_j, \theta^{(n)})}{p(SC_j, \theta^{(n)})} \\
&= \frac{p(SC_j, \theta^{(n)} | z_j = 1) p(z_j = 1)}{p(SC_j, \theta^{(n)} | z_j = 1) p(z_j = 1) + p(SC_j, \theta^{(n)} | z_j = 0) p(z_j = 0)}
\end{aligned}
$$

where

$$p(SC_j, \theta^{(n)} | z_j = 1 \text{ or } 0) = \prod_{g \in M_j} P(S_g C_j | \theta^{(n)}, z_j) \prod_{i \in c_g} P(S_i C_j | S_g C_j) \qquad (8.11)$$

where $P(S_g C_j | \theta^{(n)}, z_j)$, $P(S_i C_j | S_g C_j)$, and $P(z_j)$ are defined in Equation (8.9).

θ^* (i.e., $a_1^*, \ldots, a_m^*, b_1^*, \ldots, b_m^*, d^*$) are chosen to maximize the $Q(\theta | \theta^{(n)})$ function in each iteration to be the $\theta^{(n+1)}$ of the next iteration. To get θ^* that maximizes $Q(\theta | \theta^{(n)})$, the derivatives are set to 0: $\frac{\partial Q}{\partial a_g} = 0$, $\frac{\partial Q}{\partial a_i} = 0$, $\frac{\partial Q}{\partial b_g} = 0$, $\frac{\partial Q}{\partial b_i} = 0$, $\frac{\partial Q}{\partial d} = 0$
which yields:

$$a_g^{(n+1)} = a_g^* = \frac{\sum_{j \in SJ_g} Z(n,j)}{\sum_{j=1}^{N} Z(n,j)}$$

$$a_i^{(n+1)} = a_i^* = \frac{\sum_{j \in \overline{SJ}_g \cap SJ_i} Z(n,j)}{\sum_{j \in \overline{SJ}_g} Z(n,j)} \qquad \text{for } i \in c_g$$

$$b_g^{(n+1)} = b_g^* = \frac{\sum_{j \in SJ_g} (1 - Z(n,j))}{\sum_{j=1}^{N} (1 - Z(n,j))}$$

$$b_i^{(n+1)} = b_i^* = \frac{\sum_{j \in \overline{SJ}_g \cap SJ_i (1 - Z(n,j))}}{\sum_{j \in \overline{SJ}_g} (1 - Z(n,j))} \qquad \text{for } i \in c_g$$

$$d^{(n+1)} = d^* = \frac{\sum_{j=1}^{N} Z(n,j)}{N} \qquad (8.12)$$

where N is the total number of claims in the source claim graph SC. $Z(n,j)$ is defined in Equation (8.11). SJ_g denotes the set of claims the group parent S_g makes in SC, and $\overline{SJ}_g$ denotes the set of claims S_g does not make. Similar definitions apply to the children sources in the group (i.e., SJ_i and $\overline{SJ}_i$). One should note that the computation of *repeat ratios* (i.e., p_{ig}) falls out of the estimation step in the EM algorithm and the result is not dependent on previous values of θ during the iteration.

Given the above, The E-step and M-step of EM optimization reduce to simply calculating Equations (8.11) and (8.12) iteratively until they converge. The convergence analysis has been done for EM scheme and it is beyond the scope of this book [108]. In practice, the algorithm will run until the difference of estimation parameter between consecutive iterations becomes insignificant. Since the claim is binary, the correctness of claims can be decided based on the converged value of $Z(n,j)$. Specially, C_j is true if $Z(n,j) \geq 0.5$ and false otherwise. We summarize the resulting algorithm in the subsection below.

8.4.3 THE SOCIAL-AWARE EM ALGORITHM

In summary of the EM scheme derived above, the input is the source claim graph SC from social sensing data and the source dissemination graph SD estimated from social network, and the output is the MLE of source reliability and claim correctness. In particular, given the source claim graph SC, the algorithm begins by initializing the

---

ALGORITHM 4 EXPECTATION MAXIMIZATION ALGORITHM

1: Initialize θ with random values between 0 and 1
2: Estimate the dependent ratio (i.e., p_{ig}) from source dissemination graph SD based on Equation (8.7)
3: **while** $\theta^{(n)}$ does not converge **do**
4:     **for** $j = 1 : N$ **do**
5:         compute $Z(n,j)$ based on Equation (8.11)
6:     **end for**
7:     $\theta^{(n+1)} = \theta^{(n)}$
8:     **for** $i = 1 : M$ **do**
9:         compute $a_1^{(n+1)}, \ldots, a_m^{(n+1)}, b_1^{(n+1)}, \ldots, b_m^{(n+1)}, d^{(n+1)}$ based on Equation (8.12)
10:         update $a_1^{(n)}, \ldots, a_m^{(n)}, b_1^{(n)}, \ldots, b_m^{(n)}, d^{(n)}$ with $a_1^{(n+1)}, \ldots, a_m^{(n+1)}, b_1^{(n+1)}, \ldots, b_m^{(n+1)}, d^{(n+1)}$ in $\theta^{(n+1)}$
11:     **end for**
12:     $n = n + 1$
13: **end while**
14: Let Z_j^c = converged value of $Z(n,j)$
15: Let a_i^c = converged value of a_i^n; b_i^c = converged value of b_i^n; d^c = converged value of $d^{(n)}$
16: **for** $j = 1 : N$ **do**
17:     **if** $Z_j^c \geq 0.5$ **then**
18:         C_j^* is true
19:     **else**
20:         C_j^* is false
21:     **end if**
22: **end for**
23: Return the claim classification results.

---

parameter θ with random values between 0 and 1.[†] The dependent ratio of each non-independent source (i.e., p_{ig}) is also estimated from the source disseminate graph SD. The algorithm then iterates between the E-step and M-step until θ converges. Specifically, the conditional probability of a claim to be true (i.e., $Z(n,j)$) is computed from Equation (8.11) and the estimation parameter (i.e., $\theta^{(n+1)}$) from Equation (8.12). Finally, the correctness of each claim C_j can be decided based on the converged value of $Z(n,j)$ (i.e., Z_j^c). The pseudocode is shown in Algorithm 4.

8.5 EVALUATION

In this section, we review the evaluation of the social-aware algorithm through three real world case studies based on Twitter. Evaluation results show the viability of predominantly correct ground truth reconstruction from social sensing data. In the evaluation, the social-aware MLE algorithm, *Apollo-social*, is compared to three baselines from current literature. The first baseline is *voting*, where data credibility

---

[†]In practice, if the rough estimate of the average reliability of sources is known a priori, EM will converge faster.

is estimated by the number of times the same cluster of tweets is collected from the human network. The larger the repetition, the more credibility is attributed to the content. Considering possible retweets on Twittter, two versions of the voting scheme are considered: one that counts both retweets and original tweets as full votes (called regular Voting) and one that only counts the original tweets (called Voting-NoRT). The second baseline is the basic EM algorithm we reviewed in Chapter 5 [100]. We henceforth call it *regular EM*. The algorithm differs from the social-ware EM in that it assumes that all sources constitute independent observers. The regular EM was shown to outperform four current information ranking schemes. The last baseline is the social data cleaning scheme suggested in [127], which extends regular EM with *admission control*. The admission controller is designed to improve source independence by simply removing dependent sources using some heuristic approaches from social networks. The winning admission control scheme in [127] called Beta-1 is used.

To compare these algorithms, they were implemented inside Apollo. Three datasets were composed by Apollo by using its keyword and geographic filtering mechanism. The first was collected by Apollo during and shortly after hurricane Sandy, from around New York and New Jersey in October/November 2012. The second was collected during hurricane Irene, one of the most expensive hurricanes that hit the Northeastern United States in August 2011. The third one was collected from Cairo, Egypt during the violent events that led to the resignation of the former president in February 2011. These traces are summarized in Table 8.2.

The Apollo tool operated over each data trace above, while executing each one of the compared filtering algorithms. The output of filtering was manually graded in each case to determine match with ground truth. Due to man-power limitations, only the 150 top ranked claims were manually graded by each algorithm using the following rubric:

- *True claims:* Claims that describe a physical or social event that is generally observable by multiple independent observers and corroborated by sources external to the experiment (e.g., mainstream news media).
- *Unconfirmed claims:* Claims that do not meet the definition of true claims.

Table 8.2 Statistics of Three Traces

Trace	Sandy	Irene	Egypt Unrest
Start date	11/2/2012	8/26/2011	2/2/2011
Time duration	14 days	7 days	18 days
# of tweets	12,931	269,308	93,208
# of users twitted	7583	207,562	13,836
# of follower-followee links	37,597	3,902,713	10,490,098
# of users crawled	704,941	2,510,316	5,285,160

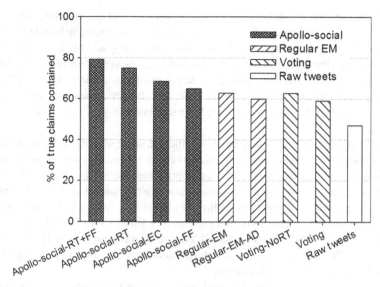

FIGURE 8.2

Evaluation on hurricane sandy trace.

Note that, the unconfirmed claims contain the false claims and some possibly true claims that cannot be independently verified by external sources. Hence, the evaluation presents a *pessimistic* performance estimates, taking all unconfirmed claims as false.

Figure 8.2 shows the result for the Hurricane Sandy trace. We observe that Apollo-social (i.e., the social-aware EM) generally outperformed the regular EM schemes in providing more true claims and suppressing the unconfirmed claims. This is achieved by incorporating the source dependency into the analytical framework of expectation maximization to better handle non-independent sources and their claims. The performance advantage of Apollo-social compared to regular EM is significant (nearly 20%) if the combined social network information (i.e., RT+FF social network) constructed from follower-followee and retweet relationship between users was used. We observed that the performance of the Apollo-social using ECs to estimate the social network is between Apollo-social using RT and FF social network. The reason is the RT social network is generated from the retweet relationship from current data interval and is very dynamic to reflect current source dependency and while FF social network is generated from the follower-followee relationship independently from the data traces and is relatively static. The dynamics of source dependency of EC social network is between RT and FF social network.

We also observe the regular EM schemes with admission control perform slightly worse than the one without admission control. The reason is: since the social network in the Sandy trace is relatively dense, the admission controller dropping some sources reduces the amount of useful information by sources that are tweeting when their parents are silent. In contrast, the Apollo-social scheme is shown to handle the social links in a more appropriate way. We also note the voting scheme has a reasonable performance on this trace. The reason is: a set of concrete key words (e.g., gas, station, fuel, etc.) were used for data collection, which results in a relatively "clean" input with less irrelevant information. As we shall see, the performance of voting drops significantly when the input tweet trace has more noise (e.g., Egypt trace as we will discuss later).

Note that, the exact recall may be of less interest, since we are usually interested in only the milestones and key moments of an event as opposed to every possible detail. Experiments were carried to evaluate an approximate recall metric. Specifically, 5 important events reported by media during Sandy were independently collected and checked to see if they are captured in the top claims. The top ranked claims for each of the algorithms were scanned to find these events. Results for selected baselines are shown in Table 8.3. We observed that all five events were covered by the top claims from the Apollo-social scheme, while two of them were missing from the top claims returned from the regular EM scheme.

The above precision and recall experiments were repeated on the Irene tweet trace and Egypt tweet trace. The precision results for Irene are shown in Figure 8.3. In Figure 8.3, we consistently observe that Apollo-social achieves non-trivial performance gain in reducing the number of unconfirmed claims and providing more useful information by using the social network information. Similar results are shown for the Egypt trace in Figure 8.4. For recall, collecting 10 media events on each case, we observed that Apollo-social found all 10 of them in the case of Irene and 9 in Egypt, compared to 7 and 7 by regular EM. Detailed results are shown in Tables 8.4 and 8.5.

Note that, in the experiments above, the number of claims that were verified to be *false* (i.e., false positives) was not reported. This is because it is easier to verify that an event occurred than it is to verify that it did not. Prominent events that are true would typically be reported in the media. Obscure events would not be. It is therefore hard to verify if they really happened or not.

There was one exception to the above. Namely, in the Sandy example, it was possible for the authors to collect ground truth on gas availability at a subset of New York and New Jersey gas stations at different points in time. This data was mainly obtained from two sources: (i) GasBuddy.com, which recruited spotters to go out and report the status of gas stations in New York and New Jersey during the gas shortage event in the aftermath of hurricane Sandy [128], and (ii) NYC_GAS_Finder, which generated updates on NYC gas stations serving gas based on credit card transaction data [129].

In order to match claims with the ground truth, tweets from the top claims were selected to meet the following criteria: (i) unambiguously mention fuel status, and (ii) explicitly describe a gas station location that matches one of the gas stations for which we have ground truth on *the day of the claim*. The claim is considered to be true if it matched ground truth status. Otherwise it was false. Thirty (30) of the top ranked Apollo claims could be verified this way. Of these, 29 were true matches, which is

Table 8.3 Ground Truth Events and Related Claims Found by Apollo-Social Versus Regular EM in Sandy

#	Media	Tweet Found by Apollo-Social	Tweet Found by Regular EM
1	Rockland County Executive C. Scott Vanderhoef is announcing a Local Emergency Order restricting the amount of fuel that an individual can purchase at a gas station.	Rockland County Orders Restrictions on Gas Sales - Nyack-Piermont, NY Patch http://t.co/cDSrqpa2	**MISSING**
2	New York City Mayor Michael Bloomberg has announced that the city will impose an indefinite program of gas rationing after fuel shortages led to long lines and frustration at the pump in the wake of superstorm Sandy.	Gas rationing plan set for New York City: The move follows a similar announcement last week in New Jersey to eas...http://t.co/nkmF7U9I	RT @nytimes: Breaking News: Mayor Bloomberg Imposes Odd-Even Gas Rationing Starting Friday, as Does Long Island http://t.co/eax7KMVi
3	New Jersey authorities filed civil suits Friday accusing seven gas stations and one hotel of price gouging in the wake of Hurricane Sandy.	RT @MarketJane: NJ plans price gouging suits against 8 businesses. They include gas stations and a lodging provider.	**MISSING**
4	The rationing system: restricting gas sales to cars with even-numbered license plates on even days, and odd-numbered on odd days will be discontinued at 6 a.m. Tuesday, Gov. Chris Christie announced on Monday.	# masdirin City Room: Gas Rationing in New Jersey to End Tuesday # news	RT @nytimes: City Room: Gas Rationing in New Jersey to End Tuesday http://t.co/pYIVOmPo
5	New Yorkers can expect gas rationing for at least five more days: Bloomberg.	Mayor Bloomberg: Gas rationing in NYC will continue for at least 5 more days. @eyewitnessnyc #SandyABC7	Bloomberg: Gas Rationing To Stay In Place At Least Through The Weekend http://t.co/mmqqjYRx

97%. Hence, it is reasonable to hypothesize that the number of unverified claims in other data sets actually contains many true claims.

Finally, we review the analysis of the average running time for the *entire* Apollo system (with different algorithms) to process and analyze data collected over a one hour window in each of three data traces. The running time is measured from the point when the first tweet of the hour is processed to the point when the results for the hour window are available. The processing times are shown in Table 8.6. We observe

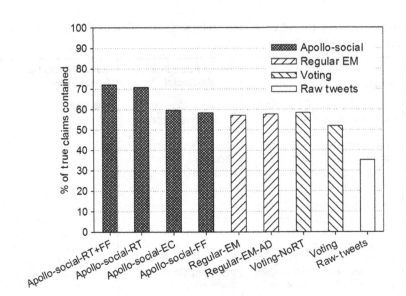

FIGURE 8.3

Evaluation on Hurricane Irene trace.

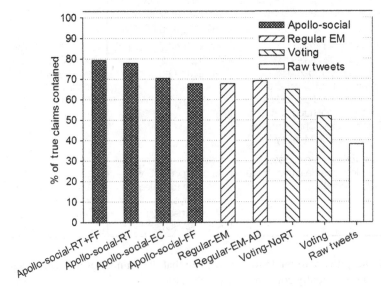

FIGURE 8.4

Evaluation on Egypt unrest trace.

Table 8.4 Ground Truth Events and Related Tweets Found by Apollo-Social Versus Original EM in Hurricane Irene

#	Media	Tweet Found by Apollo-Social	Tweet Found by Regular EM
1	East Coast Braces For Hurricane Irene; Hurricane Irene is expected to follow a path up the East Coast	RT @BBCNews: President Barack Obama has warned that Hurricane Irene, currently looming off the east coast of the US, could be a "historic" storm.	**MISSING**
2	Hurricane Irene's effects begin being felt in NC, The storm, now a Category 2, still has the East Coast on edge.	RT @kainepaine: Hurricane nears U.S.: Ferocious winds and torrential rainfall lashed coastal North Carolina early Saturday as ma…http://t.co/JDkeO58	RT @cnnbrk: Hurricane Irene make landfall near Cape Lookout, North Carolina, National Hurricane Center says http://t.co/LV7L7TX
3	NEWARK, N.J. (CBSNewYork/AP) t Officials say they will close the five New York-area airports to arriving passenger flights beginning at noon on Saturday.	RT @BreakingNews: All 5 major NYC-area airports to close to arriving flights at noon Saturday due to Hurricane Irene http://t.co/kkwvuPg	RT @BreakingNews: All 5 major NYC-area airports to close to arriving flights at noon Saturday due to Hurricane Irene http://t.co/FMOCfbF
4	Hurricane Irene charged up the U.S. East Coast on Saturday toward New York, shutting down the city, and millions of Americans sought shelter from the huge storm.	RT @AlArabiya_Eng: Hurricane # Irene rages up # US east coast, # Alarabiya http://t.co/TuvCGg4	**MISSING**
5	WASHINGTON:Obama declares emergency in New York, Virginia and Massachusetts as hurricane Irene approaches	RT @cnnbrk: President Obama declares state of emergency in Virginia and Massachusetts ahead of Hurricane Irene. http://t.co/W7f0Y3U	RT @ShantiDas404: RT @cnnbrk: President Obama declares state of emergency in Virginia and Massachusetts ahead of Hurricane Irene. http://t.co/W8wCZCp

Continued

Table 8.4 Ground Truth Events and Related Tweets Found by Apollo-Social Versus Original EM in Hurricane Irene—cont'd

#	Media	Tweet Found by Apollo-Social	Tweet Found by Regular EM
6	Irene remains a Category 1, the lowest level of hurricane classification, as it churns toward New York over the next several hours, the U.S. National Hurricane Center said on Sunday	RT @BreakingNews: Hurricane Irene speeds up as center nears New York City, maintains hurricane strength with 75 mph winds - AP	RT @BreakingNews Hurricane Irene speeds up as center nears New York City, maintains hurricane strength with 75 mph winds - AP
7	The Wall Street Journal has created a way for New Yorkers to interact with the location based social media app Foursquare to find the nearest NYC hurricane evacuation center.	Hurricane Irene: Find an NYC Evacuation Center on Foursquare: The Wall Street Journal has created a way f...http://t.co/pH2OTtk	MISSING
8	President Obama declared Wednesday what much of the state has known for days: New Jersey is a disaster area in the aftermath of Hurricane Irene.	RT @BreakingNews: President Obama signs disaster declaration for hard-hit New Jersey after Hurricane Irene	RT @BreakingNews: President Obama signs disaster declaration for hard-hit New Jersey after Hurricane Irene
9	Hurricane Irene's rampage up the East Coast has become the tenth billion-dollar weather event this year, breaking a record stretching back to 1980, climate experts said Wednesday.	Psychic Readings: Hurricane Irene: 2011s 10th Billion-dollar Disaster http://t.co/gdCotzr	RT @cnnbrk: Hurricane #Irene to join billion-dollar disaster club.
10	Hurricane Irene has led to the deaths of at least 45 people in 13 states, according to an Associated Press tally.	RT @washingtonpost: Hurricane #Irene blamed for at least 45 deaths in 13 states http://t.co/SXHckqg	RT @DMVFollowers: Hurricane Irene blamed for at least 45 deaths in 13 different state.

Table 8.5 Ground Truth Events and Related Tweets Found by Apollo-Social vs Original EM in Egypt Unrest

#	Media	Tweet Found by Apollo-Social	Tweet Found by Regular EM
1	Hundreds of thousands of Egyptians flooded into the heart of the capital, filling up Cairo's main square in the largest demonstration in a week	RT @nytimes: Pictures of the Day - Thousands gather in Tahrir Square for the largest protests yet in #Egypt http://nyti.ms/eDcBhb	RT @nytimes: Pictures of the Day - Thousands gather in Tahrir Square for the largest protests yet in #Egypt http://nyti.ms/eDcBhb
2	Google says one of its Middle East managers has gone missing in Cairo, where violent protests against the ruling regime have embroiled Egypts capital for the past week.	Egypt protest prisoner Wael Ghonim @ghonim STILL IN CUSTODY since Jan 28. He's an activist and Google exec	Egypt protest prisoner Wael Ghonim @ghonim STILL IN CUSTODY since Jan 28. He's an activist and Google exec
3	Number of protesters in Cairo's Tahir Square are revised to more than a million people	RT @amrwaked: Almost 1,000,000 already in #Tahrir! Besides immense other amounts on Kasr El Nil bridge. Historical day for sure!!	MISSING
4	Bursts of heavy gun-fire early aimed at anti-government demonstrators in Tahrir leave at least five people dead and several wounded.	RT @bencnn: Witness in #Tahrir says pro-democracy people being shot at from rooftops, several dead. #Egypt #Jan25	RT @bencnn: Witness in #Tahrir says pro-democracy people being shot at from rooftops, several dead.
5	Al Jazeera correspondent Ayman Mohyeldin is detained by the Egyptian military.	RT @evanchill: We can now tell you that our Cairo correspondent, @aymanM, has been in military custody for four hours.	RT @evanchill: We can now tell you that our Cairo correspondent, @aymanM, has been in military custody for four hours.

Continued

Table 8.5 Ground Truth Events and Related Tweets Found by Apollo-Social vs Original EM in Egypt Unrest—cont'd

#	Media	Tweet Found by Apollo-Social	Tweet Found by Regular EM
6	Ayman Mohyeldin is released seven hours later.	RT @AymanM: Safe & sound after being detained by the military Thanks 2 all for love/support Hope they Release all! Back 2 work Love Ayman	MISSING
7	Thousands of pro-democracy demonstrators have poured into Cairo's Tahrir Square, seeking president Mubarak's ouster, despite a slew of government concessions.	RT @AJEnglish: Protests swell at Tahrir Square: Tens of thousands pour into central Cairo seeking president Mubarak's ouster, http://aje.me/hltQXB	RT @AJEnglish: Protests swell at Tahrir Square: Tens of thousands pour into central Cairo seeking President Mubarak's ouster http://aje.me/gjiOsF
8	Hosni Mubarak resigns as president and hands over power to the army.	RT @3arabawy: We got rid of Mubarak. Now it's time to get rid of the Mubarak's regime.	MISSING
9	365 people, at least, were killed during the 18 days of anti-government unrest that took place in Cairo, according to the Healthy Ministry on Wednesday.	RT @AymanM: #egypt health ministry: official death toll from #jan25 protests till today is 365 dead more than 5000 injured.	RT @AymanM: #egypt health ministry: official death toll from #jan25 protests till today is 365 dead more than 5000 injured.
10	A sea of Egyptians from all walks of life packed every meter in and around Cairos Tahrir Square on Friday for a "Day of Victory"	MISSING	News - Egyptians gather for 'Day of Victory': Waving flags and beating drums, thousands gathered at Cairo's Tahr...http://bit.ly/eOMl1L

Table 8.6 Running Time (seconds) of Different Algorithms on an Hour's Trace

Algorithms	Sandy	Irene	Egypt Unrest
Apollo-social	2.06	61.1	2.67
Regular EM	1.99	47.25	2.47
Voting	1.98	33.96	2.34

that the processing time depends mainly on the size of the trace. The Voting scheme did exhibit the fastest run-time, as might one expect, at the cost of more error in classifying claims correctly. The running speed of Apollo-social is quite comparable to the regular EM scheme. We also note that the running time of Apollo-social and other baselines is well below one hour, which verified the *real-time* feature of the Apollo system on the real-world data traces.

Note that, the values reported in Table 8.6 include the time taken for computing distance functions, clustering, and running the chosen estimation algorithm (i.e., Voting, Regular EM, or Apollo-social). This explains why voting comes so close to the other two algorithms in run-time, despite the fact that they involve multiple iterations, while voting does not. A more detailed examination reveals that the bottleneck in Apollo lies in computing the distance functions between pairs of observations (as mentioned in Section 8.3). Hence, in total terms, the iterative expectation maximization algorithm described in this paper does not add too much overhead.

8.6 DISCUSSION AND LIMITATIONS

The chapter reviews encouraging results demonstrating that the accuracy of claims made by social sources can be estimated predominantly correctly even when such sources have unknown reliability and when data has uncertain provenance.

Interestingly, it was observed that the social-aware EM scheme tended to reduce the number of introspective (e.g., emotional and opinion) tweets, compared to tweets that presented descriptions of an external world. This was serendipitously quite appropriate of a "sensor network" that is not supposed to have emotions and opinions, but rather convey observations. Looking into the problem further, it was noticed that emotions and slogans tended to be retweeted along social network topology pathways and hence, tended to be suppressed by the social aware algorithm. In contrast, external facts (such as gas availability at a given location) were often observed independently by multiple sources, and hence not suppressed.

The observation offers many questions and opportunities for improvement, especially when it comes to modeling information propagation. The FF, RT, and RT+FF only provide an approximation of the actual latent social network of how sources are influencing each other. They can be improved by building information propagation models that account for topic (e.g., sensational, emotional, and other news might propagate along different models), expertise, relationship reciprocity, mutual trust, and personal bias (e.g., the claim that "police is beating up innocent demonstrators," versus "demonstrators are attacking the police"). Note that distortions and biases of human sensors are quite persistent in terms of direction and amplitude, unlike white noise distortions. In a sense, humans exaggerate information in predictable ways. Understanding more about the community of sources can help better quantify the distortion and bias, leading to more accurate formulations of the maximum likelihood model.

The source node behavior model deserves more investigation. The work presented in this chapter only considers the social network structure that can be represented by a forest of two level trees. It also assumes the child node will not independently make the same claim as its parent. Those assumptions might not hold in many real world applications. For example, the twitter user could independently tweet about a popular event with very similar content as its parent. Therefore, it is necessary to develop more comprehensive models to accurately characterize the social network structure in a more general form. The key challenge is how to integrate the new node behavior model with the maximum likelihood framework we reviewed in this chapter.

In this chapter, the social-aware EM scheme focused on a binary claim model. It is shown to be a reasonable model to represent the physical events that are either true or false. However, there is also a large number of real world applications where observations from participants are *non-binary* (e.g., on-line review systems). It is possible to generalize the fact-finding method that accounts for multiple mutually exclusive values (see Chapter 7) to incorporate the social network model. Furthermore, it is also interesting to generalize the estimation model to better handle claims that have continuous values. Probabilistic, Subjective, or Fuzzy logics could be good modeling techniques to apply in this case.

A separate problem is to deal with dynamics. When the network changes over time, how best to account for it in MLE? A better formulation is needed that puts less weight on older data. Deception and malicious users also need to be addressed. Of particular interest are sources that gain advantage by acting reliably then change their behavior to deceive the system. It is also interesting to understand the impact of distance functions inside Apollo on the accuracy of estimation results. Distance function assess how close two tweets are. Current functions are based on lexicology only (i.e., they compare words without interpreting them). How much benefit is attained by syntactic and semantic analysis of different levels of sophistication? How does that benefit depend on the properties of the trace? These issues provide directions for future work.

Finally, we should note that the human sensor model and the estimation framework reviewed in this chapter is not limited to the applications that are based on Twitter. It can also be applied to a much broader set of crowdsourcing and mobile sensing applications, where the data are collected from both human sources and the devices on their behalf. Examples include traffic condition prediction using data from in-vehicle GPS devices and geo-tagging applications using participant's smartphones. In these applications, humans or their devices represent the sources and measurements they report represent claims. The reviewed estimation approach can be used to address similar data reliability and uncertain data provenance challenges in these applications.

Understanding physical dependencies: Social meets cyber-physical

9.1 CORRELATIONS IN THE PHYSICAL WORLD

In many social applications, there exists physical constraints on both sources and observed variables. For example, in a social sensing application to report disaster status in the aftermath of a earthquake, average people normally only have opportunity to observe situations physically close to them. As another example, if we look at hurricane risk prediction map of Hurricane Sandy on the east coast, we will find the communities in nearby neighborhoods have strong correlated risk predictions. Similar observations can be found on the speed map of a city where neighboring segments of the same road often have similar speed estimation. We refer to such constraints and correlations that exist in the physical world as physical dependencies.

This chapter presents a new expectation maximization (EM) model that investigates the exploitation of physical dependencies to improve the reliability of social sensing applications. In particular, two types of physical dependencies are exploited:

- *Constraints on sources:* A source constraint simply states that a source can only observe co-located physical variables. In other words, it can only report C_j if it visited location L_j. Furthermore, claim $C_j = 1$ means that a certain event occurs at location L_j (e.g., trash is located at L_j, etc.), and $C_j = 0$ means the absence of that event). The granularity of locations is application specific. However, given location granularity in a particular application context, this constraint allows us to understand which variables a source had an opportunity to observe. Hence, for example, when a source does not report an event that others claim they observed, we can tell whether or not the silence should decrease the confidence in the reported observation, depending on whether or not the silent source was co-located with the alleged event.
- *Constraints on observed variables:* Observed variables may be correlated, which can be expressed by a joint probability distribution on the underlying variables. For example, traffic speed at different locations of the same freeway

IEEE being the copyright holder, grants permission to reprint text of the article, Dong Wang, Tarek Abdelzaher, Lance Kaplan, Raghu Ganti, Shaohan Hu and Hengchang Liu, "Exploitation of Physical Constraints for Reliable Social Sensing," Proceedings of *IEEE 34th Real-Time Systems Symposium (RTSS 13)* Vancouver, Canada, December, 2013.

may be related by a joint probability distribution that favors similar speeds. This probabilistic knowledge gives us a basis for assessing how internally consistent a set of reported observations is.

Similar as before, let S_i represent the ith source and C_j represent the jth variable. We say that S_i *observed* C_j if the source visited location L_j. We say that a source S_i made a *claim* S_iC_j if the source reported that C_j was true. $P(C_j = 1|x)$ and $P(C_j = 0|x)$ represent the conditional probability that variable C_j is indeed true or false, given x, respectively. t_i represents the (unknown) probability that a claim is correct given that source S_i reported it, $t_i = P(C_j = 1|S_iC_j)$. Different sources may make different numbers of claims. The probability that source S_i makes a claim is s_i. Formally, $s_i = P(S_iC_j|S_i$ observes $C_j)$.

a_i is redefined to be the (unknown) probability that source S_i correctly reports a claim given that the underlying variable is indeed true and the source observed it. Similarly, b_i is redefined the (unknown) probability that source S_i falsely reports a claim when the underlying variable is in reality false and the source observed it. More formally:

$$a_i = P(S_iC_j|C_j = 1, S_i \text{ observes } C_j)$$
$$b_i = P(S_iC_j|C_j = 0, S_i \text{ observes } C_j) \tag{9.1}$$

From the definitions above, the following relationships can be derived using the Bayesian theorem:

$$a_i = P(S_iC_j|C_j = 1, S_i \text{ observes } C_j)$$
$$= \frac{P(C_j = 1|S_iC_j, S_i \text{ observes } C_j)P(S_iC_j|S_i \text{ observes } C_j)}{P(C_j = 1|S_i \text{ observes } C_j)}$$
$$= \frac{P(C_j = 1|S_iC_j)P(S_iC_j|S_i \text{ observes } C_j)}{P(C_j = 1|S_i \text{ observes } C_j)}$$

$$b_i = P(S_iC_j|C_j = 0, S_i \text{ observes } C_j)$$
$$= \frac{P(C_j = 0|S_iC_j, S_i \text{ observes } C_j)P(S_iC_j|S_i \text{ observes } C_j)}{P(C_j = 0|S_i \text{ observes } C_j)}$$
$$= \frac{P(C_j = 0|S_iC_j)P(S_iC_j|S_i \text{ observes } C_j)}{P(C_j = 0|S_i \text{ observes } C_j)} \tag{9.2}$$

Let f_i be the (unknown) probability that claim C_j is true conditioned on the fact that the ith source happens to observe its location, i.e., $P(C_j = 1|S_i$ observes $C_j)$, and this value does not depend on the claim index j. Note that, the probability that a source makes a claim is proportional to the number of claims made by the source over the total number of variables observed by the source. Plugging these, together with t_i, into the definition of a_i and b_i, given in Equation (9.2), the relationship between the terms we defined above can be obtained:

$$a_i = \frac{t_i \times s_i}{f_i} \qquad b_i = \frac{(1 - t_i) \times s_i}{1 - f_i} \tag{9.3}$$

The input to the algorithm is: (i) the *claim matrix SC*, where $S_iC_j = 1$ when source S_i reports that C_j is true, and $S_iC_j = 0$ otherwise; and (ii) the source's opportunities to observe represented by a *knowledge matrix SK*, where $S_iK_j = 1$ when source S_i has the opportunity to observe C_j and $S_iK_j = 0$ otherwise. The output of the algorithm is the probability that variable C_j is true, for each j and the reliability t_i of source S_i, for each i. More formally:

$$\forall j, 1 \leq j \leq N : P(C_j = 1|SC, SK)$$

$$\forall i, 1 \leq i \leq M : P(C_j = 1|S_iC_j) \tag{9.4}$$

To account for non-independence among the observed variables, the set of all such constraints (expressed as joint distributions of dependent variables) are denoted by *JD*. The inputs to the algorithm become the *SC*, *SK* matrices and the set *JD* of constraints (joint distributions), mentioned above. The output is:

$$\forall j, 1 \leq j \leq N : P(C_j = 1|SC, SK, JD)$$

$$\forall i, 1 \leq i \leq M : P(C_j = 1|S_iC_j) \tag{9.5}$$

Below, we review the solution to the aforementioned problems using the EM algorithm. Following the approach described in Chapter 5, a latent variable z_j denotes the estimated value of variable C_j, for each j (indicating whether it is true or not). Initially, $p(z_j = 1)$ is set to f_j, which can be initialized to 0.5 in the absence of prior knowledge. This constitutes the latent vector Z above. X denotes the claim matrix *SC*, where X_j represents the jth column of the *SC* matrix (i.e., claims of the jth variable by all sources). The parameter vector to be estimated is $\theta = (a_1, a_2, \ldots, a_M; b_1, b_2, \ldots, b_M; f_1, f_2, \ldots, f_M)$. In the following sections, we review incorporation of the physical constraints into the new model.

9.2 ACCOUNTING FOR THE OPPORTUNITY TO OBSERVE

In this section, we review the incorporation of the source constraints into the EM algorithm. We call this EM scheme, EM with *opportunity to observe* (OtO EM).

9.2.1 DERIVING THE LIKELIHOOD

When source constraints are considered in the likelihood function, it is assumed that sources only claim variables they observe, and hence the probability of a source claiming a variable he/she does not have an opportunity to observe is 0. For simplicity, it is assumed that all variables are independent, then this assumption is relaxed later in Section 9.3. Under these assumptions, the new likelihood function $L(\theta; X, Z)$ that incorporates the source constraints is given by:

$$L(\theta; X, Z) = p(X, Z|\theta) = \prod_{j=1}^{N} p(z_j) \times p(X_j|z_j, \theta)$$

$$= \prod_{j=1}^{N} \prod_{i \in S_j} p(z_j) \times p(S_i C_j|z_j, S_i \text{ observes } C_j) \qquad (9.6)$$

where S_j: Set of sources observed C_j

$$p(z_j) = \begin{cases} f_j & z_j = 1 \\ (1 - f_j) & z_j = 0 \end{cases}$$

$$p(S_i C_j|z_j, S_i \text{ observes } C_j) = \begin{cases} a_i & z_j = 1, S_i C_j = 1 \\ (1 - a_i) & z_j = 1, S_i C_j = 0 \\ b_i & z_j = 0, S_i C_j = 1 \\ (1 - b_i) & z_j = 0, S_i C_j = 0 \end{cases} \qquad (9.7)$$

Note that, in the likelihood function, the probability contribution from sources who actually *observe* a variable (e.g., $i \in S_j$ for C_j) is considered. This is an important change from the reviewed maximum likelihood estimation (MLE) model in Chapter 5. This change allows the new model to nicely incorporate the source constraints (name, source opportunity to observe) into the MLE framework.

Using the above likelihood function, the corresponding E-step and M-step of OtO EM scheme can be derived. The detailed derivations are shown in Appendix of Chapter 9.

9.2.2 THE OtO EM ALGORITHM

In summary, the inputs to the OtO EM algorithm are (i) the claim matrix SC from social sensing data and (ii) the knowledge matrix SK describing the *source constraints*. The output is the MLE of source reliability and the probability of claim correctness. Compared to the regular EM algorithm from Chapter 5, source constraints are provided as a new input into the framework and imposed them on the E-step and M-step. The algorithm begins by initializing the parameter θ with random values between 0 and 1. The algorithm then performs the new derived E-steps and M-steps iteratively until θ converges. Since each observed variable is binary, variables can be classified as either true or false based on the converged value of $Z(t, j)$. Specifically, C_j is considered true if Z_j^c goes beyond some threshold (e.g., 0.5) and false otherwise. The estimated t_i of each source can also be computed from the converged values of $\theta^{(t)}$ (i.e., a_i^c, b_i^c, and d_i^c) based on Equation (9.3). Algorithm 5 provides the pseudocode of OtO EM.

ALGORITHM 5 EXPECTATION MAXIMIZATION ALGORITHM WITH SOURCE CONSTRAINTS (OtO EM)

1: Initialize θ with random values between 0 and 1
2: **while** $\theta^{(t)}$ does not converge **do**
3:    **for** $j = 1 : N$ **do**
4:       compute $Z(t,j)$ based on Equation (9.10)
5:    **end for**
6:    $\theta^{(t+1)} = \theta^{(t)}$
7:    **for** $i = 1 : M$ **do**
8:       compute $a_i^{(t+1)}, b_i^{(t+1)}, f_j^{(t+1)}$ based on Equation (9.11)
9:       update $a_i^{(t)}, b_i^{(t)}, f_i^{(t)}$ with $a_i^{(t+1)}, b_i^{(t+1)}, f_i^{(t+1)}$ in $\theta^{(t+1)}$
10:   **end for**
11:   $t = t + 1$
12: **end while**
13: Let Z_j^c = converged value of $Z(t,j)$
14: Let a_i^c = converged value of $a_i^{(t)}$; b_i^c = converged value of $b_i^{(t)}$; f_i^c = converged value of $f_j^{(t)}$ $j \in C_i$
15: **for** $j = 1 : N$ **do**
16:   **if** $Z_j^c \geq threshold$ **then**
17:     C_j is true
18:   **else**
19:     C_j is false
20:   **end if**
21: **end for**
22: **for** $i = 1 : M$ **do**
23:   calculate t_i^* from a_i^c, b_i^c and f_i^c
24: **end for**
25: Return the classification on variables and reliability estimation of sources

---

9.3 ACCOUNTING FOR PHYSICAL DEPENDENCIES

In this section, we review the incorporation of the constraints on observed variables (i.e., claims) into the EM algorithm. We refer to this EM scheme as EM with *dependent variables* (DV EM). For clarity, we first ignore the source constraints from the previous section (i.e., assume that each source observes all variables). Then, we consider the combination of the two extensions of the regular EM (i.e., OtO EM and DV EM) to obtain a comprehensive EM scheme (OtO+DV EM) that incorporates constraints on both sources and observed variables into the estimation framework.

9.3.1 DERIVING THE LIKELIHOOD

In order to derive a likelihood function that considers constraints in the form of dependencies between observed variables, N observed variables in the social sensing model are divided into G independent groups, where each independent group contains variables that are related by some local constraints (e.g., gas price of stations in the same neighborhood could be highly correlated). Consider group g, where there are k dependent variables $g_1,\ldots,g_k$. Let $p(z_{g_1},\ldots,z_{g_k})$ represent the joint probability distribution of the k variables and let $\mathcal{Y}_g$ represent all possible combinations of values of $g_1,\ldots,g_k$. For example, when there are only two variables, $\mathcal{Y}_g = [(1,1),(1,0),(0,1),(0,0)]$. Note that, it is assumed that $p(z_{g_1},\ldots,z_{g_k})$ is known or can be estimated from prior knowledge. The new likelihood function $L(\theta;X,Z)$ that considers the aforementioned constraints is:

$$L(\theta;X,Z) = \prod_{g\in G} p(X_g,Z_g|\theta) = \prod_{g\in G} p(Z_g) \times p(X_g|Z_g,\theta)$$

$$= \prod_{g\in G}\left\{ \sum_{g_1,\ldots,g_k\in\mathcal{Y}_g} p(z_{g_1},\ldots,z_{g_k}) \prod_{i\in M}\prod_{j\in c_g} p(S_i C_j|z_j)\right\} \tag{9.8}$$

where $\alpha_{i,j}$ is the same as defined in Equation (9.7) and c_g represents the set of variables belonging to the independent group g. Compared to the regular EM from Chapter 5, the new likelihood function is formulated with independent groups as units (instead of single independent variables). The joint probability distribution of all dependent variables within a group is used to replace the distribution of a single variable. This likelihood function is therefore more general, but reduces to the previous form in the special case where each group is composed of only one variable.

Using the above likelihood function, the corresponding E-step and M-step of DV EM and OtO+DV EM schemes can be derived. The detailed derivations are shown in Appendix of Chapter 9.

9.3.2 THE OtO+DV ALGORITHM

In summary, the OtO+DV EM scheme incorporates constraints on both sources and observed variables. The inputs to the algorithm are (i) the claim matrix SC, (ii) the knowledge matrix SK, and (iii) the *joint distribution* for each group of dependent variables, collectively represented by set JD. The output is the MLE of source reliability and claim correctness. The OtO+DV EM pseudocode is shown in Algorithm 6.

9.4 REAL-WORLD CASE STUDIES

In this section, we evaluate the performance of the new reliable social sensing schemes that incorporate "opportunity to observe" constraints on sources (OtO EM) and dependency constraints on observed variables (DV EM), as well as the comprehensive scheme (OtO+DV EM) that combines both. Their performance is compared to the state of the art regular EM scheme (see Chapter 5) through a real world social sensing application. The purpose of the application is to map locations of traffic lights and stop signs on the campus of the University of Illinois (in the city of Urbana-Champaign).

The SmartRoad dataset [114] is reused, where vehicle-resident Android smartphones record their GPS location traces as the cars are driven around by participants.

ALGORITHM 6 EXPECTATION MAXIMIZATION ALGORITHM WITH CONSTRAINTS ON BOTH SOURCES AND OBSERVED VARIABLES (OtO+DV EM)

1: Initialize θ with random values between 0 and 1
2: **while** $\theta^{(t)}$ does not converge **do**
3:     **for** $j = 1 : N$ **do**
4:         compute $Z(t, j)$ as the *marginal distribution* of the joint probability as shown in Equation (9.15)
5:     **end for**
6:     $\theta^{(t+1)} = \theta^{(t)}$
7:     **for** $i = 1 : M$ **do**
8:         compute $a_i^{(t+1)}, b_i^{(t+1)}, f_i^{(t+1)}$ based on Equation (9.16)
9:         update $a_i^{(t)}, b_i^{(t)}, f_i^{(t)}$ with $a_i^{(t+1)}, b_i^{(t+1)}, f_i^{(t+1)}$ in $\theta^{(t+1)}$
10:    **end for**
11:    $t = t + 1$
12: **end while**
13: Let Z_j^c = converged value of $Z(t, j)$
14: Let a_i^c = converged value of $a_i^{(t)}$; b_i^c = converged value of $b_i^{(t)}$; f_i^c = converged value of $f_j^{(t)}$ $j \in C_i$
15: **for** $j = 1 : N$ **do**
16:    **if** $Z_j^c \geq$ *threshold* **then**
17:       C_j is true
18:    **else**
19:       C_j is false
20:    **end if**
21: **end for**
22: **for** $i = 1 : M$ **do**
23:    calculate t_i^* from a_i^c, b_i^c and f_i^c
24: **end for**
25: Return the classification on variables and reliability estimation of sources

---

The GPS readings include samples of the instantaneous latitude-longitude location, speed and bearing of the vehicle, with a sampling rate of 1 s. The goal was to show that even very unreliable sensing of traffic lights and stop signs can result in a good final map once the fact-finding algorithms are applied to these claims to determine their odds of correctness. Hence, an intentionally simple-minded application scenario was designed to identify stop signs and traffic lights from GPS data.

Let us briefly review the experiment mentioned earlier: if a vehicle waits at a location for 15-90 s, the application concludes that it is stopped at a traffic light and issues a traffic-light claim (i.e., a claim that a traffic light is present at that location and bearing). Similarly if it waits for 2-10 s, it concludes that it is at a stop sign and issues a stop-sign claim (i.e., a claim that a stop sign is present at that location and bearing). If the vehicle stops for less than 2 s, for 10-15 s, or for more than 90 s, no claim is made. Claims were reported by each source to a central data collection point.

Clearly the claims defined above are very error-prone due to the simple-minded nature of the "sensor" and the complexity of road conditions and driver's behaviors.

Moreover, it is hard to quantify the reliability of sources without a training phase that compares measurements to ground truth. For example, a car can stop elsewhere on the road due to a traffic jam or crossing pedestrians, not necessarily at locations of traffic lights and stop signs. Also, a car does not stop at traffic lights that are green and a careless driver may pass stop signs without stopping. The question addressed in the evaluation is whether knowledge of constraints helps improve the accuracy of stop sign and traffic light estimation from such unreliable measurements in this case study.

Hence, different estimation approaches reviewed in this chapter were applied along with the constraints from the physical world on the noisy data to identify the correct locations of traffic lights and stop signs and compute the reliability of participants. One should note that location granularity here is of the order of half a city block. This ensures that stop sign and traffic light claims are attributed to the correct intersections. Most GPS devices easily attain such granularity. Therefore, the authors do not expect location errors to be of concern. For evaluation purposes, the ground truth locations of traffic lights and stop signs were manually collected.

In the experiment, 34 people (sources) were invited to participate and 1,048,572 GPS readings (around 300 h of driving) were collected. A total of 4865 claims were generated by the phones, of which 3303 were for stop signs and 1562 were for traffic lights, collectively identifying 369 distinct locations where claims were generated. The elements S_iC_j of the claim matrix were set according to the claims extracted from each source vehicle.

It is observed that traffic lights at an intersection are always present in all directions. Hence, when processing traffic light claims, vehicle bearing was ignored. However, stop signs at an intersection have a few possible scenarios. For example, (i) a stop sign may be present in each possible direction (e.g., All-Way stop); (ii) two stop signs may exist on one road whereas no stop sign exist on the other road (e.g., a main road intersecting with a small road); or (iii) two stop signs may exist for one road and one stop sign for the other road (e.g., a two-way road intersecting with a one way road). Hence, in claims regarding stop signs the bearing is important. Bearing was classified into four main directions. A different Boolean variable is created for each direction.

9.4.1 OPPORTUNITY TO OBSERVE

In this subsection, we first evaluate the performance of the OtO EM scheme. For the OtO EM scheme, the recorded GPS traces of each vehicle were used to determine whether it actually went to a specific location or not (i.e., decide whether a source has an opportunity to observe a given variable or not). There are 54 actual traffic lights and 190 stop signs covered by the data traces collected.

Figure 9.1 compares the source reliability estimated by both the OtO EM and regular EM schemes to the actual source reliability computed from ground truth. The source IDs are sorted by the ground truth reliability. We observed that the OtO EM scheme stays closer to the actual results for most of the sources (i.e., OtO EM estimation error is smaller than regular EM for about 74% of sources).

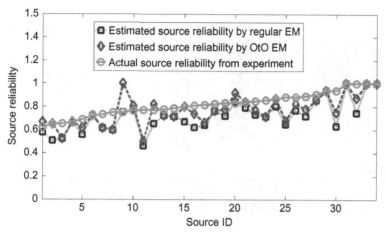

FIGURE 9.1

Source reliability estimation of OtO EM in the case of traffic lights.

Next, we review the accuracy of identifying traffic lights by the new scheme. It may be tempting to confuse the problem with one of classification and plot ROC curves or confusion matrices. This would not be appropriate, however, because the output of the algorithm is not a classification label, but rather a probability that the labeled entity (e.g., a traffic light) exists at a given location. Some locations are associated with a higher probability than others. Hence, what is needed is an estimate of how well the computed probabilities match ground truth.

Accordingly, Figures 9.2 and 9.3 show the accuracy of identifying traffic lights by the OtO EM scheme (Figure 9.2) and the regular EM scheme (Figure 9.3). The horizontal axis shows location IDs where lights were indicated by the respective schemes, sorted by their probability (as computed from the corresponding EM variant) from high to low. Hence, one should expect that lower-numbered locations be

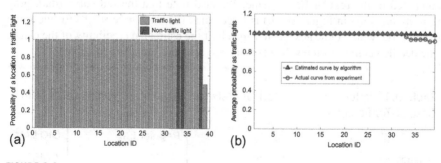

FIGURE 9.2

Claim classification of OtO EM in the case of traffic lights. (a) Locations identified as traffic lights. (b) Average probability as traffic lights.

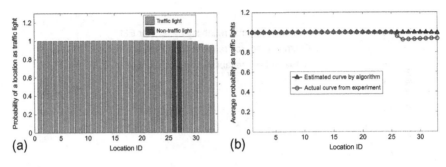

FIGURE 9.3

Claim classification of regular EM in the case of traffic lights. (a) Locations identified as traffic lights. (b) Average probability as traffic lights.

true positives, whereas high-numbered locations may contain increasingly more false positives as the scheme assigns a lower probability that those contain traffic lights.

Figure 9.2(a) shows the actual status of each location. A green (light gray in print versions) bar is a true positive, whereas a red (dark gray in print versions) one is a false positive. As expected, we observe that most of the traffic light locations identified by the OtO EM scheme are true positives. False positives occur only later on at higher-numbered (i.e., lower probability) locations. Additionally, it is interesting to compare the probability of finding traffic lights at the indicated locations, as computed by the algorithms, to the probability computed empirically for the same locations by counting how many of them have actual lights. Figure 9.2(b) shows this comparison. Specifically, it compares the average probability to the empirical probability, computed for the first n locations to have traffic lights, where n is the location index on the horizontal axis. We observe that the estimation results of OtO EM follow quite well the empirical ones.

Similarly, results for the regular EM scheme are reported in Figure 9.3. We observe that the OtO EM scheme is able to find five more traffic light locations compared to the regular EM scheme. We also note that the red curve (dark gray in print versions) in Figure 9.2(b) is larger than that of Figure 9.3(b) for the same location ID, which indicates a better match of the estimated credibility of the claim. The detailed comparison results between two schemes are given in Table 9.1.

Table 9.1 Performance Comparison Between Regular EM Versus OtO EM in Case of Traffic Lights

	Regular EM	OtO EM
Average source reliability estimation error	10.19%	7.74%
Number of correctly identified traffic lights	31	36
Number of mis-identified traffic lights	2	3

The above experiments were repeated for stop sign identification, and it is observed that the OtO EM scheme achieves a more significant performance gain in both participant reliability estimation and stop sign classification accuracy compared to the regular EM scheme. The reason is: stop signs are scattered in town and the odds that a vehicle's path covers most of the stop signs are usually small. Hence, having the knowledge of whether a source had an opportunity to observe a variable is very helpful. However, the identification of stop signs in general is found to be more challenging than that of traffic lights. There are several reasons for that. Namely, (i) the claims for stop signs are sparser because stops signs are typically located on smaller streets, so the chances of different cars visiting the same stop sign are lower than that for traffic lights, (ii) cars often stop briefly at non-stop sign locations, which the reviewed scheme mis-interpret for stop signs, and (iii) when cars want to make a turn after the stop sign, cars' bearings are often not well aligned with the directions of stop signs, which causes errors since stop-sign claims are bearing-sensitive.

Figure 9.4 compares source reliability computed by the OtO EM and regular EM schemes. The actual reliability is computed from similar experiments as traffic lights. We observe that source reliability is better estimated by the OtO EM scheme compared to the regular EM scheme.

Figures 9.5 and 9.6 show the true positives and false positives in recognizing stop signs. We observe the OtO EM scheme actually finds twelve more correct stop sign locations and reduces one false positive location compared to the regular EM scheme. The detailed comparison results are given in Table 9.2. Additionally, we observe that, for both EM schemes, the actual probability of finding stop signs at the indicated locations stays close to but slightly less than the estimated probability by the reviewed algorithms. The reasons of such deviation can be explained by the aforementioned short wait behaviors at non-stop sign locations in real world scenarios.

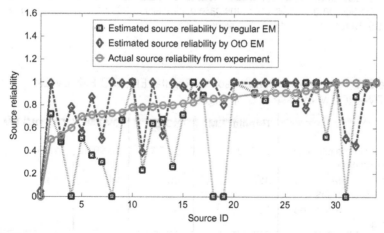

FIGURE 9.4

Source reliability estimation of OtO EM in the case of stop signs.

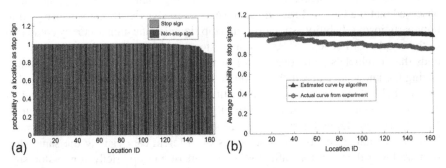

FIGURE 9.5

Claim classification of OtO EM in the case of stop signs. (a) Locations identified as stop signs. (b) Average probability as stop signs.

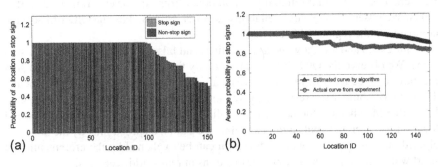

FIGURE 9.6

Claim classification of regular EM in the case of stop signs. (a) Locations identified as stop signs. (b) Average probability as stop signs.

Table 9.2 Performance Comparison of Regular EM, OtO EM, DV EM, and DV+OtO EM in Case of Stop Signs

	Regular EM	OtO EM	DV EM	DV+OtO EM
Average source reliability estimation error	25.34%	16.75%	15.99%	11.98%
Number of correctly identified stop signs	127	139	141	146
Number of mis-identified stop signs	25	24	29	25

9.4.2 DEPENDENT VARIABLES

In this subsection, we evaluate the extensions that consider dependency constraints (DV EM), and the comprehensive OtO+DV EM scheme. While the earlier discussion treated stop signs as independent variables, this is not strictly so. The existence of stop signs in different directions (bearings) is in fact quite correlated. The correlations for Urbana-Champaign were empirically computed and assumed to be known in advance. Clearly, the more "high-order" correlations are considered, the more information is given to improve performance of algorithm. To assess the effect of "minimal" information (which would be a "worst-case" improvement for the reviewed scheme), only pairwise correlations were used. Hence, the joint distribution of co-existence of (two) stop signs in opposite directions at an intersection was computed. It is presented in Table 9.3, and was used as input to the DV EM scheme.

Figure 9.7 shows the accuracy of source reliability estimation, when these constraints are used. We observe that both DV EM and DV+OtO EM scheme track the source reliability very well (the estimation error of the two EM schemes improved 9.4% and 13.4%, respectively, compared to the regular EM scheme).

The true positives and false positives for stop signs are shown in Figures 9.8 and 9.9. Observe that the DV EM scheme finds 14 more correct stop sign locations. The DV+OtO EM scheme performed the best, it finds the most stop sign locations

Table 9.3 Distribution of Stop Signs in Opposite Directions

A = stop sign 1 exists; B = stop sign 2 exists	Percentage
p(A,B)	36%
p(not A, not B)	49%
p(A,not B) = p(not A, B)	7.5%

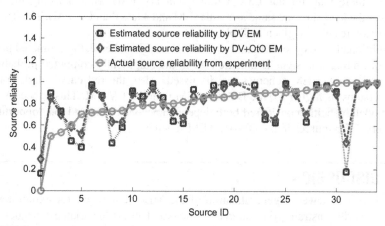

FIGURE 9.7

Source reliability estimation of DV and DV+OtO EM in the case of stop signs.

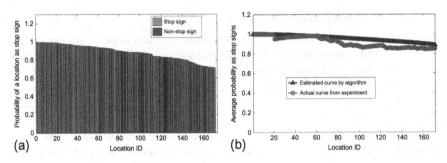

FIGURE 9.8

Claim classification of DV+OtO EM in the case of stop signs. (a) Locations identified as stop signs. (b) Average probability as stop signs.

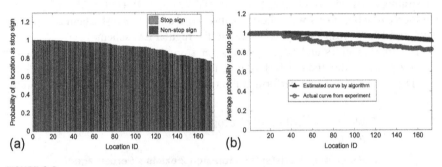

FIGURE 9.9

Claim classification of DV EM in the case of stop signs. (a) Locations identified as stop signs. (b) Average probability as stop signs.

(i.e., 19 more than regular EM, 5 more than DV EM) while keeping the false positives the least (i.e., the same as regular EM and 4 less than DV EM). The detailed comparison results are given in Table 9.2.

Additionally, we observe that, for the DV+OtO EM scheme, the estimated probability of finding stop signs is much closer to the empirically computed probability, compared to other EM schemes we discussed. Also, the red curve (dark gray in print versions) is higher for the DV+OtO EM than the DV EM. This is because the new model explicitly considered both dependency constraints and the "opportunity to observe" for sources in the DV+OtO EM scheme.

9.5 DISCUSSION

This chapter reviewed a generalization of the MLE framework for exploiting the physical world constraints (i.e., source locations and observed variable dependencies) to improve the reliability of social sensing. Some limitations exist that offer directions that deserve further discussions.

First, the framework did not explicitly model the time dimension of the problem. This is mainly because their current application involves the detection of fixed infrastructure (e.g., stop signs and traffic lights). Time is less relevant in such context. Hence, opportunity to observe is only a function of source location, and observed variable dependencies are not likely to change over time. It would be interesting to consider time constraints in future models. In systems where the state of the environment may change over time, when we consider the opportunity to observe, it is not enough for the source to have visited a location of interest. It is also important that the source visits that location within a certain time bound during which the state of the environment has not changed. Similarly, when we consider observed variable dependencies, it is crucial that dependencies of observed variables remain stable within a given time interval and that we have an efficient way to quickly update the estimation on such dependencies as time proceeds.

Second, it is assumed that sources will only report claims for the places they have been to (e.g., cars only generate stop sign claims on the streets their GPS traces covered). Hence, it makes sense to "penalize" sources for not making claims for some clearly observable variables based on their locations. However, many other factors might also influence the opportunity of users to generate claims in real-world social sensing applications. Some of these factors are out of user's control. For example, in some geo-tagging applications, participants use their phones to take photos of locations of interest. However, this approach might not work at some places due to "photo prohibited" signs or privacy concerns. Source reliability penalization based on visited locations might not be appropriate in such context. It is interesting to extend the notion of location-based opportunity-to-observe in the model to consider different types of source constrains in other social sensing applications.

Third, "Byzantine" sources are not assumed in the reviewed model (e.g., cars will not cheat in reporting the their GPS coordinates). However, in some crowd-sensing applications, sources can intentionally report incorrect locations (e.g., Google' Ingress). Different techniques have been developed to detect and address location cheating attacks on both mobile sensing applications [130] and social gaming systems [131]. These techniques can be used along with the reviewed schemes to solve the truth estimation problem in social sensing applications where source's reliability is closely related to their locations. Moreover, it is also interesting to further investigate the robustness of the scheme with respect to the percentage of cheating sources in the system.

Last, the joint probability distribution of dependent variables and knowledge about the opportunity to observe is assumed to be known or can be estimated from prior knowledge. This might not be possible for all social sensing applications. Clearly, the approach in the current paper would not apply if nothing was known about spatial correlations in environmental state. Additionally, the scale of reviewed experiment is relatively small. Recent work has developed a generative model to estimate the opportunity to observe in truth finding for spatial events [132]. More work is necessary to determine when and when not structure learning is possible within fact-finding methods for adaptive DV and OtO methods.

APPENDIX
DERIVATION OF THE E-STEP AND M-STEP OF OTO EM

After the formulation of the new likelihood function to account for the source constraints, the likelihood function can be plugged into the Q function defined in Equation (5.8) of EM. The E-step can be derived as follows:

$$Q(\theta|\theta^{(t)}) = E_{Z|X,\theta^{(t)}}[\log L(\theta; X, Z)]$$

$$= \sum_{j=1}^{N} \left\{ p(z_j = 1|X_j, \theta^{(t)}) \times \sum_{i \in S_j} (\log((a_i)^{S_i C_j}(1 - a_i)^{(1-S_i C_j)}) + \log f_j) \right.$$

$$\left. + p(z_j = 0|X_j, \theta^{(t)}) \times \sum_{i \in S_j} (\log((b_i)^{S_i C_j}(1 - b_i)^{(1-S_i C_j)}) + \log(1 - f_j)) \right\} \quad (9.9)$$

where $p(z_j = 1|X_j, \theta^{(t)})$ represents the conditional probability of the variable C_j to be true given the claim matrix related to the jth claim and current estimate of θ. $p(z_j = 1|X_j, \theta^{(t)})$ is represented by $Z(t, j)$ since it is only a function of t and j. $Z(t, j)$ can be further computed as:

$$Z(t, j) = p(z_j = 1|X_j, \theta^{(t)})$$

$$= \frac{p(z_j = 1; X_j, \theta^{(t)})}{p(X_j, \theta^{(t)})}$$

$$= \frac{p(X_j, \theta^{(t)}|z_j = 1)p(z_j = 1)}{p(X_j, \theta^{(t)}|z_j = 1)p(z_j = 1) + p(X_j, \theta^{(t)}|z_j = 0)p(z_j = 0)}$$

$$= \frac{\prod_{i \in S_j} (a_i)^{S_i C_j}(1 - a_i)^{(1-S_i C_j)} \times f_j^{(t)}}{\prod_{i \in S_j} (a_i)^{S_i C_j}(1 - a_i)^{(1-S_i C_j)} \times f_j^{(t)} + \prod_{i \in S_j} (b_i)^{S_i C_j}(1 - b_i)^{(1-S_i C_j)} \times (1 - f_j^{(t)})}$$

$$(9.10)$$

Note that, in the E-step, only sources who observe a given variable are considered while computing the likelihood of reports regarding that variable.

In the M-step, the derivatives are set to 0: $\frac{\partial Q}{\partial a_i} = 0$, $\frac{\partial Q}{\partial b_i} = 0$, and $\frac{\partial Q}{\partial f_j} = 0$. This gives us the θ^* (i.e., $a_1^*, a_2^*, \ldots, a_M^*; b_1^*, b_2^*, \ldots, b_M^*; f_1^*, f_2^*, \ldots, f_M^*$) that maximizes the $Q(\theta|\theta^{(t)})$ function in each iteration and is used as the $\theta^{(t+1)}$ of the next iteration.

$$a_i^{(t+1)} = a_i^* = \frac{\sum_{j \in SJ_i} Z(t, j)}{\sum_{j \in C_i} Z(t, j)}$$

$$b_i^{(t+1)} = b_i^* = \frac{\sum_{j \in SJ_i} (1 - Z(t, j))}{\sum_{j \in C_i} (1 - Z(t, j))}$$

$$f_j^{t+1} = f_j^* = Z(t, j)$$

$$f_i^{t+1} = f_i^* = \frac{\sum_{j \in C_i} Z(t, j)}{|C_i|} \quad (9.11)$$

where C_i is set of variables source S_i observes according to the knowledge matrix SK and $Z(t,j)$ is defined in Equation (9.10). SJ_i is the set of variables the source S_i actually claims in the claim matrix SC. We note that, in the computation of a_i and b_i, the silence of source S_i regarding some variable C_j is interpreted differently depending on whether S_i *observed* it or not. This reflects that the opportunity to observe has been incorporated into the M-step when the estimation parameters of sources are computed. The resulting OtO EM algorithm is summarized in the subsection below.

DERIVATION OF E-STEP AND M-STEP OF DV AND OtO+DV EM

Given the new likelihood function of the DV EM scheme defined in Equation (9.8), the E-step becomes:

$$Q(\theta|\theta^{(t)}) = E_{Z|X,\theta^{(t)}}[\log L(\theta; X, Z)]$$

$$= \sum_{g \in G} p(z_{g_1}, \ldots, z_{g_k}|X_g, \theta^{(t)})$$

$$\times \left\{ \sum_{i \in M} \sum_{j \in c_g} \log p(S_i C_j|z_j) + \log p(z_{g_1}, \ldots, z_{g_k}) \right\} \quad (9.12)$$

where $p(z_{g_1}, \ldots, z_{g_k}|X_g, \theta^{(t)})$ represents the conditional joint probability of all variables in independent group g (i.e., $g_1, \ldots, g_k$) given the observed data regarding these variables and the current estimation of the parameters. $p(z_{g_1}, \ldots, z_{g_k}|X_g, \theta^{(t)})$ can be further computed as follows:

$$p(z_{g_1}, \ldots, z_{g_k}|X_g, \theta^{(t)}) = \frac{p(z_{g_1}, \ldots, z_{g_k}; X_g, \theta^{(t)})}{p(X_g, \theta^{(t)})}$$

$$= \frac{p(X_g, \theta^{(t)}|z_{g_1}, \ldots, z_{g_k})p(z_{g_1}, \ldots, z_{g_k})}{\sum_{g_1, \ldots, g_k \in \mathcal{Y}_g} p(X_g, \theta^{(t)}|z_{g_1}, \ldots, z_{g_k})p(z_{g_1}, \ldots, z_{g_k})}$$

$$= \frac{\prod_{i \in M} \prod_{j \in c_g} p(S_i C_j|z_j)p(z_{g_1}, \ldots, z_{g_k})}{\sum_{g_1, \ldots, g_k \in \mathcal{Y}_g} \prod_{i \in M} \prod_{j \in c_g} p(S_i C_j|z_j)p(z_{g_1}, \ldots, z_{g_k})} \quad (9.13)$$

We note that $p(z_j = 1|X_j, \theta^{(t)})$ (i.e., $Z(t,j)$), defined as the probability that C_j is true given the observed data and the current estimation parameters, can be computed as the *marginal distribution* of the joint probability of all variables in the independent claim group g that variable C_j belongs to (i.e., $p(z_{g_1}, \ldots, z_{g_k}|X_g, \theta^{(t)})j \in c_g$). We also note that, for the worst case where N variables fall into one independent group, the computational load to compute this marginal grows exponentially with respect to N. However, as long as the constraints on observed variables are localized, the reviewed approach stays scalable, independently of the total number of estimated variables.

In the M-step, as before, θ^* is chosen to maximize the $Q(\theta|\theta^{(t)})$ function in each iteration to be the $\theta^{(t+1)}$ of the next iteration. Hence:

$$a_i^{(t+1)} = a_i^* = \frac{\sum_{j \in SJ_i} Z(t,j)}{\sum_{j=1}^N Z(t,j)}$$

$$b_i^{(t+1)} = b_i^* = \frac{\sum_{j \in SJ_i} (1 - Z(t,j))}{\sum_{j=1}^N (1 - Z(t,j))}$$

$$f_j^{t+1} = f_j^* = Z(t,j) \tag{9.14}$$

where $Z(t,j) = p(z_j = 1 | X_j, \theta^{(t)})$. We note that for the estimation parameters, a_i and b_i, the same expression as for the case of independent variables is obtained. The reason is that sources report variables independently of the form of constraints between these variables.

Next, the two EM extensions (i.e., OtO EM and DV EM) derived so far are combined to obtain a comprehensive EM scheme (OtO+DV EM) that considers constraints on both sources and observed variables. The corresponding E-step and M-step are shown below:

$$
\begin{aligned}
p(z_{g_1}, \ldots, z_{g_k} | X_g, \theta^{(t)}) &= \frac{p(z_{g_1}, \ldots, z_{g_k}; X_g, \theta^{(t)})}{p(X_g, \theta^{(t)})} \\[2mm]
&= \frac{p(X_g, \theta^{(t)} | z_{g_1}, \ldots, z_{g_k}) p(z_{g_1}, \ldots, z_{g_k})}{\sum_{g_1, \ldots, g_k \in \mathcal{Y}_g} p(X_g, \theta^{(t)} | z_{g_1}, \ldots, z_{g_k}) p(z_{g_1}, \ldots, z_{g_k})} \\[2mm]
&= \frac{\prod_{i \in S_j} \prod_{j \in c_g} p(S_i C_j | z_j, S_i \text{ observes } C_j) \times p(z_{g_1}, \ldots, z_{g_k})}{\sum_{g_1, \ldots, g_k \in \mathcal{Y}_g} \prod_{i \in S_j} \prod_{j \in c_g} p(S_i C_j | z_j, S_i \text{ observes } C_j) \times p(z_{g_1}, \ldots, z_{g_k})}
\end{aligned}
\tag{9.15}
$$

where S_j: Set of sources observes C_j

$$a_i^{(t+1)} = a_i^* = \frac{\sum_{j \in SJ_i} Z(t,j)}{\sum_{j \in C_i} Z(t,j)}$$

$$b_i^{(t+1)} = b_i^* = \frac{\sum_{j \in SJ_i} (1 - Z(t,j))}{\sum_{j \in C_i} 1 - Z(t,j)}$$

$$f_j^{t+1} = f_j^* = Z(t,j)$$

$$f_i^{t+1} = f_i^* = \frac{\sum_{j \in C_i} Z(t,j)}{|C_i|} \tag{9.16}$$

where C_i is set of variables source S_i observes.

Recursive fact-finding

10.1 REAL TIME SOCIAL SENSING

This chapter presents a recursive fact-finding solution to the real-time social sensing problem. We introduced the reliable social sensing problem in Chapter 5. An iterative EM algorithm was developed to solve the reliable sensing problem under the assumption that all data are collected a priori. However, in many real world social sensing applications, data arrives as a stream. A key challenge emerge in this real-time context: how could we solve the reliable social sensing problem as data stream in? In particular, how could we develop an efficient scheme to update the estimation parameters of maximum likelihood estimation (MLE) model for the streaming data? We call this problem *real time social sensing* problem. A naive approach to solve the above problem is to re-run the iterative EM solution whenever new data arrive. The obvious deficiency of such an approach is that it is not scalable over the time dimension. In this chapter, we review a new recursive solution to solve this real time social sensing problem.

Reputation systems [18] have been successful at assessing quality of *providers* (e.g., the reliability of data sources) when the same providers repeatedly execute transactions that can be scored by others. In contrast to such scenarios, the reviewed work is specially interested in short-lived crowdsourcing campaigns (e.g., to support post-disaster recovery and rescue missions, which may last for only a few days), where anyone can volunteer and where there is not enough history to accumulate meaningful reputations. For example, consider the severe gas shortage around New York City in the aftermath of hurricane Sandy in November 2012. Social networks, such as Twitter carried tens of thousands of tweets on the availability of gas at different stations, but the reliability of the corresponding tweeters remained unknown.

Fact-finder algorithms [37, 44, 100] have been proposed that use unsupervised machine learning techniques to assess data reliability directly from multitudes of unreliable claims, whose sources may not have a known history in advance. The problem was also explored in data mining literature [35, 36, 133], with intuitions tracing back to Google's original PageRank [34, 134]. These solutions iteratively rank claims and sources to jointly assess the reliability of both, without requiring sources to explicitly comment on each other's performance. Unfortunately, they use batch algorithms, designed to run on a static dataset. As such, they are not well-suited

IEEE being the copyright holder, grants permission to reprint text of the article, Dong Wang, Tarek Abdelzaher, Lance Kaplan, and Charu Aggarwal, "Recursive Fact-finding: A Streaming Approach to Truth Estimation in Crowdsourcing Applications," In Proceedings of *2013 IEEE 33rd International Conference on Distributed Computing Systems (ICDCS 13)* Philadelphia, PA, July 2013.

to processing streaming data for applications such as crowdsourcing, where new observations continue to arrive over time. The batch algorithms will either need to operate on a growing data set as new data arrive (which does not scale), or ignore some previously computed results and run from scratch on a sliding recent data window (which does not exploit all available data).

In contrast, the main contribution of the reviewed model in this chapter is to develop a *recursive* fact-finder, based on expectation maximization (EM) that updates on new data, as it arrives, updating previous truth estimates (i.e., estimates of correctness of reported data) in a manner that approximates running an optimal batch algorithm on the entire augmented dataset [107]. The streaming EM scheme reviewed in this chapter is considered as one of the first *online* fact-finding approaches designed to solve the real time social sensing problem, where there is no prior knowledge on source reliability and no immediate way to verify the correctness of the collected data. The streaming EM scheme is derived by formulating an optimization problem (in the sense of maximum-likelihood estimation) and approximating the optimal solution using results from estimation theory.

10.2 A STREAMING TRUTH ESTIMATION MODEL

Real time social sensing addresses the challenge of estimating some pertinent "state of the world" from source's reported observations that come continuously over time. The streaming model represents the state of the world by a set of true/false statements (e.g., "The Golden Gate bridge is on fire," "The 435 Main Street gas station is out of power," or "The 5th Avenue and 34th Street intersection is flooded"). Such a binary approach, while simple, is a powerful tool to articulate arbitrarily complex conditions. It is also well-suited to geotagging campaigns that mark locations of some conditions of interest (e.g., locations of street flooding after a thunderstorm). For example, each location may be associated with a number of Booleans indicating the presence or absence of different types of damage. A report from a source conveys one or more claims, each presenting the value of one of these Booleans. The values of claims are assumed to not change over the period of study. The "ground truth" state is unknown and needs to be reconstructed as accurately as possible from claims by different sources, whose reliability is unknown.

More formally, let us first review the social sensing application model discussed in Chapter 5, where a group of M sources (sources), $S_1, \ldots, S_M$, collectively make observations about N measured Boolean variables, $C_1, \ldots, C_N$, which are of interest to the application. It is assumed, without loss of generality, that the "normal" state of each (Boolean) variable is negative (e.g., a place is not damaged). Hence, sources only report when the positive state of the claim (repair is needed) is encountered. Each source generally reports only a subset of the variables (e.g., those at the places they have been to). The goal of reliable social sensing is to jointly calculate the reliability of sources (i.e., the probability that a source reports correct observations) and the correctness of observations, given only the record of who reported what.

Importantly, in crowdsourcing applications, the observations from sources do not come all at once. Instead, updates are reported over the course of the campaign, lending themselves better to the abstraction of a *data stream* arriving from the community of sources. In Chapter 5, we reviewed a batch EM (expectation maximization) algorithm to solve the reliable sensing problem based on a MLE hypothesis [100]. As its name suggests, the batch EM scheme is designed to run in a batch mode, which is not suitable for continuously arriving data. This is because, every time a new report arrives, the batch EM algorithm needs to be re-run on the whole data set from scratch. Considering such inefficiency, this chapter reviews a new fact-finding approach based on a recursive EM algorithm to update estimation results on the fly in view of newly arriving data.

Following the terminology of previous chapters, let us review a few notations we will use in the following sections. Let S_i denote the ith source and C_j denote the jth claim. Let $X_{i,j}$ denote whether source S_i reports claim C_j. The matrix representing who reported what is called the observation matrix X, where $X_{i,j} = 1$ when source S_i reports that C_j is true, and $X_{i,j} = 0$ otherwise. Let T_j represent the ground truth value of C_j (i.e., T_j is 1 if C_j is true and 0 otherwise). Source reliability t_i is defined as the probability that the source is right in a randomly chosen claim he/she reported. Formally, t_i is defined as:

$$t_i = P(T_j = 1 | X_{i,j} = 1) \tag{10.1}$$

Let us also review two more important conditional probabilities: a_i is the (unknown) probability that source S_i reports a variable to be true when it is indeed true, and b_i is the (unknown) probability that source S_i reports a variable to be true when it is in reality false. Formally, a_i and b_i are defined as follows:

$$a_i = P(X_{i,j} = 1 | T_j = 1) \quad b_i = P(X_{i,j} = 1 | T_j = 0) \tag{10.2}$$

As we discussed before, the relationship between t_i, a_i, and b_i can be derived by the Bayes' theorem:

$$a_i = \frac{t_i \times s_i}{d} \quad b_i = \frac{(1 - t_i) \times s_i}{1 - d} \tag{10.3}$$

where d is the overall background prior that a randomly chosen claim is true. Note that, this value does not indicate, however, whether any particular report about a specific claim is true or not. d can be either chosen from the prior knowledge or jointly estimated in the EM scheme [100]. Finally, s_i denotes the probability that source S_i reports an observation.

Starting with a log-likelihood function that describes the likelihood of the observed data (i.e., who said what) given the estimation parameter defined in Equation (10.2), the batch EM algorithm converges to the MLE of the variables in question (in this case, the truth values of claims and the reliability of sources). The likelihood function can be given by:

$$L = \prod_{j=1}^{N} \left\{ \prod_{i=1}^{M} a_i^{X_{i,j}} (1 - a_i)^{(1-X_{i,j})} \times d \times z_j \right.$$

$$\left. + \prod_{i=1}^{M} b_i^{X_{i,j}} (1 - b_i)^{(1-X_{i,j})} \times (1 - d) \times (1 - z_j) \right\} \qquad (10.4)$$

where N and M are the numbers of claims and sources, respectively, z_j is 1 if claim C_j is true (and 0 otherwise). The optimal estimation of the parameters in the batch EM algorithm [100] are given by:

$$a_i^* = \frac{\sum_{j \in SJ_i} Z_j}{\sum_{j=1}^{N} Z_j}$$

$$b_i^* = \frac{K_i - \sum_{j \in SJ_i} Z_j}{N - \sum_{j=1}^{N} Z_j} \qquad (10.5)$$

where SJ_i is the set of claims the source S_i actually observes and K_i is its size. Z_j is the probability of C_j to be true given current estimation and observed data.

In this chapter, we review a new streaming fact-finder based on a recursive EM algorithm to accurately estimate the above parameters in *real time* from streaming data.

10.3 DYNAMICS AND THE RECURSIVE ALGORITHM

In the following subsections, we derive the recursive formulas for the fact-finder to account for the staggered data in the stream and provide the resulting algorithm.

10.3.1 THE DERIVATION

In estimation theory, a recursive formula of the EM scheme estimates parameters of the model in consecutive time intervals as follows [91]:

$$\hat{\theta}_{k+1} = \hat{\theta}_k + \{(k+1)I_c(\hat{\theta}_k)\}^{-1} V_n(X_{k+1}, \hat{\theta}_k) \qquad (10.6)$$

where $\hat{\theta}_k$ is the estimation parameter by observing the data up to the time interval k, $I_c(\hat{\theta}_k)$ represents the "complete" Fisher information matrix, which is the expected value of Fisher information matrix average over the missing data at time k. In this work, we take the asymptotic CRLB from Chapter 6, which is slightly different than the inverse of the "complete" Fisher information matrix. This is one of the key distinctions of the approach in [91] vice using the actual Fisher information. $V_n(X_{k+1}, \hat{\theta}_k)$ is the score function (defined in Equation (3.10)) of the observed data at time interval $k+1$ w.r.t. the estimation parameter $\hat{\theta}_k$. Authors in [91] state that we can take expectation of the score function over the missing data instead of the score function itself. The above formula basically provides us a recursive way to compute the estimation parameter in the new time interval (i.e., $\hat{\theta}_{k+1}$) based on its estimation value in the previous time interval (i.e., $\hat{\theta}_k$), the complete CRLB of the estimation (i.e., $I_c^{-1}(\hat{\theta}_k)$) and the score function of the updated data observed in the new interval (i.e., $V_n(X_{k+1}, \hat{\theta}_k)$). Based on the results are from Chapter 6 (under the assumption that the number of sources is sufficiently large to reach this asymptotic results) of the EM scheme, $\hat{\theta}_k$ is the estimation vector defined as $\hat{\theta}_k = (\hat{a}_1^k, \hat{a}_2^k, \ldots, \hat{a}_M^k; \hat{b}_1^k, \hat{b}_2^k, \ldots, \hat{b}_M^k)$. $I_c^{-1}(\hat{\theta}_k)$ and $\psi(X_{k+1}, \hat{\theta}_k)$ are given by the asymptotic CRLB from Chapter 6 (see Equation (6.16)):

$$I_c^{-1}(\hat{\theta}_k)_{i,j} = \begin{cases} 0 & i \neq j \\ \dfrac{\hat{a}_i^k \times (1 - \hat{a}_i^k)}{\sum_j Z_j} & i = j \in [1, M] \\ \dfrac{\hat{b}_i^k \times (1 - \hat{b}_i^k)}{\sum_j (1 - Z_j)} & i = j \in (M, 2M] \end{cases} \tag{10.7}$$

and the score function is:

$$V_n(X_{k+1}, \hat{\theta}_k)_j = \begin{cases} \sum_{j=1}^N \hat{Z}_j^{k+1} \left(\dfrac{X_{i,j}}{\hat{a}_i^k} - \dfrac{1 - X_{i,j}}{1 - \hat{a}_i^k} \right) & i = j \text{ for } i \in [1, M] \\ \sum_{j=1}^N (1 - \hat{Z}_j^{k+1}) \left(\dfrac{X_{i,j}}{\hat{b}_i^k} - \dfrac{1 - X_{i,j}}{1 - \hat{b}_i^k} \right) & i = j - M \text{ for } i \in [M+1, 2M] \end{cases} \tag{10.8}$$

where $\hat{Z}_j^{k+1}$ is the probability of the jth claim to be true in the $k+1$ time interval. Plugging Equations (10.7) and (10.8) into (10.6), the recursive formula to update the estimation parameters is given by:

$$\hat{a}_i^{k+1} = \hat{a}_i^k + \frac{1}{Nd(k+1)} \times \left[\sum_{j \in SJ_i^{k+1}} \hat{Z}_j^{k+1}(1 - \hat{a}_i^k) - \sum_{j \in S\bar{J}_i^{k+1}} \hat{Z}_j^{k+1} \hat{a}_i^k \right]$$

$$\hat{b}_i^{k+1} = \hat{b}_i^k + \frac{1}{Nd(k+1)} \times \left[\sum_{j \in SJ_i^{k+1}} (1 - \hat{Z}_j^{k+1})(1 - \hat{b}_i^k) - \sum_{j \in S\bar{J}_i^{k+1}} (1 - \hat{Z}_j^{k+1}) \hat{b}_i^k \right] \tag{10.9}$$

From above equations, one can observe that the estimation of the parameters related with reliability of each source in current time interval can be computed from their estimations in the past and the observed data in the new interval. Moreover, $\hat{Z}_j^{k+1}$ is unknown and can be estimated by its approximation $\tilde{Z}_j^{k+1}$, which can be computed as follows:

$$\tilde{Z}_j^{k+1} = f(\tilde{a}_i^{k+1}, \tilde{b}_i^{k+1}, X_{k+1})$$

$$= \frac{A_j^{k+1} \times d}{A_j^{k+1} \times d + B_j^{k+1} \times (1 - d)}$$

where

$$A_j^{k+1} = \prod_{i=1}^{M} (\tilde{a}_i^{(k+1)})^{X_{i,j}^{k+1}} (1 - \tilde{a}_i^{(k+1)})^{(1-X_{i,j}^{k+1})}$$

$$B_j^{k+1} = \prod_{i=1}^{M} (\tilde{b}_i^{(k+1)})^{X_{i,j}^{k+1}} (1 - \tilde{b}_i^{(k+1)})^{(1-X_{i,j}^{k+1})}$$

$$\tilde{a}_i^{k+1} = \hat{a}_i^{k} \times \frac{s_i^{k+1}}{s_i^{k}} \quad \tilde{b}_i^{k+1} = \hat{b}_i^{k} \times \frac{s_i^{k+1}}{s_i^{k}} \tag{10.10}$$

where s_i^{k+1} and s_i^{k} are the frequencies of source S_i reports a claim after iteration $k + 1$ and k (i.e., at time $k + 1$ and k). Note that s_i^{k} can be computed as the percentage of all claims made by S_i relative to the total number of claims that it could have made, which is known from the observed data. For the above equation to hold, it is assumed that source reliability changes slowly over time and can be treated unchanged over two consecutive time intervals.

Based on the definition of $\tilde{Z}_j^{k+1}$, it can be further represented as a function of $\hat{a}_i^{k}, \hat{b}_i^{k}, X_k, X_{k+1}$, the values of which are known at time interval $k + 1$:

$$\tilde{Z}_j^{k+1} = g(\hat{a}_i^{k}, \hat{b}_i^{k}, X_k, X_{k+1})$$

$$= \frac{C_j^{k+1} \times d}{C_j^{k+1} \times d + D_j^{k+1} \times (1 - d)}$$

where

$$C_j^{k+1} = \prod_{i=1}^{M} \left(\hat{a}_i^{k} \times \frac{s_i^{k+1}}{s_i^{k}} \right)^{X_{i,j}^{k+1}} \left(1 - \hat{a}_i^{k} \times \frac{s_i^{k+1}}{s_i^{k}} \right)^{(1-X_{i,j}^{k+1})}$$

$$D_j^{k+1} = \prod_{i=1}^{M} \left(\hat{b}_i^{k} \times \frac{s_i^{k+1}}{s_i^{k}} \right)^{X_{i,j}^{k+1}} \left(1 - \hat{b}_i^{k} \times \frac{s_i^{k+1}}{s_i^{k}} \right)^{(1-X_{i,j}^{k+1})} \tag{10.11}$$

Plugging Equation (10.11) into Equation (10.9), the following recursive computation of the estimation parameters can be obtained:

$$\hat{a}_i^{k+1} = \hat{a}_i^{k} + \frac{1}{Nd(k+1)}$$

$$\times \left[\sum_{j \in SJ_i^{k+1}} g(\hat{a}_i^{k}, \hat{b}_i^{k}, X_k, X_{k+1})(1 - \hat{a}_i^{k}) \right.$$

$$\left. - \sum_{j \in S\bar{J}_i^{k+1}} g(\hat{a}_i^{k}, \hat{b}_i^{k}, X_k, X_{k+1})\hat{a}_i^{k} \right]$$

$$\hat{b}_i^{k+1} = \hat{b}_i^{k} + \frac{1}{Nd(k+1)}$$

$$\times \left[\sum_{j \in SJ_i^{k+1}} (1 - g(\hat{a}_i^{k}, \hat{b}_i^{k}, X_k, X_{k+1}))(1 - \hat{b}_i^{k}) \right.$$

$$\left. - \sum_{j \in S\bar{J}_i^{k+1}} (1 - g(\hat{a}_i^{k}, \hat{b}_i^{k}, X_k, X_{k+1}))\hat{b}_i^{k} \right] \tag{10.12}$$

Additionally, the updated correctness of claims (i.e., $\hat{Z}_j^{k+1}$) can also be computed as follows:

$$\hat{Z}_j^{k+1} = f(\hat{a}_i^{k+1}, \hat{b}_i^{k+1}, X_{k+1}) \tag{10.13}$$

where function f is the same as the one in Equation (10.10).

This gives us the recursive equations to compute the estimation parameters of the model in the current time interval based on the estimations from the previous time interval and the observed data up to now. Therefore, Equation (10.12) can be utilized to keep track of the estimation parameter of the sources that report new observations consecutively over time. We also note that the estimation parameter change of the updated sources will affect the credibility of claims they report, which in turn will affect the credibility of other sources asserting the same claim. We call this credibility update propagation "ripple effect." To capture such an effect, a simple trick was designed: only run one EM iteration after applying the recursive formula (as compared to running the full version of EM from scratch). This turns out to be an efficient heuristic based on the following observations: (i) the recursive estimation already offers us a reasonably good initialization on the estimation parameter; (ii) the credibility change of sources by a few updates in a short time interval is usually slight. This allows the recursive EM to converge much faster than the batch algorithm that starts from a random point.

10.3.2 THE RECURSIVE EM ALGORITHM

In summary of the recursive EM algorithm derived above, the pseudocode of the algorithm is given in Algorithm 7. The algorithm runs when a new update X_{k+1} arrives and it first computes the recursive update on the estimation parameter (i.e., $\hat{a}_i^{k+1}, \hat{b}_i^{k+1}$) based on Equation (10.12). The correctness of claims are consequently updated from the estimation parameters based on Equation (10.13). The recursive algorithm runs one EM iteration to capture the "ripple effect" of the credibility prorogation as we discussed in the previous subsection. Thus the iteration only consider who are making the claims as the current time. After that, once can decide the truthfulness of each claim C_j at current time slot based on the updated value of $\hat{Z}_j^{k}$ (i.e., Z_j^r). One can also compute the reliability of each source from the updated values of $\hat{a}_i^{k+1}, \hat{b}_i^{k+1}$ (i.e., a_i^r and b_i^r) based on Equation (10.3).

ALGORITHM 7 RECURSIVE EXPECTATION MAXIMIZATION ALGORITHM

1: **while** new update X_{k+1} arrives **do**
2:   **for** $i = 1 : M$ **do**
3:       compute $\hat{a}_i^{k+1}, \hat{b}_i^{k+1}$ based on Equation (10.12)
4:       update $\hat{a}_i^k, \hat{b}_i^k$ with $\hat{a}_i^{k+1}, \hat{b}_i^{k+1}$
5:   **end for**
6:   **for** $j = 1 : N$ **do**
7:       compute $\hat{Z}_j^{k+1}$ based on Equation (10.13)
8:   **end for**
9:   run one EM iteration to capture the "ripple effect"
10:   Let $Z_j^r = $ the value of $\hat{Z}_j^{k+1}$ after the iteration
11:   Let $a_i^r = $ the value of $\hat{a}_i^{k+1}$ after the iteration
12:   Let $b_i^r = $ the value of $\hat{b}_i^{k+1}$ after the iteration
13:   **for** $j = 1 : N$ **do**
14:       **if** $Z_j^r \geq 0.5$ **then**
15:           C_j is true
16:       **else**
17:           C_j is false
18:       **end if**
19:   **end for**
20:   **for** $i = 1 : M$ **do**
21:       calculate t_i^r from a_i^r, b_i^r based on Equation (10.3)
22:   **end for**
23:   $k = k + 1$
24: **end while**

10.4 PERFORMANCE EVALUATION

In this section, we review the evaluation of the performance of the proposed recursive EM algorithm compared to the batch EM algorithm (see Chapter 5) and three state-of-art fact-finders; namely, Sums [35], Average-Log [37], and Truthfinder [36]. For the batch EM algorithm, there are two ways for parameter initialization: one way is to statically initialize the estimation parameters based on the observed data and run EM from scratch for each time epoch [100] and the other way is to use the values computed from the previous updates for the current initialization (denoted as EM-P). Below, We first review the evaluation of estimation accuracy and algorithm execution time through an extensive simulation study. The recursive EM algorithm is shown to achieve a better performance tradeoff compared to the batch EM algorithm and other state-of-art baselines. Then, we present an empirical study that demonstrates convergence of the recursive EM algorithm to results of the (optimal but slower) batch EM algorithm through a real-world social sensing application.

10.4.1 SIMULATION STUDY

We begin by reviewing the evaluation of the performance of the proposed recursive EM algorithm in simulation by measuring (i) the accuracy of source reliability estimation, (ii) the false positive and false negative rates (i.e., claims misclassified as true or false), and (iii) the average time the algorithm takes to process an update in different conditions.

A similar simulator as the one we discussed in Chapter 5 was built to generate a random number of sources and measured (Boolean) variables. A random probability P_i is assigned to each source S_i representing his/her reliability (i.e., the ground truth probability that they report correct observations). A "reporting rate" of a source is defined as the probability that the source reports an observation at a given time slot, reflecting the source's willingness to report. At a given time slot, for each source S_i, the simulator decides whether or not the source reports an observation based on its reporting rate. If a measured variable is true, the S_i reports with probability $P_i \times$ reporting rate and if it is false then S_i speaks with $(1 - P_i) \times$ reporting rate. P_i is uniformly distributed between 0.5 and 1 in the experiments.* The fact-finder is executed as reports arrive to update estimates of source reliability and truth values of reported data. Each point on the following curves is an average of 50 experiments.

The first experiment evaluated the performance of recursive EM, the batch EM, and other baselines while varying the number of sources in the system. The total number of reported variables was set to 2000, half of which were reported correctly. The reporting rate of sources was fixed at 0.5. The number of sources was varied from 60 to 150. 100 time slots were simulated for the data stream generation. The observation updates of the last 20 slots were used to evaluate the algorithm performance. Reported results were averaged 50 experiments that differ in source reliability distributions. Results are shown in Figure 10.1. Observe that the recursive EM algorithm takes the shortest time to process an update while keeping the estimation accuracy (in terms of both source reliability estimation and claim classification) only slightly worse than the batch EM algorithm.

The second experiment compares the recursive EM to baseline algorithms when the source reporting rate changes from 0.1 to 1. Reported results are averaged over 50 experiments. The results are shown in Figure 10.2. We observe that the recursive EM algorithm continues to achieve a better trade-off between estimation accuracy and execution time: it runs fastest while offering comparable quality to the batch algorithm. Note also that both estimation accuracy and execution time of the studied algorithms improve as the source reporting rate increases. The reason is that a higher reporting rate leads to more data, which eventually allows faster convergence of the algorithm to a more accurate point.

---

*In principle, there is no incentive for a source to lie more than 50% of the time, since negating their statements would then give a more accurate truth.

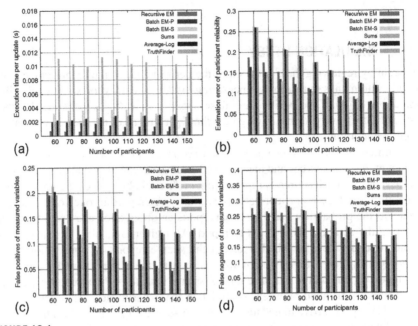

FIGURE 10.1

Algorithm performance versus number of sources. (a) Algorithm execution time.
(b) Source reliability estimation accuracy. (c) Measured variable estimation: false positives.
(d) Measured variable estimation: false negatives.

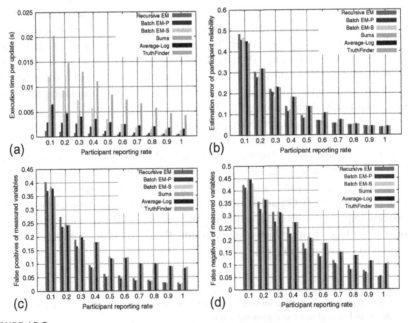

FIGURE 10.2

Algorithm performance versus source chat rate. (a) Algorithm execution time.
(b) Source reliability estimation accuracy. (c) Measured variable estimation: false positives.
(d) Measured variable estimation: false negatives.

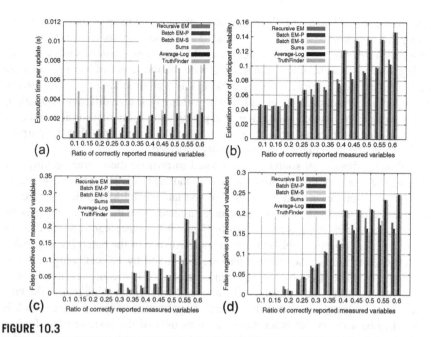

FIGURE 10.3

Algorithm performance versus ratio of correctly reported measured variables. (a) Algorithm execution time. (b) Source reliability estimation accuracy. (c) Measured variable estimation: false positives. (d) Measured variable estimation: false negatives.

The third and last experiment examined the effect of changing the claim mix on the performance of all algorithms. The total number of claims to was fixed at 2000 and the ratio of the number of correctly reported claims to the total number of reported variables was varied from 0.1 to 0.6. The number of sources is set to 120 and source reporting rate is fixed at 0.5. Reported results are averaged over 50 experiments. The results are shown in Figure 10.3. As before, one can observe that the recursive EM algorithm has the shortest execution time and does almost as well as the batch EM algorithm.

The simulation results show that the proposed recursive EM algorithm succeeds at offering similar estimation accuracy to its best batch counterpart while running significantly faster.

10.4.2 A REAL WORLD CASE STUDY

In this section, we review the evaluation of the performance of the proposed recursive EM algorithm compared to the batch EM algorithm through a real world social sensing application. The application targets at finding the free parking lots on the campus of University of Illinois at Urbana-Champaign (UIUC). The "free parking lots" are defined as the parking lots that are free of charge after 5pm daily in this application. The goal here was to see if the recursive EM algorithm can track the performance of the batch EM algorithm and correctly find the real locations of free parking lot on campus. Specially, 106 parking lots on campus were selected and volunteers were asked to mark the ones they believe as "Free." Sources marked those parking lots they have been to or are familiar with. Various types of parking lots were observed to exist on campus: enforced parking lots with time limits, parking meters, permit parking, street parking, etc. Different parking lots have different regulations for free parking. Moreover, instructions and permit signs often read similar and easy to miss. Hence, sources are prone to make mistakes in their marks. For the purpose of evaluation, the ground truth were manually collected.

In the experiment, 30 sources were invited to provide their "free parking lot" marks on the 106 parking lots (46 of which are indeed free). There were 340 marks collected from sources in total. Both the recursive and batch EM algorithms were ran on the collected marks and their performance on identifying the correct free parking lots were compared. Results are shown in Figure 10.4. Once can observe that the recursive EM algorithm is able to track the performance of the batch EM algorithm and converge to the number of free parking lots found by the batch algorithm as the amount of marks used by the algorithm increases. This result verified the nice convergence property of the developed recursive EM algorithm using real world data.

It should be emphasized that the choice of application of the reviewed work is intended to be a proxy for other more pertinent uses of the reviewed fact-finding tool that are harder to experiment with in a paper (due to absence of ground truth). For example, "free parking lots" may stand for "operational gas stations" in a post-disaster scenario (such as the New York gas crisis in the aftermath of recent hurricane Sandy).

It should also highlight that the reviewed evaluation chose an application where ground truth *does not change*. This is claimed to be intentional, in order to favor their competition (the batch algorithms) that operate on the entire data set at once and hence have difficulty handling dynamic changes. It is expected the advantages of the recursive algorithm to be more pronounced if ground truth did change during the

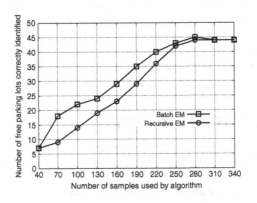

FIGURE 10.4

Recursive EM algorithm convergence.

experiment (e.g., a gas station runs out of gas), since it is easy to adapt them to give more weight to more recent measurements.

Finally, one should note that the reviewed work kept its data sets small enough such that running the batch algorithm upon every update remained feasible (for evaluation purposes, where each point needs 50 runs). The real advantage of the recursive scheme, however, becomes clear when the input volume is scaled up. For example, hundreds of thousands of tweets may be received in the aftermath of real disaster events. Interpreting individual tweets as claims, a recursive fact-finder can rank the claims by credibility in real-time as events unfold, which would be much less time consuming than if a batch fact-finder is re-run continuously as new tweets arrive.

10.5 DISCUSSION

This chapter reviewed a streaming fact-finding approach to address the real time social sensing problem on the fly. Several limitations exist that offer directions for future work.

The recursive EM algorithm is sensitive to the dynamics in the source membership (e.g., new sources join and old sources leave). This is because the recursive model is continuously updating the estimation vector, which is related to the set of sources who are involved in the application. When few sources join or leave the applications, the algorithm is able to infer the reliability of new sources based on the corroboration between their claims and claims made by other sources who are already in the system. However, in the case where a large number of sources change their membership over a short period of time, it is challenging for the recursive algorithm to converge to a stable point quickly. One possible solution is to re-run the batch algorithm when such large dynamics in sources happen. Then, the next challenge is to find the appropriate threshold to invoke the batch algorithm so that the algorithm achieves a nice tradeoff between time and estimation accuracy. It would also be interesting to extend the reviewed recursive model to enhance its robustness against the membership changes in participating sources.

The values of claims are not assumed to change over time. However, in some real world social sensing applications, such assumption may not hold. For example, in a geotagging application to find litter locations in a neighborhood, the litter could be cleaned up periodically by a group of cleaning crew. Hence, the claim of a certain place to have litter may change over time. It is very interesting to further extend our model to consider the dynamics in the values of the same claim. The authors have recently applied the DV EM algorithm discussed in Chapter 9 to handle the dependency between instances of the same claim over different time slots [135]. In this way, one could leverage the results of DV EM to solve this interesting real time social sensing problem where the values of claims change over time. It would also be interesting to further extend this recursive model to consider more complex dynamics. For example, how could one extend the recursive model to apply in the cases where the dependency between sources and correlations between claims also evolve as time proceeds?

Further readings

11.1 ESTIMATION THEORY

In estimation theory, expectation maximization (EM) is a general optimization technique for finding the maximum likelihood estimation (MLE) of parameters in a statistic model where the data are "incomplete" or involve latent variables in addition to estimation parameter and observed data [93]. That is, either there are some missing value among the data, or the model can be formulated more simply by assuming the existence of some unobserved data. In many cases, the EM is used for parameter estimation of mixture distributions where the latent variable inform which mixture is active [136]. The general EM algorithm iterates between two main steps: the Expectation step (E-step) and the Maximization step (M-step) until the estimation converges (i.e., the likelihood function reaches the maximum). In the E-step, the algorithm computes the expectation of the log-likelihood function (so-called Q-function) of complete data w.r.t. the conditional distribution of the latent variables given the current settings of the parameters and the observed data. In the M-step, it re-estimates the parameters in the next iteration that maximizes the expectation of the log-likelihood function defined in the E-step. EM is frequently used for data clustering in data mining and machine learning because the collection of clusters can be modeled as one mixture distribution. For language modeling, the EM is often used to estimate parameters of a mixed model where the exact model from which the data is generated is unobservable [137]. EM has also been used in PLSA [138, 139] and community detection [140, 141]. There are also many good tutorials on EM algorithms [142–144]. In this book, we showed that social sensing applications lend themselves nicely to an EM formulation because it is natural to think that each individual source speaks out different for true claims as compared to untrue ones. In other words, a source's willingness to espouse a claims is drawn from a mixture distribution, where the possible ground truths form the mixtures. The optimal solution, in the sense of MLE, directly leads to an accurate quantification of measurement correctness as well as participant reliability.

The Cramer-Rao lower bound (CRLB) is a fundamental bound used in estimation theory to characterize the lower bound on the estimation variance of a deterministic parameter [109]. The Fisher information is defined as the second moment of the score vector of random variable and estimation parameter [111]. Intuitively, if the Fisher information is large, the distribution with the θ_0 (i.e., true value) of the estimation parameter will be different and well distinguished from the distributions with a parameter that is not so close to θ_0. This means we are able to estimate θ_0 well (hence a small variance) based on the data. If the Fisher information is small, our estimation will be worse due to the similar reason. We reviewed the basics of CRLB and Fisher information in Chapter 3. CRLB has been used to study the performance of estimators in different applications such as range estimation [145], sinusoidal parameter estimation [146], and bearing estimation [147]. For example, Wang et al. leveraged CRLB to estimate the accuracy of time-based range estimation (TBRE) using Orthogonal frequency-division multiplexing (OFDM) [145]. Qian et al. used CRLB to show a frequency domain nonlinear least squares estimation algorithm achieved the near-optimal performance for noisy damped sinusoidal signals [146]. Wang et al. analyzed the performance bounds (i.e., CRLB) of a location-penalized MLE for bearing-only target localization [147]. One of the key properties of MLE is the asymptotic normality. This property basically states that the MLE estimator is asymptotically distributed with a normal distribution as the data sample size increases [112]. The mean of the normal distribution is the MLE of the estimation parameter and the variance is given by the CRLB of the estimation. The asymptotic normality has been recently studied in various contexts such as stochastic blockmodels [148], maximum entropy models [149], Markov jump process [150], and binary neural networks [151]. The EM scheme we reviewed in this book provides the MLE of source reliability for social sensing applications. We also reviewed an quantification approach to compute the *confidence interval* for source reliability estimation based on both the actual and asymptotic CRLB by leveraging the asymptotic normality of our MLE estimator.

11.2 DATA QUALITY AND TRUST ANALYSIS

Data quality and integration is a critical problem in the database communities and a number of techniques have been developed. These techniques include methods for detecting erroneous values [152, 153], entity resolution [154, 155], information extraction [156, 157], type inference [158, 159], and schema matching [160, 161]. Besides, an end-to-end data curation system (Data Tamer) has been developed to perform data cleaning and reusable transformation [162]. Direct manipulation and programming-by-demonstration (PBD) methods have been applied to specific cleaning tasks in many data cleaning applications [163–165]. Supervised learning presumes the existence of labeled data for training. Because it is difficult to collect ground truthed data, many researchers have turned to crowd sourcing to label the data. There exists a significant literature in the machine learning community to improve data quality and identify low quality labelers in a multi-labeler environment. In such context, multiple non-expert sources could offer cheap but noisy labels at scale for supervised modeling. Robust techniques have been developed to improve the data quality of using noisy labels. Sheng et al. proposed a repeated labeling scheme to improve label quality by selectively acquiring multiple labels and empirically comparing several models that aggregate responses from multiple labelers [166].

Dekel et al. applied a classification technique to simulate aggregate labels and prune low-quality labelers in a crowd to improve the label quality of the training dataset [167]. However, all of the above approaches made explicit or implicit assumptions that are not appropriate in the social sensing context. For example, the work in [166] assumed labelers were known a priori and could be explicitly asked to label certain data points. The work in [167] assumed most of labelers were reliable and the simple aggregation of their labels would be enough to approximate the ground-truth. In contrast, participants in social sensing usually upload their measurements based on their own observations and the simple aggregation technique (e.g., majority voting) was shown to be inaccurate when the reliability of participant is not sufficient [37]. The MLE approach reviewed in this book addressed these challenges by intelligently casting the reliable social sensing problem into an optimization problem that can be efficiently solved by the EM scheme.

We reviewed several important trust analysis schemes developed to solve fact-finding problems in information networks (i.e., fact-finders) in Chapter 4. They normally depend on the source and claim networks that describe "who said what" to make the trust decision. In addition to those schemes, there exists a large amount of literature on trust analysis that look into attributes of the sources as well as the lexicon, syntax, and semantics of the claims to improve the analysis performance. For example, Pasternack et al. proposed a generalized fact-finding framework that incorporates a wealth of background knowledge and contextual information such as source attributes (e.g., age, educational attainment, groups), claim similarity and the uncertainty in the information extraction of claims [44]. Amin et al. designed an extended version of the MLE based fact-finding framework by explicitly considering source's bias in their model and showed performance improvement over the state-of-the-art schemes in scenarios where source opinions are polarized [168]. Gupta et al. developed a credibility analysis scheme based on Twitter to identify credible events [169]. Their scheme explored attributes/features of both sources (e.g., number of friends, followers, status updates, profile) and claims (e.g., existence of slang words, supportive URLs, words in first/second/third person pronouns, number of named entities related to the event, sentiment analysis). Vydiswaran et al. developed a content-driven trust propagation framework that helps ascertain the veracity of free-text claims and estimate the trustworthiness of their sources. Their approach explored the evidence related with a claim, uncertainty in the quality of those evidence artifacts, and the information network structure [170]. Finally, Castillo et al. and O'Donovan et al. investigated a combination of different content, social, and behavioral features to assess the credibility of Twitter messages [171, 172].

11.3 OUTLIER ANALYSIS AND ATTACK DETECTION

Several previous efforts on data cleaning and outlier analysis from data mining and noise removal from statistics addressed some notion of noisy data [115, 116, 173–176]. They differ in the assumption made, the modeling approach applied and the targeted objective. For example, Bayesian inference and decision tree induction techniques are applied to fill the missing values of data by predictions from their constructed model [173]. Binning and linear regression techniques are used to smooth the noisy data by either using bin means or fitting data into some linear functions [174, 175]. Clustering techniques are widely used to detect outliers by organizing similar data values into clusters and identifying the ones that fall outside the clusters as outliers [176]. Other approaches are used in statistics to estimate model parameters or filter noises from continuous data [115, 116, 177]. Random Sample Consensus (RANSAC) algorithm is a widely used robust parameter estimation algorithm can potentially deal with a large outlier contamination rate [177]. Kalman filter is an efficient reclusive filter that estimates some latent variables of a linear dynamic system from a series of noisy measurements [115]. It produces estimations of the measurements by computing a weighted average of the predicted values based on their uncertainty. Particle filters are more sophisticated filters that are based on Sequential Monte Carlo methods. They are often used to determine the distribution of a latent variable whose state space is not restricted to Gaussian distribution [116]. Our work is complementary to the above efforts. On one hand, an appropriately cleaned and outlier-removed dataset will likely result in a better estimation of our scheme. On the other hand, outliers or noises may not be completely (or even possibly) removed by the data cleaning and outlier analysis techniques mentioned above due to their own limitations (e.g., linear model assumption, continuous data assumption, known data distribution assumption, etc.). The quantifiable and confident estimation provided by our approach on both information source and observed data could actually help the data cleaning and outlier analysis tools do a better job.

In intrusion detection, one critical task is to detect (or identify) the malicious nodes (or sources) accurately and confidently. Two main kinds of detection techniques exist: signature-based detection and anomaly-based detection [176, 178]. The signature-based detection takes the predefined attack patterns (by domain experts) as signatures and monitor the node's behavior (or network traffic) for matches to report the anomaly [176]. The anomaly-based detection builds profiles of normal node's (or network) behavior and use the profiles to detect new patterns that have remarkable deviation [178]. For the reliable social sensing problem in our work, it is not obvious what behavior patterns the malicious (unreliable) sources will have without knowing the correctness of their measurements. Hence, there might not be an easy way to apply the intrusion techniques mentioned above to discover malicious sources for social sensing applications. Instead, given the MLE on participant reliability and the corresponding confidence interval provided by our scheme, we are able to both identify unreliable sources and quantify their reliability with certain confidence without prior knowledge of their behavior patterns.

Since people are an indispensable element in social sensing, some popular attacks originated from human (or source) interactions are interesting to investigate. Collusion attack is carried out by a group of colluded attackers who collectively perform some malicious (sometimes illegal) actions based on their agreement to defraud honest sources or obtain objective forbidden by the system. This attack could be mitigated by monitoring the interactions or relationships among colluded attackers or identifying the abnormal behavior from the group [179]. Sybil attack is another related attack carried out by a single attacker who intentionally create a large number of pseudonymous entities and use them to gain a disproportionately large influence on the system. This attack could be mitigated by certifying trust of identity assignment, increasing the cost of creating identities, limiting the resource the attacker can use to create new identities, etc. [180]. By handling reports from colluded or duplicate sources in a way that takes care of the source dependency, we will be able to address the above attacks to some extent. For example, by identifying duplicate sources, we can remove them along with their reports from the observed dataset, which is expected to improve the estimation performance. Problems become more interesting when sources are not just duplicates but actually linked through some orthogonal information network (e.g., social network). Recent work has investigated theory to characterize ones ability to identify and compensate for attacked nodes within a large scale sensor network performing target detection [181]. These principles may provide a starting point to analyze and characterize sensing over social networks.

11.4 RECOMMENDER SYSTEMS

Our work is related with a type of information filtering system called recommender systems, where the goal is usually to predict a user's rating or preference to an item using the model built from the characteristics of the item and the behavioral pattern of the user [182]. EM has been used in either collaborative recommender systems as a clustering module [183] to mine the usage pattern of users or in a content-based recommender systems as a weighting factor estimator [184] to infer the user context. However, the reliable social sensing problem targets a different goal: we try to quantify how reliable a source is and identify whether a measured variable is true or not rather than predict how likely a user would choose one item compared to another. Moreover, users in recommender systems are commonly assumed to provide reasonably good data while the sources in social sensing are in general unreliable and the likelihood of the correctness of their measurements is unknown a priori. There appears no straightforward use of methods in the recommender systems regime for the target problem with unpredictably unreliable data. Additionally, the rating or preference we get from users in the recommender systems are sometimes *subjective* [185]. For example, some people may prefer Ford car to Toyota while others prefer exactly the opposite. It is hard to say who is right and who is wrong due to the fact that there is no universal ground truth on the items to be evaluated. We note that the work in this book may not be directly applicable to handle the above case due to the different assumptions made in models for truth finding. In social sensing applications, we aim to leverage the data contributed by common individuals and reconstruct the *state of the physical world*, where we usually do have the universal ground truth associated with the assertions that describe those physical states (e.g., a building is either on fire or not). The techniques reviewed in our book make much more sense under this assumption of social sensing applications. It enables the application to not only obtain the optimal estimation (in MLE sense) on source and information reliability, but also assess the quality of the estimation compared to the ground truth.

11.5 SURVEYS AND OPINION POLLING

Surveys and influence analysis are often subjective [186]. They tend to survey personal facts, or individual emotions and sentiments [187]. This is as opposed to assessing physical state that is external to the human (sensor). For example, a survey question may ask "Was the customer service representative knowledgeable?" or it may ask "Do you support government's decision to increase tax?" Survey participants answer the questions with their own ideas independently, and the responses are often private [188]. Source dependency is not the main issue in these studies [189]. In contrast, in this book, it is not our goal to determine what individuals feel, think, or support, or to extract who is influential, popular, or trending. Instead of assessing humans' own beliefs, opinions, popularity, or influence, we focus on applications concerned with the *observation and state estimation of an external environment*. That external state has a *unique ground truth* that is independent of human beliefs. Humans act merely as sensors of that state. There is therefore an objective and unambiguous notion of *sensing error*, leading to a clear optimization problem whose goal is to reconstruct ground truth with minimum error from reported human observations.

The work reviewed in this book should not be confused with work from sociology and statistics on opinion polling, opinion sampling, influence analysis, and surveys. Opinion polling and sampling are usually carefully designed and engineered by the experts to create appropriate questionnaires and select representative partici-pants [190, 191]. These are often controlled experiments, and the provenance of the information is also controllable [192]. Moreover, data cleaning is domain specific and semantic knowledge is required [193]. In contrast, in the reliable sensing problem studied in this book, the data collection is open to all. We assume *no control* over both the participants (data sources) and the measurements in their reports. The *reliability of sources* and their *data provenance* is usually unknown to the applications. The approaches reviewed in this book are designed to be *general* and not require domain specific knowledge to clean the data.

Conclusions and future challenges

12

12.1 SUMMARY AND CONCLUSIONS

In this book, we reviewed a set of recently developed theories and methodologies to build reliable systems on unreliable data in social sensing. Social sensing has emerged as a new paradigm of sensing and data collection due to the proliferation of mobile devices owned by common individuals, fast data sharing, and large scale information dissemination opportunities. A key challenge in social sensing applications lies in *data reliability*. Solutions to address this key challenge is non-trivial given the reliability of participants (sources) is usually unknown a priori and there is no independent way to verify the correctness of their measurements. In this section, we briefly summarized the contents and key points presented in each chapter of the book.

In Chapter 1, we started the book with an introduction to the emerging research field called *social sensing*. It is a multi-disciplinary research field that is situated at the intersection of networked sensing, data mining, statistics, and cyber-physical systems. We summarized a few main technical enablers and fundamental motivations for research in social sensing and pointed out several key challenges in social sensing are centered around the problem of data reliability. We also outlined the organization of this book at the end of the chapter.

In Chapter 3, we summarized the mathematical foundations that are used in this book. These foundations include concepts and basic principles in statistics, data mining, and estimation theory such as information networks, Bayesian analysis, maximum likelihood estimation (MLE), expectation maximization (EM), confidence intervals, and Cramer-Rao lower bound (CRLB). We reviewed the above math foundations with some simple examples to help readers understand and digest the underlying principles. We concluded this chapter with an information network abstraction that allows us to leverage the math tools we reviewed to efficiently solve the data reliability problem in social sensing.

In Chapter 4, we reviewed a Bayesian interpretation scheme that offered a probability semantic to interpret the ranking outputs of the basic fact-finder used in trust analysis in information networks. This interpretation leads to a direct quantification of the accuracy of the conclusions obtained from information network analysis. Hence it provides a general foundation for using information network analysis not only to heuristically extract likely facts, but also to quantify, in analytical founded manner, the probability each source is correct. Such quantification is critical to analyze source reliability and correctness of their measurements in the social sensing context. We also pointed out the Bayesian interpretation remains to be an approximation scheme due to the heuristic nature of fact-finders and is sensitive to the priors of initialization.

In Chapter 5, we considered the limitation of Bayesian interpretation and reviewed a MLE to obtain the optimal estimation on participant (source) reliability and the correctness of their measurements in social sensing applications. We called the above estimation problem *reliable social sensing*. In this chapter, we showed that the reliable social sensing problem lend themselves nicely to an EM formulation. The MLE we reviewed makes inference regarding both source reliability and measurement correctness by observing how observations are corroborated by the sources. The EM based approach was shown to outperform the state of the art fact-finding heuristics as well as simple baselines such as majority voting.

In Chapter 6, we considered an important issue for fact-finding methods: what is the confidence bound of the resulting participant reliability estimation? To answer this question, we reviewed a MLE quantification scheme that derived both real and asymptotic confidence bounds for participant reliability estimation in EM scheme. The confidence bounds are obtained by leveraging the asymptotic normality of the MLE and computing the CRLB for the estimation parameters. We studied the limitation of the real and asymptotic CRLBs and demonstrated the trade-offs they offer between computation complexity and estimation scalability. We also examined the robustness of these bounds to changes in the number of sources. The results offered us an understanding of attainable estimation accuracy of source reliability in social sensing applications that rely on un-vetted sources whose reliability is not known in advance.

In Chapter 7, we extend the fact finding work to address two important simplifying assumptions made in the basic MLE model in Chapter 5: (i) observations from different participants on the same measured variable are assumed to be corroborating; (ii) values of measured variables are assumed to be binary (i.e., true or false). We reviewed generalizations of the MLE model to remove the above two assumptions and make the EM scheme applicable to a much wider range of social sensing applications. First, we extended the estimation parameter to incorporate the conflicting observations from different participants on the same measured variable. The corresponding likelihood function and E-step and M-step were re-derived to obtain the extended MLE to handle conflicting observations. Second, we generalized the model for conflicting observations to incorporate non-binary values of measured variables and similarly derived the MLE for non-binary measured variables.

In Chapter 8, we explored the *social aspect* of the reliable social sensing problem presented in Chapter 5. Specifically, we provided a social-aware MLE model that explicitly considers the source dependency between non-independent sources in social sensing. This is a critical model when we consider humans as data sources ("human sensors") and their potential information dissemination throughout the social network. This model bridges the human (cyber) world with the physical (sensor) world, while offering rigorous guarantees on the reliability of fusion results. We compared the performance of the new social-aware EM scheme with the regular EM that ignores source dependencies through several real world case studies using human observations in the field. The results showed that the social-aware approach outperformed the regular EM and other baselines such as majority voting.

In Chapter 9, we explored the *physical aspect* of the reliable sensing problem. In particular, we considered the correlations and constraints on both sources and variables imposed by the physical world. We reviewed several generalizations of the basic EM approach to consider the source constraints (i.e., sources could only report observations from the places they have been to) and claim/variable constraints (i.e., claims could be non-independent). These generalizations are important because they allow social sensing applications to explicitly incorporate various variable correlations and dependencies that exist in real world scenarios. We compared the new generalized EM schemes with the regular EM that ignores these constraints in a real world crowd-sensing application. The generalized EM schemes showed good performance improvement by considering the constraints from the physical world.

In Chapter 10, we presented a recursive EM algorithm to better handle streaming data in social sensing. The iterative EM algorithm reviewed in previous chapters is mainly designed for static dataset and not necessarily efficient for the streaming data. In contrast, the recursive EM algorithm computes the updated estimations from the previous results and the new observed data in a recursive way. We studied the performance of the recursive EM algorithm over different problem dimensions and the recursive EM algorithm was shown to achieve nice performance trade-offs.

In Chapter 11, we recommended a few directions of related work for further readings. These directions include estimation theory, trust analysis in information networks, outlier detection and attack detection, recommender and reputation systems, and surveys and opinion polling.

In essence, the belief theory community is trying to determine how to fuse opinion of claims from different sources when the claims are conflicting. Fact-finding can provide a mechanism to filter and discount claims to remove the conflicts before fusion. Furthermore, fact-finding provides a decision maker with valuable information about the confidence one should have in the fused information or even the raw data. This books represents the first steps to estimate truth in the wild via statistical principles.

More can be done to improve the estimates including understanding the social network channels that connect the sources to each other and to the decision makers. For instance, sources influence each other through direct interaction and through social norms. Furthermore, sources will reveal different thoughts depending on who they perceive will be the audience. For instance, when a person requests a response from a particular source, that source will probably provide a guarded response if he/she does not have a good rapport with the information requester.

12.2 REMAINING CHALLENGES AND FUTURE WORK

The theories, methods, and techniques reviewed in this book can be used to develop the analytic foundations for a new science of summarizing information from a large collection of real-time, heterogeneous, and dynamic information sources, and to build the next generation of information distillation system that extracts useful information with time and quality guarantees by exploring the collective wisdom of common individuals. To achieve this long-term goal, there exists significant challenges for future work. We outline some of these challenges as follows.

Generalized Assured Knowledge Discovery: Future information distillation tasks require solutions with assured quality to a broad set of knowledge discovery problems such as clustering, classification, ranking, community discovery, link prediction, etc. Our hypothesis is that a variety of knowledge discovery problems can be solved under a unified theoretical foundation. The key insight is that knowledge discovery problems are often modeled as network attribute estimations, which determine the "best" assignment of attribute values to network nodes and/or links, subject to problem constraints. These problems essentially share the same underlying estimation principle as the analytical framework we developed for reliable social sensing. It is hoped that one can develop new theories and modeling techniques that compute *confidence levels* of analysis results, which has rarely been studied in the state of the art. This work will be fundamental to the future information distillation service in that it will, for the first time, guarantee *assured* quality of knowledge discovery on a unified foundation. To achieve this goal, numerous questions need to be answered. For example, how to build the general theoretical framework of quality estimation that works for different knowledge discovery problems? When is it possible to give reliable confidence estimates in results? Recently, authors have made some progress toward this direction: a provenance-assisted classifier has been developed based on the basic fact-finding framework to significantly improve the classification accuracy of social signals by leveraging the source identity information [194]. Moreover, researchers from information extraction (IE) also uses the fact-finding research to develop a new multi-dimensional fact-finding framework that integrates signals from multiple sources and multiple systems through knowledge graphs [48].

Real-Time Data Analytics: The real-time feature is a must-have for future information distillation system. Making sense of huge volumes of global data streams coming from a complex and highly dynamic environment in a timely manner is a big challenge. Many of current research efforts focus on boosting the processing power of facilities (e.g., supercomputers) and designing efficient paradigms for parallel and distributed computing (e.g., Hadoop). In contrast, we are very interested in looking at the core of real-time data analytics for the purpose of reliable information distillation. We would like to build a new data analysis engine that efficiently organizes a firehose of streaming and heterogeneous data feeds and delivers reliable information with real-time guarantees. In the process of building Apollo, we discovered several interesting questions for future research. For example, how to distribute data streams over clusters and compute results in a way that optimizes the estimation accuracy while minimizing the analysis time?

Enhanced Fact-finders: In this book, we present a set of fact-finders that can be used toward addressing the reliable social sensing problem. A simplified bipartite graph describing sources, claims, and their relations represents our basic problem abstraction. However, there still exists a rich set of information related with both source attributes and claim contexts that can be further explored to develop enhanced versions of fact-finders in the future research. On one hand, sources attributes need more investigations. For example, sources in social sensing applications have different religious, social, political, and economic backgrounds that can color how they report their observations of the world. Moreover, the observations sources report may contain different degrees of uncertainty and such uncertainty could be affected by source's physical location, expertise, and prior knowledge. It will be very interesting to generalize the fact-finders presented in this book to incorporate various source attributes to further improve the algorithms' performance. On the other hand, the context information of claims can also be analyzed to better process the claims. For example, the data clustering module in Apollo system is syntax-based and does not explore the semantics of claims. In such context, two pieces of tweets reporting the same event with different words (e.g., "huge explosion" vs "big blast") may be considered as two independent claims and lose credibility boost they would have enjoyed had they been considered as the same one. Understanding the sentiments of the claims can also be very helpful since they are strong indicators of the attitudes of sources toward a given topic and overall contextual polarity of their reports. Therefore, it will also be very interesting to enhance the fact-finders with deeper analysis of the claims in terms of their semantics, contexts, and sentiments.

Future Assured Medical Diagnosis: The reliable social sensing framework I built can be generalized and applied in future medical applications to provide *assured diagnosis* for various kinds of diseases. In the context of medical applications, the observed data usually take the form of "symptoms" or "indicators" of diseases and the sources of the data are normally the "causes" of such diseases. The reliable estimation approach I developed can be used to jointly estimate the best indicators and the most indicated causes of a set of diseases of interests. While traditional diagnosis methods provide "best effort" analysis results for doctors, these techniques usually do not offer a confident assessment of *quality of results*. In contrast, this analytic approach not only provides the best hypothesis but also rigorously quantifies how accurate it is compared to the ground truth by giving concrete confidence bounds on the estimation results. This assured quality of diagnosis result is particularly important in medical applications where a small error could lead to the loss of lives.

Online Disaster Report and Crisis Tracking Systems: Disaster report and crisis tracking applications using online social media represent a set of very broad, distributed, and collaborative information distillation paradigms that feature the most versatile platform, *the humans, as the sensors*. A unique feature of using humans as sensors is the notion of *uncertain data provenance*. Namely, it is not unusual for a person to report observations they received from others as if they were his/her own. Such rumor spreading behavior has no analogy in correctly functioning physical sensors. From an information system perspective, this means that errors in "measurements" across "sensors" may be non-independent, as one erroneous observation may be propagated by other sources without being verified. We are interested in understanding several important problems along this direction: How to model humans as sensors with uncertain data provenance? Given the complex nature of humans, how good is such model when tested with real human observations in the field? We believe solving the uncertain data provenance problem will enable humans as powerful sensors for tasks unachievable by traditional data collection and information processing systems. The work in Chapter 8 represents our initial progress to tackle these problems. Much work is necessary to accommodate arbitrary social network structures.

Multi-genre Network Analysis: Comprehensive understandings of multi-genre networks play a critical role in future information distillation systems. For example, on June 9th, 2013, an anomalous 10-mile traffic jam was detected (by the deployed sensor network) on a major Southern California freeway. At the same time, there as a unusual bursts of traffic on Twitter around the same location. The contents of tweets actually offered a very clear and first-time explanation that the traffic jam was caused by a rally organized by the Tea Party. This example shows that analyzing data across multi-genre networks will not only detect abnormal phenomenon but also extract useful information to identify the underlying causes. We expect more exciting work in multi-genre network research to develop techniques that will automatically unearth new information, evaluate its reliability, and provide more effective solutions for decision makers.

References

[1] J. Surowiecki, *The wisdom of crowds*. Random House LLC, 2005.

[2] C. R. Sunstein, *Infotopia: How many minds produce knowledge*. Oxford University Press, 2006.

[3] R. R. Rajkumar, I. Lee, L. Sha, and J. Stankovic, "Cyber-physical systems: the next computing revolution," in *Proceedings of the 47th Design Automation Conference*. ACM, 2010, pp. 731–736.

[4] L. Sha, S. Gopalakrishnan, X. Liu, and Q. Wang, "Cyber-physical systems: A new frontier," in *Machine Learning in Cyber Trust*. Springer, 2009, pp. 3–13.

[5] E. A. Lee, "Cyber physical systems: Design challenges," in *Object Oriented Real-Time Distributed Computing (ISORC), 2008 11th IEEE International Symposium on*. IEEE, 2008, pp. 363–369.

[6] N. D. Lane, S. B. Eisenman, M. Musolesi, E. Miluzzo, and A. T. Campbell, "Urban sensing systems: Opportunistic or participatory," in *In Proc. ACM 9th Workshop on Mobile Computing Systems and Applications (HOTMOBILE '08)*, 2008.

[7] Y. Bar-Shalom and X. R. Li, *Multisensor, Multitarget Tracking: Principles and Techniques*. Storrs, CT: YBS Publishing, 1995.

[8] H. Chen, T. Kirubarajan, and Y. Bar-Shalom, "Performance limits of track-to-track fusion versus centralized estimation: Theory and application," *IEEE Transactions on Aerospace and Electronic Systems*, vol. 39, no. 2, pp. 386–400, Apr. 2003.

[9] C.-Y. Chong, S. Mori, and K.-C. Chang, "Distributed multitarget multisensor tracking," in *Multitarget Multisensor Tracking: Advanced Applications*, Y. Bar-Shalom, Ed. Norwood, MA: Artech House, 1990, pp. 247–295.

[10] C.-Y. Chong, S. Mori, W. H. Barker, and K.-C. Chang, "Architectures and algorithms for track association and fusion," *IEEE Aerospace and Electronic Systems Magazine*, vol. 15, no. 1, pp. 5–13, Jan. 2000.

[11] B. S. Rao and H. F. Durrant-Whyte, "Fully decentralized algorithm for multisensor Kalman filtering," *IEE Proceedings-D*, vol. 138, no. 5, pp. 413–420, 1991.

[12] Y. Bar-Shalom and H. Chen, "Multisensor track-to-track association for tracks with dependent errors," in *Proc. of the 43rd IEEE Conf. on Decision and Control*, Paradise Island, Bahamas, Dec. 2004.

[13] L. M. Kaplan, Y. Bar-Shalom, and W. D. Blair, "Assignment costs for multiple sensor track-to-track association," *IEEE Transactions on Aerospace and Electronic Systems*, vol. 44, no. 2, pp. 655–677, Apr. 2008.

[14] G. Shafer, *A Mathematical Theory of Evidence*. Princeton University Press, 1976.

[15] R. R. Yager, J. Kacprzyk, and M. Fedrizzi, Eds., *Advances in the Dempster-Shafer Theory of Evidence*. New York: John Wiley & Sons, Inc., 1994.

[16] F. Smarandache and J. Dezert, Eds., *Advances and Applications of DSmT for Information Fusion: Collected Works*. Infinite Study, 2004.

[17] A. Jøsang, S. Marsh, and S. Pope, "Exploring different types of trust propagation," in *Proc. of the 4th International Conference on Trust Management (iTrust)*, Pisa, Italy, May 2006.

[18] A. Jøsang, R. Ismail, and C. Boyd, "A survey of trust and reputation systems for online service provision," *Decision Support Systems*, vol. 43, no. 2, pp. 618–644, Mar. 2007. [Online]. Available: http://dx.doi.org/10.1016/j.dss.2005.05.019.

[19] D. Artz and Y. Gil, "A survey of trust in computer science and the semantic web," *Web Semantics: Science, Services and Agents on the World Wide Web*, vol. 5, no. 2, pp. 58–71, 2007.

[20] Y. Wang and J. Vassileva, "A review on trust and reputation for web service selection," in *Distributed Computing Systems Workshops, 2007. ICDCSW'07. 27th International Conference on*. IEEE, 2007, pp. 25–25.

[21] L. Cabral and A. Hortacsu, "The dynamics of seller reputation: Evidence from eBay," *The Journal of Industrial Economics*, vol. 58, no. 1, pp. 54–78, 2010.

[22] T. D. Huynh, N. R. Jennings, and N. R. Shadbolt, "An integrated trust and reputation model for open multi-agent systems," *Autonomous Agents and Multi-Agent Systems*, vol. 13, no. 2, pp. 119–154, Sep. 2006. [Online]. Available: http://dx.doi.org/10.1007/s10458-005-6825-4.

[23] T. D. Huynh, "Trust and reputation in open multi-agent systems," Ph.D. dissertation, University of Southampton, 2006.

[24] K. Aberer and Z. Despotovic, "Managing trust in a peer-2-peer information system," in *CIKM '01: Proceedings of the tenth international conference on Information and knowledge management*. New York, NY, USA: ACM, 2001. [Online]. Available: http://dx.doi.org/10.1145/502585.502638 pp. 310–317.

[25] D. Houser and J. Wooders, "Reputation in auctions: Theory, and evidence from eBay," *Journal of Economics & Management Strategy*, vol. 15, no. 2, pp. 353–369, 2006. [Online]. Available: http://dx.doi.org/10.1111/j.1530-9134.2006.00103.x.

[26] W. Zheng and L. Jin, "Online reputation systems in web 2.0 era," in *Value Creation in E-Business Management*. Springer, 2009, pp. 296–306.

[27] R. Farmer and B. Glass, *Building web reputation systems*. O'Reilly Media, Inc.", 2010.

[28] B. Yu and M. P. Singh, "Detecting deception in reputation management," in *Proceedings of the second international joint conference on Autonomous agents and multiagent systems*. ACM, 2003, pp. 73–80.

[29] W. T. Teacy, J. Patel, N. R. Jennings, and M. Luck, "TRAVOS: Trust and reputation in the context of inaccurate information sources," *Autonomous Agents and Multi-Agent Systems*, vol. 12, no. 2, pp. 183–198, Mar. 2006. [Online]. Available: http://dx.doi.org/10.1007/s10458-006-5952-x.

[30] L. Xiong and L. Liu, "Peertrust: Supporting reputation-based trust for peer-to-peer electronic communities," *IEEE Transactions on Knowledge and Data Engineering*, vol. 16, no. 7, pp. 843–857, 2004.

[31] I. Pinyol and J. Sabater-Mir, "Computational trust and reputation models for open multi-agent systems: a review," *Artificial Intelligence Review*, vol. 40, no. 1, pp. 1–25, 2013.

[32] M. Sensoy, G. de Mel, L. Kaplan, T. Pham, and T. J. Norman, "Tribe: Trust revision for information based on evidence," in *Information Fusion (FUSION), 2013 16th International Conference on*. IEEE, 2013, pp. 914–921.

[33] L. Kaplan, M. Scensoy, and G. de Mel, "Trust estimation and fusion of uncertain information by exploiting consistency," in *Information Fusion (FUSION), 2014 17th International Conference on*. IEEE, 2014, pp. 1–8.

[34] S. Brin and L. Page, "The anatomy of a large-scale hypertextual web search engine," in *7th international conference on World Wide Web (WWW'07)*, 1998. [Online]. Available: http://portal.acm.org/citation.cfm?id=297805.297827 pp. 107–117.

[35] J. M. Kleinberg, "Authoritative sources in a hyperlinked environment," *Journal of the ACM*, vol. 46, no. 5, pp. 604–632, 1999.

[36] X. Yin, J. Han, and P. S. Yu, "Truth discovery with multiple conflicting information providers on the web," *IEEE Trans. on Knowl. and Data Eng.*, vol. 20, pp. 796–808, June 2008. [Online]. Available: http://portal.acm.org/citation.cfm?id=1399100.1399392.

[37] J. Pasternack and D. Roth, "Knowing what to believe (when you already know something)," in *International Conference on Computational Linguistics (COLING)*, 2010.

[38] A. Galland, S. Abiteboul, A. Marian, and P. Senellart, "Corroborating information from disagreeing views," in *WSDM*, 2010, pp. 131–140.

[39] D. Wang, T. Abdelzaher, H. Ahmadi, J. Pasternack, D. Roth, M. Gupta, J. Han, O. Fatemieh, and H. Le, "On Bayesian interpretation of fact-finding in information networks," in *14th International Conference on Information Fusion (Fusion 2011)*, 2011.

[40] L. Berti-Equille, A. D. Sarma, X. Dong, A. Marian, and D. Srivastava, "Sailing the information ocean with awareness of currents: Discovery and application of source dependence," in *CIDR'09*, 2009.

[41] X. Dong, L. Berti-Equille, and D. Srivastava, "Truth discovery and copying detection in a dynamic world," *VLDB*, vol. 2, no. 1, pp. 562–573, 2009. [Online]. Available: http://portal.acm.org/citation.cfm?id=1687627.1687691.

[42] X. Dong, L. Berti-Equille, Y. Hu, and D. Srivastava, "Global detection of complex copying relationships between sources," *PVLDB*, vol. 3, no. 1, pp. 1358–1369, 2010.

[43] G.-J. Qi, C. C. Aggarwal, J. Han, and T. Huang, "Mining collective intelligence in diverse groups," in *Proceedings of the 22nd international conference on World Wide Web*. International World Wide Web Conferences Steering Committee, 2013, pp. 1041–1052.

[44] J. Pasternack and D. Roth, "Making better informed trust decisions with generalized fact-finding," in *Proceedings of the Twenty-Second international joint conference on Artificial Intelligence - Volume Three*, ser. IJCAI'11. AAAI Press, 2011. [Online]. Available: http://dx.doi.org/10.5591/978-1-57735-516-8/IJCAI11-387 pp. 2324–2329.

[45] J. Pasternack and D. Roth, "Generalized fact-finding," in *Proceedings of the 20th international conference companion on World wide web*. ACM, 2011, pp. 99–100.

[46] B. Zhao, B. I. P. Rubinstein, J. Gemmell, and J. Han, "A Bayesian approach to discovering truth from conflicting sources for data integration," *Proc. VLDB Endow.*, vol. 5, no. 6, pp. 550–561, Feb. 2012. [Online]. Available: http://dl.acm.org/citation.cfm?id=2168651.2168656.

[47] J. Pasternack and D. Roth, "Latent credibility analysis," in *Proceedings of the 22nd international conference on World Wide Web*. International World Wide Web Conferences Steering Committee, 2013, pp. 1009–1020.

[48] D. Yu, H. Huang, T. Cassidy, H. Ji, C. Wang, S. Zhi, J. Han, C. Voss, and M. Magdon-Ismail, "The wisdom of minority: Unsupervised slot filling validation based on multi-dimensional truth-finding." in *The 25th International Conference on Computational Linguistics (COLING)*, 2014.

[49] M. Gupta and J. Han, "Heterogeneous network-based trust analysis: a survey," *ACM SIGKDD Explorations Newsletter*, vol. 13, no. 1, pp. 54–71, 2011.

[50] D. Wang, "On quantifying the quality of information in social sensing," Ph.D. dissertation, University of Illinois at Urbana-Champaign, 2013.

[51] C. Aggarwal and T. Abdelzaher, "Social sensing," Managing and Mining Sensor Data, Kluwer Academic Publishers, 2013.

[52] T. F. Abdelzaher, Y. Anokwa, P. Boda, J. Burke, D. Estrin, L. J. Guibas, A. Kansal, S. Madden, and J. Reich, "Mobiscopes for human spaces," *IEEE Pervasive Computing*, vol. 6, no. 2, pp. 20–29, 2007.

[53] T. Yan, V. Kumar, and D. Ganesan, "Crowdsearch: Exploiting crowds for accurate real-time image search on mobile phones," in *8th Annual International Conference on Mobile Systems, Applications and Services (MobiSys 2010)*, 2010.

[54] B. Hull, V. Bychkovsky, Y. Zhang, K. Chen, M. Goraczko, A. Miu, E. Shih, H. Balakrishnan, and S. Madden, "Cartel: a distributed mobile sensor computing system," in *Proceedings of the 4th international conference on Embedded networked sensor systems*, ser. SenSys '06. New York, NY, USA: ACM, 2006. [Online]. Available: http://doi.acm.org/10.1145/1182807.1182821 pp. 125–138.

[55] S. B. Eisenman, E. Miluzzo, N. D. Lane, R. A. Peterson, G.-S. Ahn, and A. T. Campbell, "The bikenet mobile sensing system for cyclist experience mapping," in *Proceedings of the 5th international conference on Embedded networked sensor systems*, ser. SenSys '07. New York, NY, USA: ACM, 2007. [Online]. Available: http://doi.acm.org/10.1145/1322263.1322273 pp. 87–101.

[56] J.-H. Huang, S. Amjad, and S. Mishra, "CenWits: a sensor-based loosely coupled search and rescue system using witnesses," in *SenSys'05*, 2005, pp. 180–191.

[57] T. Abdelzaher, Y. Anokwa, P. Boda, J. Burke, D. Estrin, L. Guibas, A. Kansal, S. Madden, and J. Reich, "Mobiscopes for human spaces," *IEEE Pervasive Computing*, vol. 6, no. 2, pp. 20–29, 2007.

[58] Sense Networks, "Cab Sense," http://www.cabsense.com.

[59] A. Thiagarajan, J. Biagioni, T. Gerlich, and J. Eriksson, "Cooperative transit tracking using smart-phones," in *SenSys'10*, 2010, pp. 85–98.

[60] B. Longstaff, S. Reddy, and D. Estrin, "Improving activity classification for health applications on mobile devices using active and semi-supervised learning," in *Pervasive Computing Technologies for Healthcare (PervasiveHealth), 2010 4th International Conference on-NO PERMISSIONS*. IEEE, 2010, pp. 1–7.

[61] A. Helal, D. J. Cook, and M. Schmalz, "Smart home-based health platform for behavioral monitoring and alteration of diabetes patients." *Journal of diabetes science and technology*, vol. 3, no. 1, pp. 141–148, Jan. 2009. [Online]. Available: http://www.ncbi.nlm.nih.gov/pmc/articles/PMC2769843/.

[62] A. Madan, M. Cebrian, D. Lazer, and A. Pentland, "Social sensing for epidemiological behavior change," in *Proceedings of the 12th ACM international conference on Ubiquitous computing*, ser. Ubicomp '10. New York, NY, USA: ACM, 2010. [Online]. Available: http://doi.acm.org/10.1145/1864349.1864394 pp. 291–300.

[63] A. Madan, S. T. Moturu, D. Lazer, and A. S. Pentland, "Social sensing: obesity, unhealthy eating and exercise in face-to-face networks," in *Wireless Health 2010*. ACM, 2010, pp. 104–110.

[64] D. J. Cook and L. B. Holder, "Sensor selection to support practical use of health-monitoring smart environments," *Wiley Interdisciplinary Reviews: Data Mining and Knowledge Discovery*, vol. 1, no. 4, pp. 339–351, 2011. [Online]. Available: http://dx.doi.org/10.1002/widm.20.

[65] R. K. Ganti, S. Srinivasan, and A. Gacic, "Multisensor fusion in smartphones for lifestyle monitoring," in *Proceedings of the 2010 International Conference on Body Sensor Networks*, ser. BSN '10. Washington, DC, USA: IEEE Computer Society, 2010. [Online]. Available: http://dx.doi.org/10.1109/BSN.2010.10 pp. 36–43.

[66] H. Ahmadi, N. Pham, R. Ganti, T. Abdelzaher, S. Nath, and J. Han, "Privacy-aware regression modeling of participatory sensing data," in *Proceedings of the 8th ACM Conference on Embedded Networked Sensor Systems*, ser. SenSys '10. New York, NY, USA: ACM, 2010. [Online]. Available: http://doi.acm.org/10.1145/1869983.1869994 pp. 99–112.

[67] N. Pham, R. K. Ganti, Y. S. Uddin, S. Nath, and T. Abdelzaher, "Privacy-preserving reconstruction of multidimensional data maps in vehicular participatory sensing," in *Proceedings of the 7th European conference on Wireless Sensor Networks*, ser. EWSN'10. Berlin, Heidelberg: Springer-Verlag, 2010, pp. 114–130.

[68] S. Nath, "Ace: Exploiting correlation for energy-efficient and continuous context sensing," in *Proceedings of the tenth international conference on Mobile systems, applications, and services (MobiSys'12)*, 2012.

[69] T. Park, J. Lee, I. Hwang, C. Yoo, L. Nachman, and J. Song, "E-gesture: a collaborative architecture for energy-efficient gesture recognition with hand-worn sensor and mobile devices," in *Proceedings of the 9th ACM Conference on Embedded Networked Sensor Systems*, ser. SenSys '11. New York, NY, USA: ACM, 2011. [Online]. Available: http://doi.acm.org/10.1145/2070942.2070969 pp. 260–273.

[70] H. Ahmadi, T. Abdelzaher, J. Han, N. Pham, and R. Ganti, "The sparse regression cube: A reliable modeling technique for open cyber-physical systems," in *Proc. 2nd International Conference on Cyber-Physical Systems (ICCPS'11)*, 2011.

[71] D. Wang, H. Ahmadi, T. Abdelzaher, H. Chenji, R. Stoleru, and C. Aggarwal, "Optimizing quality-of-information in cost-sensitive sensor data fusion," in *IEEE 7th International Conference on Distributed Computing in Sensor Systems (DCoSS 11)*, June 2011.

[72] S. Reddy, K. Shilton, G. Denisov, C. Cenizal, D. Estrin, and M. Srivastava, "Biketastic: sensing and mapping for better biking," in *Proceedings of the 28th international conference on Human factors in computing systems*, ser. CHI '10. New York, NY, USA: ACM, 2010. [Online]. Available: http://doi.acm.org/10.1145/1753326.1753598 pp. 1817–1820.

[73] M. Mun, S. Reddy, K. Shilton, N. Yau, J. Burke, D. Estrin, M. Hansen, E. Howard, R. West, and P. Boda, "Peir, the personal environmental impact report, as a platform for participatory sensing systems research," in *Proceedings of the 7th international conference on Mobile systems, applications, and services*, ser. MobiSys '09. New York, NY, USA: ACM, 2009. [Online]. Available: http://doi.acm.org/10.1145/1555816.1555823 pp. 55–68.

[74] S. Reddy, D. Estrin, and M. Srivastava, "Recruitment framework for participatory sensing data collections," in *Proceedings of the 8th International Conference on Pervasive Computing*. Springer Berlin Heidelberg, May 2010, pp. 138–155.

[75] S. A. Delre, W. Jager, and M. A. Janssen, "Diffusion dynamics in small-world networks with heterogeneous consumers," *Comput. Math. Organ. Theory*, vol. 13, pp. 185–202, June 2007. [Online]. Available: http://portal.acm.org/citation.cfm?id=1210317.1210335.

[76] C. Hui, M. K. Goldberg, M. Magdon-Ismail, and W. A. Wallace, "Simulating the diffusion of information: An agent-based modeling approach." *IJATS*, pp. 31–46, 2010.

[77] J. Xie, S. Sreenivasan, G. Korniss, W. Zhang, C. Lim, and B. K. Szymanski, "Social consensus through the influence of committed minorities," *CoRR*, vol. abs/1102.3931, 2011.

[78] P. Gilbert, L. P. Cox, J. Jung, and D. Wetherall, "Toward trustworthy mobile sensing," in *Proceedings of the Eleventh Workshop on Mobile Computing Systems & Applications*, ser. HotMobile '10. New York, NY, USA: ACM, 2010, pp. 31–36.

[79] P. Gilbert, J. Jung, K. Lee, H. Qin, D. Sharkey, A. Sheth, and L. P. Cox, "Youprove: authenticity and fidelity in mobile sensing," in *Proceedings of the 9th ACM Conference on Embedded Networked Sensor Systems*, ser. SenSys '11. New York, NY, USA: ACM, 2011. [Online]. Available: http://doi.acm.org/10.1145/2070942.2070961 pp. 176–189.

[80] J. Han, "Mining heterogeneous information networks by exploring the power of links," in *Discovery Science*. Springer, 2009, pp. 13–30.

[81] Y. Sun and J. Han, "Mining heterogeneous information networks: Principles and methodologies," *Synthesis Lectures on Data Mining and Knowledge Discovery*, vol. 3, no. 2, pp. 1–159, 2012.

[82] S. Brin and L. Page, "The anatomy of a large-scale hypertextual web search engine," *Computer Networks and ISDN Systems*, vol. 30, no. 1–7, pp. 107–117, 1998.

[83] S. Fortunato, "Community detection in graphs," *Physics Reports*, vol. 486, no. 3, pp. 75–174, 2010.

[84] D. Liben-Nowell and J. Kleinberg, "The link-prediction problem for social networks," *Journal of the American society for information science and technology*, vol. 58, no. 7, pp. 1019–1031, 2007.

[85] J. Tang, J. Sun, C. Wang, and Z. Yang, "Social influence analysis in large-scale networks," in *Proceedings of the 15th ACM SIGKDD international conference on Knowledge discovery and data mining*. ACM, 2009, pp. 807–816.

[86] Y. Sun, J. Han, P. Zhao, Z. Yin, H. Cheng, and T. Wu, "RankClus: integrating clustering with ranking for heterogeneous information network analysis," in *Proceedings of the 12th International Conference on Extending Database Technology: Advances in Database Technology*. ACM, 2009, pp. 565–576.

[87] Y. Sun, J. Han, C. C. Aggarwal, and N. V. Chawla, "When will it happen?: Relationship prediction in heterogeneous information networks," in *Proceedings of the fifth ACM international conference on Web search and data mining*. ACM, 2012, pp. 663–672.

[88] Y. Sun, J. Tang, J. Han, M. Gupta, and B. Zhao, "Community evolution detection in dynamic heterogeneous information networks," in *Proceedings of the Eighth Workshop on Mining and Learning with Graphs*. ACM, 2010, pp. 137–146.

[89] S. M. Lynch, "Basics of Bayesian statistics," in *Introduction to Applied Bayesian Statistics and Estimation for Social Scientists*. Springer, 2007, pp. 47–75.

[90] R. J. A. Little and D. B. Rubin, *Statistical Analysis with Missing Data*. New York, NY, USA: John Wiley & Sons, Inc., 1986.

[91] D. M. Titterington, "Recursive parameter estimation using incomplete data," *Journal of the Royal Statistical Society. Series B (Methodological)*, vol. 46, no. 2, pp. pp. 257–267, 1984. [Online]. Available: http://www.jstor.org/stable/2345509.

[92] A. Papoulis and S. U. Pillai, *Probability, random variables, and stochastic processes*. Tata McGraw-Hill Education, 2002.

[93] A. P. Dempster, N. M. Laird, and D. B. Rubin, "Maximum likelihood from incomplete data via the EM algorithm," *Journal of The Royal Statistical Society, Series B*, vol. 39, no. 1, pp. 1–38, 1977.

[94] T. K. Moon and W. C. Stirling, *Mathematical methods and algorithms for signal processing*. Prentice hall New York, 2000, vol. 1.

[95] D. R. Cox and D. V. Hinkley, *Theoretical statistics*. CRC Press, 1979.

[96] C. R. Rao, *Information and the accuracy attainable in the estimation of statistical parameters*. Bulletin of the Calcutta Mathematical Society, 1945.

[97] X. L. Dong, L. Berti-Equille, Y. Hu, and D. Srivastava, "SOLOMON: Seeking the truth via copying detection," *Proceedings of the VLDB Endowment*, vol. 3, no. 1–2, pp. 1617–1620, 2010.

[98] S. Sikdar, B. Kang, J. ODonovan, T. Hollerer, and S. Adah, "Understanding information credibility on twitter," in *Social Computing (SocialCom), 2013 International Conference on*. IEEE, 2013, pp. 19–24.

[99] S. Sikdar, S. Adah, T. Amin, T. Abdelzaher, K. Chan, J.-H. Cho, B. Kang, and J. ODonovan, "Finding true and credible information on twitter," in *17th International Conference on Information Fusion (Fusion 2014)*, 2014.

[100] D. Wang, L. Kaplan, H. Le, and T. Abdelzaher, "On truth discovery in social sensing: A maximum likelihood estimation approach," in *The 11th ACM/IEEE Conference on Information Processing in Sensor Networks (IPSN 12)*, April 2012.

[101] D. Wang, L. Kaplan, and T. Abdelzaher, "Maximum likelihood analysis of conflicting observations in social sensing," *ACM Transactions on Sensor Networks (ToSN)*, Vol. 10, No. 2, Article 30, January, 2014.

[102] D. Wang, T. Abdelzaher, L. Kaplan, and C. C. Aggarwal, "On quantifying the accuracy of maximum likelihood estimation of participant reliability in social sensing," in *DMSN11: 8th International Workshop on Data Management for Sensor Networks*, August 2011.

[103] D. Wang, L. Kaplan, T. Abdelzaher, and C. C. Aggarwal, "On scalability and robustness limitations of real and asymptotic confidence bounds in social sensing," in *The 9th Annual IEEE Communications Society Conference on Sensor, Mesh and Ad Hoc Communications and Networks (SECON 12)*, June 2012.

[104] D. Wang, L. Kaplan, T. Abdelzaher, and C. C. Aggarwal, "On credibility estimation tradeoffs in assured social sensing," *IEEE Journal on Selected Areas in Communications*, vol. 31, no. 6, pp. 1026–1037, 2013.

[105] D. Wang, T. Amin, S. Li, T. Abdelzaher, L. Kaplan, S. Gu, C. Pan, H. Liu, C. Aggrawal, R. Ganti, X. Wang, P. Mohapatra, B. Szymanski, and H. Le, "Humans as sensors: An estimation theoretic perspective," in *The 13th ACM/IEEE International Conference on Information Processing in Sensor Networks (IPSN 14)*, April 2014.

[106] D. Wang, T. Abdelzaher, L. Kaplan, R. Ganti, S. Hu, and H. Liu, "Exploitation of physical constraints for reliable social sensing," in *The IEEE 34th Real-Time Systems Symposium (RTSS'13)*, 2013.

[107] D. Wang, T. Abdelzaher, L. Kaplan, and C. C. Aggarwal, "Recursive fact-finding: A streaming approach to truth estimation in crowdsourcing applications," in *The 33rd International Conference on Distributed Computing Systems (ICDCS'13)*, July 2013.

[108] C. F. J. Wu, "On the convergence properties of the EM algorithm," *The Annals of Statistics*, vol. 11, no. 1, pp. 95–103, 1983. [Online]. Available: http://dx.doi.org/10.2307/2240463

[109] H. Cramer, *Mathematical Methods of Statistics*. Princeton Univ. Press., 1946.

[110] T. Pang-Ning, M. Steinbach, V. Kumar et al., "Introduction to data mining," in *Library of Congress*, 2006.

[111] R. V. Hogg and A. T. Craig, *Introduction to mathematical statistics*. Prentice Hall, 1995.

[112] G. Casella and R. Berger, *Statistical Inference*. Duxbury Press, 2002.

[113] R. K. Ganti, N. Pham, H. Ahmadi, S. Nangia, and T. F. Abdelzaher, "GreenGPS: a participatory sensing fuel-efficient maps application," in *MobiSys '10: Proceedings of the 8th international conference on Mobile systems, applications, and services*. New York, NY, USA: ACM, 2010, pp. 151–164.

[114] S. Hu, H. Liu, L. Su, H. Wang, and T. Abdelzaher, "SmartRoad: A Mobile Phone Based Crowd-Sourced Road Sensing System," University of Illinois at Urbana-Champaign, Tech. Rep., 08 2013, https://www.ideals.illinois.edu/handle/2142/45699.

[115] R. E. Kalman, "A New Approach to Linear Filtering and Prediction Problems," *Transactions of the ASME Journal of Basic Engineering*, no. 82 (Series D), pp. 35–45, 1960. [Online]. Available: http://www.cs.unc.edu/~welch/kalman/media/pdf/Kalman1960.pdf.

[116] A. Doucet, N. De Freitas, and N. Gordon, Eds., *Sequential Monte Carlo methods in practice*. Springer, 2001. [Online]. Available: http://www.worldcatlibraries.org/wcpa/top3mset/839aaf32b6957a10a19afeb4da09e526.html.

[117] P. Netrapalli and S. Sanghavi, "Learning the graph of epidemic cascades," in *Proceedings of the 12th ACM SIGMETRICS/PERFORMANCE joint international conference on Measurement and Modeling of Computer Systems*, ser. SIGMETRICS '12. New York, NY, USA: ACM, 2012. [Online]. Available: http://doi.acm.org/10.1145/2254756.2254783 pp. 211–222.

[118] W. Galuba, K. Aberer, D. Chakraborty, Z. Despotovic, and W. Kellerer, "Outtweeting the twitterers-predicting information cascades in microblogs," in *Proceedings of the 3rd conference on Online social networks*. USENIX Association, 2010, pp. 3–3.

[119] E. Sun, I. Rosenn, C. Marlow, and T. M. Lento, "Gesundheit! Modeling contagion through facebook news feed." in *ICWSM*, 2009.

[120] M. Cha, A. Mislove, B. Adams, and K. P. Gummadi, "Characterizing social cascades in Flickr," in *Proceedings of the first workshop on Online social networks*. ACM, 2008, pp. 13–18.

[121] G. Szabo and B. A. Huberman, "Predicting the popularity of online content," *Communications of the ACM*, vol. 53, no. 8, pp. 80–88, 2010.

[122] A. Susarla, J.-H. Oh, and Y. Tan, "Social networks and the diffusion of user-generated content: Evidence from YouTube," *Information Systems Research*, vol. 23, no. 1, pp. 23–41, 2012.

[123] C. Hui, Y. Tyshchuk, W. A. Wallace, M. Magdon-Ismail, and M. Goldberg, "Information cascades in social media in response to a crisis: a preliminary model and a case study," in *Proceedings of the 21st international conference companion on World Wide Web*. ACM, 2012, pp. 653–656.

[124] H. Le, D. Wang, H. Ahmadi, M. Y. S. Uddin, Y. H. Ko, T. Abdelzaher, O. Fatemieh, J. Pasternack, D. Roth, J. Han, H. Wang, L. Kaplan, B. Szymanski, S. Adali, C. Aggarwal, and R. Ganti, "Apollo: A data distillation service for social sensing," University of Illinois Urbana-Champaign, Tech. Rep., 2012.

[125] "Apollo:towards fact-finding for human centric sensing," http://apollo.cse.nd.edu/index.html.

[126] A. P. Dawid and A. M. Skene, "Maximum likelihood estimation of observer Error-Rates using the EM algorithm," *Journal of the Royal Statistical Society. Series C (Applied Statistics)*, vol. 28, no. 1, pp. 20–28, 1979. [Online]. Available: http://dx.doi.org/10.2307/2346806

[127] M. Uddin, M. Amin, H. Le, T. Abdelzaher, B. Szymanski, and T. Nguyen, "On diversifying source selection in social sensing," in *2012 Ninth International Conference on Networked Sensing Systems (INSS)*, June 2012, pp. 1–8.

[128] GasBuddy, http://gasbuddy.com/.

[129] NYC Gas Finder, https://github.com/hirefrank/nycgasfinder.

[130] W. He, X. Liu, and M. Ren, "Location cheating: A security challenge to location-based social network services," in *2011 31st International Conference on Distributed Computing Systems (ICDCS)*, 2011, pp. 740–749.

[131] J. Martın de Valmaseda, G. Ionescu, and M. Deriaz, "TrustPos model: Trusting in mobile users? location," in *Mobile Web Information Systems*, ser. Lecture Notes in Computer Science, F. Daniel, G. Papadopoulos, and P. Thiran, Eds. Springer Berlin Heidelberg, 2013, vol. 8093, pp. 79–89.

[132] W. Ouyang, M. B. Srivastava, A. Toniolo, and T. J. Norman, "Truth discovery in crowd-sourced detection of spatial events," in *In International conference on information and knowledge management (CIKM)*. ACM, 2014.

[133] J. Han, "Mining heterogeneous information networks by exploring the power of links," in *Proceedings of the 20th international conference on Algorithmic learning theory, ser. ALT'09. Berlin, Heidelberg: Springer-Verlag*, 2009. [Online]. Available: http://portal.acm.org/citation.cfm?id=1813231.1813235 pp. 3–3.

[134] L. Page, S. Brin, R. Motwani, and T. Winograd, "The pagerank citation ranking: Bringing order to the web." Stanford InfoLab, Technical Report 1999-66, November 1999, previous number = SIDL-WP-1999-0120. [Online]. Available: http://ilpubs.stanford.edu:8090/422/.

[135] S. Wang, D. Wang, L. Su, T. Abdelzaher, and L. Kaplan, "Towards cyber-physical systems in social spaces: The data reliability challenge," in *The IEEE 35th Real-Time Systems Symposium (RTSS'14)*, 2014.

[136] N. Shental, A. Bar-Hillel, T. Hertz, and D. Weinshall, "Computing gaussian mixture models with EM using equivalence constraints," *Advances in neural information processing systems*, vol. 16, no. 8, pp. 465–472, 2004.

[137] R. Samdani, M.-W. Chang, and D. Roth, "Unified expectation maximization," in *Proceedings of the 2012 Conference of the North American Chapter of the Association for Computational Linguistics: Human Language Technologies*. Association for Computational Linguistics, 2012, pp. 688–698.

[138] T. Hofmann, "Probabilistic latent semantic indexing," in *Proceedings of the 22Nd Annual International ACM SIGIR Conference on Research and Development in Information Retrieval*, ser. SIGIR '99. New York, NY, USA: ACM, 1999. [Online]. Available: http://doi.acm.org/10.1145/312624.312649 pp. 50–57.

[139] M. Masseroli, D. Chicco, and P. Pinoli, "Probabilistic latent semantic analysis for prediction of gene ontology annotations," in *Neural Networks (IJCNN), The 2012 International Joint Conference on*. IEEE, 2012, pp. 1–8.

[140] B. Ball, B. Karrer, and M. Newman, "Efficient and principled method for detecting communities in networks," *Physical Review E*, vol. 84, no. 3, p. 036103, 2011.

[141] S. Bhattacharyya and P. J. Bickel, "Community detection in networks using graph distance," *arXiv preprint arXiv:1401.3915*, 2014.

[142] J. Bilmes, "A gentle tutorial on the EM algorithm and its application to parameter estimation for Gaussian mixture and hidden Markov models," *Technical Report, University of Berkeley, ICSI-TR-97-021*, 1997.

[143] G. J. McLachlan and T. Krishnan, "The EM algorithm and extensions." *John Wiley and Sons, Inc.,* 1997.

[144] C. Zhai, "A note on the expectation maximization (EM) algorithm," *Department of Computer Science, University of Illinois at Urbana Champaign,* 2007.

[145] D. Wang and M. Fattouche, "OFDM transmission for time-based range estimation," *Signal Processing Letters, IEEE,* vol. 17, no. 6, pp. 571–574, 2010.

[146] F. Qian, S. Leung, Y. Zhu, W. Wong, D. Pao, and W. Lau, "Damped sinusoidal signals parameter estimation in frequency domain," *Signal Processing,* vol. 92, no. 2, pp. 381–391, 2012.

[147] Z. Wang, J.-A. Luo, and X.-P. Zhang, "A novel location-penalized maximum likelihood estimator for bearing-only target localization," *Signal Processing, IEEE Transactions on,* vol. 60, no. 12, pp. 6166–6181, 2012.

[148] P. Bickel, D. Choi, X. Chang, H. Zhang et al., "Asymptotic normality of maximum likelihood and its variational approximation for stochastic blockmodels," *The Annals of Statistics,* vol. 41, no. 4, pp. 1922–1943, 2013.

[149] T. Yan, Y. Zhao, and H. Qin, "Asymptotic normality in the maximum entropy models on graphs with an increasing number of parameters," *arXiv preprint arXiv:1308.1768,* 2013.

[150] A. Kremer and R. Weißbach, "Asymptotic normality for discretely observed Markov jump processes with an absorbing state," *Statistics & Probability Letters,* vol. 90, pp. 136–139, 2014.

[151] H. D. Nguyen and I. A. Wood, "Asymptotic normality of the maximum pseudolikelihood estimator for fully visible Boltzmann machines," *arXiv preprint arXiv:1409.8047,* 2014.

[152] J. M. Hellerstein, "Quantitative data cleaning for large databases," *United Nations Economic Commission for Europe (UNECE),* 2008.

[153] V. J. Hodge and J. Austin, "A survey of outlier detection methodologies," *Artificial Intelligence Review,* vol. 22, no. 2, pp. 85–126, 2004.

[154] A. K. Elmagarmid, P. G. Ipeirotis, and V. S. Verykios, "Duplicate record detection: A survey," *Knowledge and Data Engineering, IEEE Transactions on,* vol. 19, no. 1, pp. 1–16, 2007.

[155] H. Köpcke and E. Rahm, "Frameworks for entity matching: A comparison," *Data & Knowledge Engineering,* vol. 69, no. 2, pp. 197–210, 2010.

[156] A. Arasu and H. Garcia-Molina, "Extracting structured data from web pages," in *Proceedings of the 2003 ACM SIGMOD international conference on Management of data.* ACM, 2003, pp. 337–348.

[157] S. Soderland, "Learning information extraction rules for semi-structured and free text," *Machine learning,* vol. 34, no. 1–3, pp. 233–272, 1999.

[158] K. Fisher and R. Gruber, "Pads: a domain-specific language for processing ad hoc data," in *ACM Sigplan Notices,* vol. 40, no. 6. ACM, 2005, pp. 295–304.

[159] Y. Mandelbaum, K. Fisher, D. Walker, M. Fernandez, and A. Gleyzer, "Pads/ml: A functional data description language," in *ACM SIGPLAN Notices,* vol. 42, no. 1. ACM, 2007, pp. 77–83.

[160] L. M. Haas, M. A. Hernández, H. Ho, L. Popa, and M. Roth, "Clio grows up: from research prototype to industrial tool," in *Proceedings of the 2005 ACM SIGMOD international conference on Management of data.* ACM, 2005, pp. 805–810.

[161] E. Rahm and P. A. Bernstein, "A survey of approaches to automatic schema matching," *the VLDB Journal,* vol. 10, no. 4, pp. 334–350, 2001.

[162] M. Stonebraker, D. Bruckner, I. F. Ilyas, G. Beskales, M. Cherniack, S. B. Zdonik, A. Pagan, and S. Xu, "Data curation at scale: The data tamer system." in *CIDR*, 2013.

[163] D. F. Huynh, R. C. Miller, and D. R. Karger, "Potluck: semi-ontology alignment for casual users," in *The Semantic Web*. Springer, 2007, pp. 903–910.

[164] S. Kandel, A. Paepcke, J. Hellerstein, and J. Heer, "Wrangler: Interactive visual specification of data transformation scripts," in *PART 5——Proceedings of the 2011 annual conference on Human factors in computing systems*. ACM, 2011, pp. 3363–3372.

[165] J. Lin, J. Wong, J. Nichols, A. Cypher, and T. A. Lau, "End-user programming of mashups with vegemite," in *Proceedings of the 14th international conference on Intelligent user interfaces*. ACM, 2009, pp. 97–106.

[166] V. S. Sheng, F. Provost, and P. G. Ipeirotis, "Get another label? Improving data quality and data mining using multiple, noisy labelers," in *Proceedings of the 14th ACM SIGKDD international conference on Knowledge discovery and data mining*, ser. KDD '08. New York, NY, USA: ACM, 2008. [Online]. Available: http://doi.acm.org/10.1145/1401890.1401965 pp. 614–622.

[167] O. Dekel and O. Shamir, "Vox populi: Collecting high-quality labels from a crowd," in *In Proceedings of the 22nd Annual Conference on Learning Theory*, 2009.

[168] M. T. A. Amin, T. Abdelzaher, D. Wang, and B. Szymanski, "Crowd-sensing with polarized sources," in *Distributed Computing in Sensor Systems (DCOSS), 2014 IEEE International Conference on*. IEEE, 2014, pp. 67–74.

[169] M. Gupta, P. Zhao, and J. Han, "Evaluating event credibility on twitter." in *SDM*. SIAM, 2012, pp. 153–164.

[170] V. Vydiswaran, C. Zhai, and D. Roth, "Content-driven trust propagation framework," in *Proceedings of the 17th ACM SIGKDD international conference on Knowledge discovery and data mining*. ACM, 2011, pp. 974–982.

[171] C. Castillo, M. Mendoza, and B. Poblete, "Information credibility on twitter," in *Proceedings of the 20th international conference on World wide web*. ACM, 2011, pp. 675–684.

[172] J. O'Donovan, B. Kang, G. Meyer, T. Hollerer, and S. Adalii, "Credibility in context: An analysis of feature distributions in twitter," in *Privacy, Security, Risk and Trust (PASSAT), 2012 International Conference on and 2012 International Conference on Social Computing (SocialCom)*. IEEE, 2012, pp. 293–301.

[173] R. O. Duda, P. E. Hart, and D. G. Stork, *Pattern Classification (2nd Edition)*, 2nd ed. Wiley-Interscience, Nov. 2001. [Online]. Available: http://www.worldcat.org/isbn/0471056693.

[174] U. T. Inc and U. T. I. Staff, *Solving Data Mining Problems Using Pattern Recognition Software with Cdrom*, 1st ed. Upper Saddle River, NJ, USA: Prentice Hall PTR, 1997.

[175] R. A. Johnson and D. W. Wichern, *Applied multivariate statistical analysis*. Upper Saddle River, NJ, USA: Prentice-Hall, Inc., 2002.

[176] J.Han, M.Kamber, and J. Pei, *Data Mining: Concepts and Techniques, Third Edition*. Morgan Kaufman, 2011.

[177] Z. Yaniv, "Random sample consensus (ransac) algorithm, a generic implementation," *Imaging*, 2010.

[178] M. E. Whitman and H. J. Mattord, *Principles of Information Security*. Boston, MA, United States: Course Technology Press, 2004.

[179] Q. Lian, Z. Zhang, M. Yang, B. Y. Zhao, Y. Dai, and X. Li, "An empirical study of collusion behavior in the Maze P2P file-sharing system," in *Proceedings of the*

27th International Conference on Distributed Computing Systems, ser. ICDCS '07. Washington, DC, USA: IEEE Computer Society, 2007, pp. 56–.

[180] H. Yu, M. Kaminsky, P. B. Gibbons, and A. Flaxman, "SybilGuard: defending against Sybil attacks via social networks," *SIGCOMM Comput. Commun. Rev.*, vol. 36, pp. 267–278, August 2006.

[181] J. Zhang and R. S. Blum, "Distributed estimation in the presence of attacks for large scale sensor networks," in *Information Sciences and Systems (CISS), 2014 48th Annual Conference on.* IEEE, 2014, pp. 1–6.

[182] G. Adomavicius and A. Tuzhilin, "Toward the next generation of recommender systems: A survey of the state-of-the-art and possible extensions," *IEEE Transactions on Knowledge and Data Engineering*, vol. 17, no. 6, pp. 734–749, 2005.

[183] N. Mustapha, M. Jalali, and M. Jalali, "Expectation maximization clustering algorithm for user modeling in web usage mining systems," *European Journal of Scientific Research*, vol. 32, no. 4, pp. 467–476, 2009.

[184] D. Pomerantz and G. Dudek, "Context dependent movie recommendations using a hierarchical Bayesian model," in *Proceedings of the 22nd Canadian Conference on Artificial Intelligence: Advances in Artificial Intelligence*, ser. Canadian AI '09. Berlin, Heidelberg: Springer-Verlag, 2009, pp. 98–109.

[185] G. Adomavicius and Y. Kwon, "New recommendation techniques for multicriteria rating systems," *IEEE Intelligent Systems*, vol. 22, no. 3, pp. 48–55, May 2007. [Online]. Available: http://dx.doi.org/10.1109/MIS.2007.58

[186] A. E. Cano, S. Mazumdar, and F. Ciravegna, "Social influence analysis in microblogging platforms–a topic-sensitive based approach," *Semantic Web*, 2011.

[187] K.-w. Fu and C.-h. Chan, "Analyzing online sentiment to predict telephone poll results," *Cyberpsychology, Behavior, and Social Networking*, 2013.

[188] E. Toch, Y. Wang, and L. F. Cranor, "Personalization and privacy: A survey of privacy risks and remedies in personalization-based systems," *User Modeling and User-Adapted Interaction*, vol. 22, no. 1–2, pp. 203–220, 2012.

[189] J. Blair, R. F. Czaja, and E. A. Blair, *Designing surveys: A guide to decisions and procedures*. SAGE Publications, Incorporated, 2013.

[190] J. R. Lax and J. H. Phillips, "How should we estimate public opinion in the states?" *American Journal of Political Science*, vol. 53, no. 1, pp. 107–121, 2009. [Online]. Available: http://dx.doi.org/10.1111/j.1540-5907.2008.00360.x

[191] S. Splichal, "Public opinion and opinion polling: Contradictions and controversies," *Opinion Polls and the Media: Reflecting and Shaping Public Opinion*, p. 25, 2012.

[192] J. Zhu, H. Wang, M. Zhu, B. K. Tsou, and M. Ma, "Aspect-based opinion polling from customer reviews," *IEEE Trans. Affect. Comput.*, vol. 2, no. 1, pp. 37–49, Jan. 2011. [Online]. Available: http://dx.doi.org/10.1109/T-AFFC.2011.2

[193] R. M. Gardner, D. L. Brown, and R. Boice, "Using Amazon's Mechanical Turk website to measure accuracy of body size estimation and body dissatisfaction," *Body Image*, 2012.

[194] D. Wang, M. Amin, T. Abedlzaher, D. Roth, C. Voss, L. Kaplan, S. Tratz, J. Laoudi, and D. Briesch, "Provenance-assisted classification in social networks," *IEEE Journal of Selected Topics in Signal Processing (J-STSP)*, 2014.

Index

Note: Page numbers followed by *f* indicate figures and *t* indicate tables.

Printed in the United States
By Bookmasters